STUDIES IN ECONOMICS OF MICROFINANCE

Pankaj Gupta

CYBER TECH PUBLICATIONS
4264/3, Ansari Road, Daryaganj, New Delhi-110002 (India)
Ph.: 011-23244078, 011-43559448 Fax: 011-23280028
E-Mail: cyberpublicationsdelhi@yahoo.com
Website: www.cybertechpublications.com

STUDIES IN ECONOMICS OF MICROFINANCE

Pankaj Gupta

Edition 2026

Published by :

G.S. Rawat for **Cyber Tech Publications**
4264/3, Ansari Road, Daryaganj, New Delhi-110002 (India)
Ph.: 011-23244078, 011-43559448 Fax: 011-23280028
E-Mail: cyberpublicationsdelhi@yahoo.com
Website: www.cybertechpublications.com

CONTENTS

Preface

TAccess to finance by the poor and vulnerable groups is a prerequisite for poverty reduction and social cohesion. This has to become an integral part of our efforts to promote inclusive growth. In fact, providing access to finance is a form of empowerment of the vulnerable groups. Financial inclusion denotes delivery of financial services at an affordable cost to the vast sections of the disadvantaged and low-income groups. The various financial services include credit, savings, insurance and payments and remittance facilities. The objective of financial inclusion is to extend the scope of activities of the organized financial system to include within its ambit people with low incomes. Through graduated credit, the attempt must be to lift the poor from one level to another so that they come out of poverty.

NSSO data reveal that 45.9 million farmer households in the country (51.4%), out of a total of 89.3 million households do not access credit, either from institutional or noninstitutional sources. Further, despite the vast network of bank branches, only 27% of total farm households are indebted to formal sources (of which one-third also borrow from informal sources). Farm households not accessing credit from formal sources as a proportion to total farm households is especially high at 95.91%, 81.26% and 77.59% in the North Eastern, Eastern and Central Regions respectively. Thus, apart from the fact that exclusion in general is large, it also varies widely across regions, social groups and asset holdings. The poorer the group, the greater is the exclusion. While financial inclusion can be substantially enhanced by improving the supply side or the delivery systems, it is also important to note that many regions, segments of the population and sub-sectors of the economy have a limited or weak demand for financial services. In order to improve their level of inclusion, demand side efforts need to be undertaken including improving human and physical resource endowments, enhancing productivity, mitigating risk and strengthening market linkages. However, the primary focus of the Committee has been on improving the delivery systems, both conventional and innovative.

The Committee feels that the task of financial inclusion must be taken up in a mission mode as a financial inclusion plan at the national level. A National Mission on Financial Inclusion (NaMFI) comprising representatives from all stakeholders may be constituted to aim at achieving universal financial inclusion within a specific time frame. The Mission should be responsible for suggesting the overall policy changes required for achieving the desired level of financial inclusion, and for supporting a range of stakeholders - in the domain of public, private and NGO sectors - in undertaking promotional initiatives.

— *Author*

1

Introduction

Every day about a hundred people go to work in an unassuming brick office building in the Mohammedpur neighborhood of Dhaka, the main office of ASA—the Bengali word for hope and the acronym of the Association for Social Advancement. ASA is a nongovernmental organ-ization (NGO) that at the end of 2003 provided banking services to nearly 2.3 million customers in Bangladesh. Unlike many commercial banks, ASA's present headquarters contains no marble floors and no plush rugs. Accounting procedures are so streamlined that the account-ing department is housed in a single room where thirteen staff members keep an eye on the numbers for the entire operation. If the headquarters is surprising, the clients are even more so. Target clients are the wives and mothers of landless laborers and small-scale farmers with average monthly incomes around $50, borrowing on average around $120 per loan. Traditional commercial banks avoid this popu-lation. First, the loans are so small that profits are typically hard to find, and, second, lending seems risky since the borrowers are too poor to offer much in the way of collateral. But in 2003 ASA reported loan recovery rates of 99.9 percent, and their reported revenues have fully covered costs in every year since 1993.

ASA and institutions like it challenge decades of thinking about markets and social policy in low-income communities. For many observers, microfinance—a collection of banking practices built around providing small loans (typically without collateral) and accepting tiny savings deposits—is nothing short of a revolution or a paradigm shift (Robinson 2001). To others, microfinance is still to be fully developed and tested by time. Few will disagree, though, that microfinance has already shaken up the world of international development. One of the most striking elements is that the pioneering models grew out of experiments in low-income countries like Bolivia and Bangladesh—rather than from adaptations of standard banking models in richer countries.

Entrepreneurs, academics, social activists, and development experts from around the world have been drawn to microbanks and NGOs like ASA. They are attracted by the lessons about retail banking through microfinance, as well as by the promise that banks like ASA hold for getting much-needed resources to underserved populations. Scores of doctoral dissertations, master's theses, and academic studies have now been written on microfinance. Some focus on the nontraditional con-tracts used to compensate for risks and to address information prob-lems faced by the microlenders. Others focus on microfinance as a way to better understand the nature of markets in low-income economies— with possible lessons for how to supply insurance, water, and electric-ity through markets rather than through inefficient state-owned companies. Still others focus on the ways that microfinance promises to reduce poverty, fight gender inequality, and strengthen communi-ties. This book provides a critical guide to some of the most important new ideas.

The ideas give reasons for hope. Banks and NGOs like ASA are flour-ishing at a time when the effectiveness of foreign aid to ease the burdens of the world's poor faces fundamental questions (e.g., Boone 1996; Easterly 2001). Governments around the world routinely face crit-icism for at times being corrupt, bloated, and uninterested in reform. Against this background, banks and NGOs like ASA offer innovative, cost-effective paths to poverty reduction and social change.

ASA is not the only microlender flourishing in rural Bangladesh. ASA's management could learn from the experiences of the pioneering Grameen Bank and from BRAC (formerly the Bangladesh Rural Advancement Committee), now Bangladesh's largest microlender. By the end of 2003, Grameen had 3.1 million members and BRAC had 3.9 million. In Bangladesh, microlenders collectively serve roughly 10–12 million clients, nearly all of which had been written off by commercial banks as being "unbankable."

The institutions anchor a movement that is global and growing. Microfinance programs have created new opportunities in contexts as diverse as villages along the Amazon, inner-city Los Angeles, and war-ravaged Bosnia. Programs are well-established in Bolivia, Bangladesh, and Indonesia, and momentum is gaining in Mexico, China, and India.

Table 1.1: Growth of microfinance coverage as reported to the Microcredit Summit Campaign, 1997–2001

End of year	Total number of institutions	Total number of clients reached (millions)	Number of "poorest" clients reported (millions)
1997	618	13.5	7.6
1998	925	20.9	12.2
1999	1,065	23.6	13.8
2000	1,567	30.7	19.3
2001	2,186	54.9	26.8
2002	2,572	67.6	41.6

Source: Daley-Harris 2003, Table 1.

Table 1.1 shows the results of a survey conducted by the Microcredit Summit Campaign. By the end of 2002, the campaign had reports of 67.6 million microfinance clients served worldwide by over 2,500 microfinance institutions. Of these clients, 41.6 million were in the bottom half of those living below their nation's poverty line (defined as "the poorest"; Microcredit Summit 2003). Between 1997 and 2002, the numbers grew on average by about 40 percent per year, and the movement's leaders expect to continue expanding as credit unions, commercial banks, and others enter the market.

Microfinance presents a series of exciting possibilities for extending markets, reducing poverty, and fostering social change. But it also pres-ents a series of puzzles, many of which have not yet been widely dis-cussed. One aim of this book is to describe the innovations that have created the movement. Another aim is to address and clarify the puzzles, debates, and assumptions that guide conversations but that are too often overlooked. Debates include whether the poorest are best served by loans or by better ways to save, whether subsidies are a help or a hindrance, whether providing credit without training and other complements is enough, and which aspects of lending mechanisms have driven successful performances. Many of the insights from the microfinance experience can be seen fruitfully through the lens of recent innovations in economics (especially the economics of informa-tion, contract theory, and the mechanism design approach). Other microfinance insights point to areas where new research is needed, especially around possibilities and constraints for saving by the poor and for estimating social impacts.

Another aim of the book is to tackle the myths that have made their way into conversations on microfinance. The first myth is that micro-finance is essentially about providing loans. But we take issue with the argument that, for the poorest, saving is *more* important. The second myth is that the secret to the high repayment rates on loans is tied closely to the use of the group lending contracts made famous by Bangladesh's Grameen Bank and Bolivia's BancoSol. Group lending has indeed been a critical innovation, but we note emerging tensions, and in chapter 5 we describe a series of innovations in contracts and banking pactices that go beyond group lending. We believe that the future of microfinance lies with these less-heralded innovations—along with the focus on female customers and the improved management practices.

The third myth is that microfinance has a clear record of social impacts and has been shown to be a major tool for poverty reduction and gender empowerment. We believe that microfinance can make a real difference in the lives of those served (otherwise we would not have written this book), but microfinance is neither a panacea nor a magic bullet, and it cannot be expected to work everywhere or for everyone. Relatively few rigorous studies of impacts have been com-pleted, and the evidence on statistical impacts has been mixed so far. There is not yet a widely acclaimed study that robustly shows strong impacts, but many studies suggest the possibility. Better impact studies can help resolve debates, and chapter 8 describes approaches and chal-lenges to be confronted in pushing ahead.

The final myth is that most microlenders today are both serving the poor and making profits. We show in chapter 9 that profitability has been elusive for most institutions, and we describe why good banking practices matter—and how subsidies can be deployed strategically to move microfinance forward.

Unlike most discussions of microfinance oriented toward practition-ers, we do not begin by describing new microfinance institutions. We will have much to say about recent innovations later, but our approach begins instead with the nature of poverty and the markets and institutions that currently serve poor households. By beginning with households, communities, and markets, we develop analytical tools and insights that can then be used to think about the new institutions, as well as to think about directions that go beyond current approaches.

Why Doesn't Capital Naturally Flow to the Poor?

From the viewpoint of basic economics, the need for microfinance is somewhat surprising. One of the first lessons in introductory econom-ics is the principle of diminishing marginal returns to capital, which says that enterprises with relatively little capital should be able to earn higher returns on their investments than enterprises with a great deal of capital. Poorer enterprises should thus be able to pay banks higher interest rates than richer enterprises. Money should flow from rich depositors to poor entrepreneurs.

The "diminishing returns principle" is derived from the assumed concavity of production functions. Concav-ity is a product of the very plausible assumption that when an enter-prise invests more (i.e., uses more capital), it should expect to produce more output, but each additional unit of capital will bring smaller and smaller incremental ("marginal") gains. When a tailor buys his first $100 sewing machine, production can rise quickly relative to output possible when using only a needle and thread. The next $100 invest-ment, say for a set of electric scissors, will also bring gains, but the incremental increase is not likely to be as great as that generated by the sewing machine. After all, if buying the scissors added more to output than the sewing machine, the wise tailor would have bought the scis-sors first. The size of the incremental gains matter since the marginal return to capital determines the borrowers' ability to pay. As figure 1.1 shows, concavity implies that the poor entrepreneur has a higher mar-ginal return to capital (and thus a higher ability to repay lenders) than a richer entrepreneur.

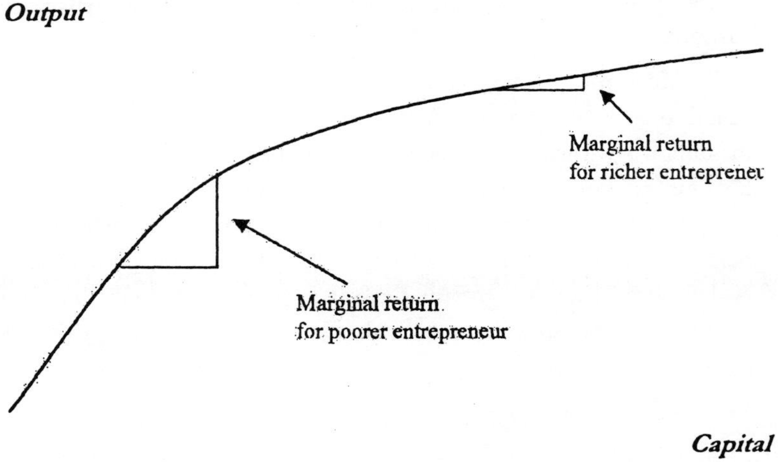

Figure 1.1: Marginal returns to capital with a concave production function. The poorer entrepreneur has a greater return on his next unit of capital and is willing to pay higher interest rates than the richer entrepreneur.

On a larger scale, if this basic tool of introductory economics is correct, global investors have got it all wrong. Instead of investing more money in New York, London, and Tokyo, wise investors should direct their funds toward India, Kenya, Bolivia, and other low-income countries where capital is relatively scarce. Money should move from North to South, not out of altruism but in pursuit of profit. The Nobel-winning economist Robert Lucas Jr. has measured the extent of the expected difference in returns across countries (assuming that marginal returns to capital depend just on the amount of capital rela-tive to other productive inputs). Based on his estimates of marginal returns to capital, Lucas (1990) finds that borrowers in India should be willing to pay fifty-eight times as much for capital as borrowers in the United States. Money should thus flow from New York to New Delhi.

The logic can be pushed even further. Not only should funds move from the United States to India, but also, by the same argument, capital should naturally flow from rich to poor borrowers *within* any given country. Money should flow from Wall Street to Harlem and to the poor mountain communities of Appalachia, from New Delhi to villages throughout India. The principle of diminishing marginal returns says that a simple cobbler working on the streets or a woman selling flowers in a market stall should be able to offer investors higher returns than General Motors or IBM or the Tata Group can—and banks and investors should respond accordingly.

Lucas's ultimate aim is to point to a puzzle: Given that investors are basically prudent and self-interested, how has introductory economics got it wrong? Why are investments in fact far more likely to flow from poor to rich countries, and not in the other direction? Why do large cor-porations have a far easier time obtaining financing from banks than self-employed cobblers and flower sellers?

The first place to start in sorting out the puzzle is with risk. Invest-ing in Kenya, India, or Bolivia is for many a far riskier prospect than investing in U.S. or European equities, especially for global investors without the time and resources to keep up-to-date on shifting local conditions. The same is true of lending to cobblers and flower sellers versus lending to large, regulated corporations. But why can't cobblers and flower sellers in the hinterlands offer such high returns to investors that their risk is well compensated for?

One school argues that poor borrowers can pay high interest rates in principle but that government-imposed interest rate restrictions prevent banks from charging the interest rates required to draw capital from North to South and from cities to villages. If this is so, the challenge for microfinance is wholly political. Advocates must only convince governments to remove usury laws and other restrictions on banks, then sit back and watch the banks flood into poor regions. That is easier said than done of course, especially since usury laws (i.e., laws that put upper limits on the interest rates that lenders can charge) have long histories and strong constituencies.

Reality is both more complicated and more interesting. Even if usury laws could be removed, providing banks with added freedom to serve the poor and cover costs is not the only answer. Indeed, as we show in chapter 2, raising interest rates can undermine institutions by weaken-ing incentives for borrowers. Once (lack of) information is brought into the picture (together with the lack of collateral), we can more fully explain why lenders have such a hard time serving the poor, even households with seemingly high returns. The important factors are the bank's incomplete information about poor borrowers and the poor bor-rowers' lack of collateral to offer as security to banks.

The first problem—adverse selection—occurs when banks cannot easily determine which customers are likely to be more risky than others. Banks would like to charge riskier customers more than safer customers in order to compensate for the added probability of default. But the bank does not know who is who, and raising average interest rates for everyone often drives safer customers out of the credit market. The second problem, moral hazard, arises because banks are unable to ensure that customers are making the full effort required for their investment projects to be successful. Moral hazard also arises when customers try to abscond with the bank's money. Both problems are made worse by the difficulty of enforcing contracts in regions with weak judicial systems.

These problems could potentially be eliminated if banks had cheap ways to gather and evaluate information on their clients and to enforce contracts. But banks typically face relatively high transactions costs when working in poor communities since handling many small trans-actions is far more expensive than servicing one large transaction for a richer borrower. Another potential solution would be available if borrowers had marketable assets to offer as collateral. If that were so, banks could lend without risk, knowing that problem loans were covered by assets. But the starting point for microfinance is that new ways of delivering loans are needed precisely because borrowers are too poor to have much in the way of marketable assets. In this sense, for generations poverty has reproduced poverty—and microfinance is seen as a way to break the vicious circle by reducing transactions costs and overcoming information problems.

GOOD INTENTIONS GONE AWRY: THE FAILURES OF STATE-OWNED DEVELOPMENT BANKS

The lack of banks does not mean that poor individuals are unable to borrow. They do—but from informal sources such as moneylenders, neighbors, relatives, and local traders. Such lenders often have the rich information (and effective means of enforcing contracts) that banks lack. Their resources, however, are limited. Microfinance presents itself as the latest solution to the age-old challenge of finding a way to combine the banks' resources with the local informational and cost advantages of neighbors and moneylenders. Like traditional banks, microfinance institutions can bring in resources from outside the com-munity. Microfinance is not the first attempt to do this, but it is by far the most successful.

The success of microfinance depends in part on studiously avoiding the mistakes of the past. As low-income countries attempted to develop their agricultural sectors after World War II, rural finance emerged as a large concern then too. Large state agricultural banks were given the responsibility for allocating funds, with the hope that providing sub-sidized credit would induce farmers to irrigate, apply fertilizers, and adopt new crop varieties and technologies (e.g., Reserve Bank of India 1954). The hope was to increase land productivity, increase labor demand, and thereby to increase agricultural wages.

Heavy subsidies were also deployed to compensate the banks for entering into markets where they feared taking huge losses due to high transactions costs and inherent risks. The subsidies were also used to keep interest rates low for poor borrowers. In the Philippines, for example, interest rates charged to borrowers were capped at 16 percent before a reform in 1981, while inflation rates were around 20 percent annually (David 1984). The negative real interest rates created excess demand for loans, adding pressure to allocate loans to politically favored residents, rather than to target groups. Meanwhile, the inter-est rates offered to rural depositors were only about 6 percent per year, so inflation eroded the purchasing power of savings at a rate of about 14 percent per year. The policies, not surprisingly, turned out disastrously. David (1984, 222) concludes that in the Philippines "credit subsidies through low interest rates worsen income distribution because only a few, typically well-off farmers, receive the bulk of the cheap credit. When interest rates are not allowed to reflect costs of financial intermediation, wealth and political power replace profitabil-ity as the basis of allocating credit." Rather than delivering access, the policies have been blamed for creating financial repression (McKinnon 1973). India's Integrated Rural Development Program (IRDP) is, to many, a too perfect example of inefficient subsidized credit. The program allo-cated credit according to "social targets" that in principle pushed 30 percent of loans toward socially excluded groups (as signified by being a member of a "scheduled" tribe or caste) and 30 percent toward women. Achieving social goals became as important as achieving effi-ciency.

Under the system, capital was allocated according to a series of nested planning exercises, with village plans aggregating to block plans aggregating to district plans aggregating to state plans. Subsidies between 1979 and 1989, a period of rapid IRDP growth, amounted to $6 billion (roughly 25 percent to 50 percent of loan volume made to weak sectors). Those resources did not generate good institutional per-formance.

According to Pulley (1989), IRDP repayment rates fell below 60 percent, and just 11 percent of borrowers took out a second loan after the first (which is particularly striking given the importance accorded to repeat lending by microfinance practitioners). In 2000, the IRDP loan recovery rate fell to just 31 percent (Meyer 2002). As institutional per-formance dramatically weakened, the IRDP failed to be a reliable and meaningful source of services for the poor.

In the late 1970s and early 1980s, the Rural Finance Program at Ohio State University launched a devastating critique of government-led development banks like the IRDP and the Philippine programs. Its starting point was that credit is not like fertilizer or seeds. Instead, the critics argued, credit should be thought of as a fungible tool of finan-cial intermediation (with many uses) and not as a specific input into particular production processes.

Thus one problem, according to the critics, came from mistakenly believing that credit could be "directed" to particular ends favored by policymakers (e.g., expanding the use of high-yielding crop varieties). And that, coupled with cheap credit policies, created havoc in rural financial markets and ultimately under-mined attempts to reduce poverty (Adams, Graham, and Pischke 1984). The story hinges on a failure to adequately account for the incentive effects and politics associated with subsidies. Subsidizing banks, it was argued, made those banks flabby by creating monopolies and remov-ing market tests.

Thus, critics of the subsidized state banks argue that poor house-holds would often have been better off *without* the subsidies. This is in part because, first, subsidized banks pushed out informal credit sup-pliers on which the poor rely. Second, the market rate of interest is a rationing mechanism—those who are willing to pay for credit are only those with projects that are most worthy. But with subsidies driving interest rates well below market rates of interest, the rationing mecha-nism broke down. Credit was no longer allocated to the most produc-tive recipients, but instead was often allocated on the basis of politics or social concerns. Good projects thus went unfunded. Third, bankers' incentives to collect savings deposits were diminished by the steady flow of capital from the government, so poor households were left with relatively unattractive and inefficient ways to save. Fourth, the fact that the banks were state banks led to pressure to forgive loans just before elections, to privilege the powerful with access to cheap funds meant for the poor, and to remove incentives for management to build tight, efficient institutions. Braverman and Guasch (1986) conclude that government credit programs in Africa, the Middle East, Latin America, South Asia, and Southeast Asia have, "with a few exceptions," ended up with default rates between 40 percent to 95 percent. And at such rates, borrowers can be excused for seeing the credit programs as pro-viding grants rather than loans. The misallocation of resources hap-pened so regularly that Gonzalez-Vega (1984) dubs it the "iron law of interest rate restrictions."

Critics hold that these kinds of subsidies undermined the poor, although the evidence from India at least provides a more nuanced picture. New empirical work by Burgess and Pande (2002), for example, shows net positive average impacts on the poor in India. Similarly, Binswanger and Khandker (1995) find that between 1972–1973 and 1980–1981 the state banks in India increased nonfarm growth, employment, and rural wages. Still, the Indian programs have been clearly inefficient, and a great deal of money that was originally targeted to the poor ended up being wasted or going into the wrong hands. As a result, Binswanger and Khandker find only modest impacts on agricultural output and none on agricultural employment, and they conclude that the costs of the government programs were so high that they nearly swamped the economic benefits. More than any positive historical precedent, it is the repudiation of these negative legacies that has driven the microfinance movement to look to the private sector for inspiration.

The Grameen Bank and the Beginnings of Microfinance

The roots of microfinance can be found in many places, but the best-known story is that of Muhammad Yunus and the founding of Bangladesh's Grameen Bank. We briefly tell the story now and return to Grameen's experience in later chapters.

In the middle of the 1970s, Bangladesh was starting down the long road to build a new nation. The challenges were great: Independence from Pakistan had been won in December 1971 after a fierce war, and two years later widespread flooding brought on a famine that killed tens of thousands (Sen 1981). Government surveys found over 80 percent of the population living in poverty in 1973–1974 (Bangladesh Bureau of Statistics 1992).

Muhammad Yunus, an economist trained at Vanderbilt University, was teaching at Chittagong University in southeast Bangladesh. The famine, though, brought him disillusionment with his career as an eco-nomics professor. In 1976, Yunus started a series of experiments lending to poor households in the nearby village of Jobra. Even the little money he could lend from his own pocket was enough for villagers to run simple business activities like rice husking and bamboo weaving. Yunus found that borrowers were not only profiting greatly by access to the loans but that they were also repaying reliably, even though the villagers could offer no collateral. Realizing that he could only go so far with his own resources, in 1976 Yunus convinced the Bangladesh Bank, the central bank of Bangladesh, to help him set up a special branch that catered to the poor of Jobra. That soon spawned another trial project, this time in Tangail in North-Central Bangladesh. Assured that the successes were not flukes or region-specific, Grameen went nation-wide. One innovation that allowed Grameen to grow explo-sively was group lending, a mechanism that essentially allows the poor borrowers to act as guarantors for each other. With group lending in place, the bank could quickly grow village by village as funding per-mitted. And funding—supplied in the early years by the International Fund for Agriculture and Development, the Ford Foundation, and the governments of Bangladesh, Sweden, Norway, and the Netherlands— permitted rapid growth indeed. As figure 1.2 shows, the bank grew by 40 percent per year at its peak. By 1991 the Grameen bank had over one million members in Bangladesh, and by 2002 the number had swollen to 2.4 million. Today, replications exist in thirty countries, from East Timor to Bosnia. Group lending programs also operate in thirty of the fifty states in the United States.

Grameen's group lending contract works very differently than a standard banking contract for small business. In a standard relation-ship, the borrower gives the bank collateral as security, gets a loan from the bank, invests the capital to generate a return, and finally pays the loan back with interest. If borrowers cannot repay, their collateral is seized. But Grameen clients are most often too poor to be able to offer collateral; instead, the Grameen contract takes advantage of the client's close ties within their community. To take advantage of those relation-ships, the loan contract involves groups of customers, not individuals acting on their own. The groups form voluntarily, and, while loans are made to individuals within groups, all members are expected to support the others when difficulties arise.

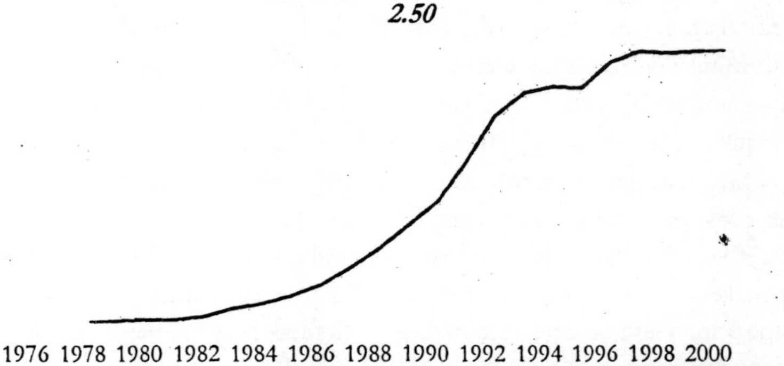

Figure 1.2: Growth in Grameen Bank membership, 1976–2001.
Source: *Grameen Bank,* Annual Reports *(various years).*

The groups consist of five borrowers each; loans go first to two members, then to another two, and then to the fifth group member. As long as loans are being repaid, the cycle of lending continues. But, according to the rules, if one member defaults and fellow group members do not pay off the debt, all in the group are denied subsequent loans. This feature gives customers important incentives to repay promptly, to monitor their neighbors, and to select responsible partners when forming groups (Fugelsang and Chandler 1993). Moreover, the five-member group is part of a "center" composed of eight groups. Repayments are made in public, that is, before the forty members of the center, in weekly installments. Group lending thus takes advantage of local information, peer support, and, if needed, peer pressure. The mechanisms rely on informal relation-ships between neighbors that facilitate borrowing for households lacking collateral (Besley and Coate 1995; Armendáriz de Aghion 1999a). The program thus combines the scale advantages of a standard bank with mechanisms long used in traditional modes of informal finance.

The "joint liability" condition is the most celebrated feature of the Grameen contract, and it is why microfinance is so closely associated with the idea of group lending. Economic theorists have been intrigued by Grameen's contracts, and there has been an outpouring of research, beginning with Stiglitz (1990), on how joint liability works. Through-out the 1990s, however, we have witnessed a growing diversity of approaches that go well beyond group lending with joint liability. As we argue in chapter 5, although Grameen Bank's "joint liability" con-tract gets much attention, there are other, often overlooked, features of the lending relationship that make the Grameen model different from the textbook bank example. In particular, Grameen creates "dynamic incentives" and generates information by starting with very small loans and gradually increasing loan size as customers demonstrate reliability. In addition, the bank uses an unusual repayment schedule: Repayments usually begin just a week after the initial loan disbursal and continue weekly after that; this makes the contract look much closer to a consumer loan than a business loan and changes the nature of the risk that the bank is taking on—and the service that it is pro-viding. Beyond these economic mechanisms, Grameen has found that not only does having a customer base that is 95 percent female improve social impacts, but it may also reduce the financial risk for the bank, an issue to which we return in chapters 5 and 7. While traditional banks have historically lent nearly exclusively to men, women make up the bulk of Grameen borrowers and they are often more reliable customers than their husbands (Khandker 1998).

Disentangling how the various mechanisms work matters, since what works in Bangladesh may work less well in Brazil or Uganda. Even in rural Bangladesh a variety of approaches are being employed. ASA, for example, started with group lending in 1991, with twenty-person groups (rather than five-person groups) and a highly stan-dardized process. In the beginning, ASA's members took loans in the same amount as one another and thus repaid the same each week, and also saved the same amount. But ASA's program has become far more flexible, one outcome of which has been to reduce reliance on the joint liability contract. ASA's repayment rates have not suffered at all. In other countries different methods are used, including the use of collateral—but often on more flexible terms than a standard bank would use. In general, the use of "individual lending" (as opposed to group lending) methods is gaining ground.

A MICROFINANCE REVOLUTION? FROM "MICROCREDIT" TO "MICROFINANCE"

One of the most important departures has involved the shift from "microcredit"—which refers specifically to small loans—to "microfinance." The broader term embraces efforts to collect savings from low-income households, to provide insurance ("microinsurance"), and, in some places (BRAC in Bangladesh has pioneered here), to also help in distributing and marketing clients' output. Robinson (2001) provides a rich description of a "microfinance revolution" that is just beginning.

While the words *microcredit* and *microfinance* are often used inter-changeably, they have different resonances and are loosely attached to contrasting beliefs about the state of rural finance and the nature of poverty. The small difference in language signals, for some, a big dif-ference in opinion. Microcredit was coined initially to refer to insti-tutions like the Grameen Bank that were focusing on getting loans to the very poor. The focus was explicitly on poverty reduction and social change, and the key players were NGOs. The push to "microfinance" came with recognition that households can benefit from access to finan-cial services more broadly defined (at first the focus was mainly on savings) and not just credit for microenterprises. With the change in language has come a change in orientation, toward "less poor" house-holds and toward the establishment of commercially oriented, fully regulated financial entities.

The push to embrace savings is a welcome one, because it recognizes the pent-up demand for secure places to save, and in that context, the shift from microcredit to microfinance should not be contentious. Debate arises, though, with the relatively new (and wrongheaded in our belief) argument that in fact the poorest customers need savings facilities *only*—that making loans to the poorest is a bad bet. (So much for the principle of diminishing returns to capital!)

The debate drags up the legacy of the "exploitative moneylender" on one side and the legacy of the subsidized state banks on the other. In the process it also brings out tensions that run through academic work on household consumption patterns in rural areas. Those who see informal moneylenders as exploitative are sensitive to the powerlessness of poor borrowers (e.g., Bhaduri 1973, 1977). But, as Basu (1997) argues, the question then becomes: Why do the poor remain powerless? If only borrowers could tuck away a bit of money at regular intervals, eventually they would accumulate enough to get out from under the clutches of the moneylender. Bhaduri's response is that the very poor are so close to subsistence that saving is impossible—all extra resources need to go into consumption. Loans not savings, are thus essential.

Against this is the argument that, to the contrary, even the very poor can save in quantity if only given the chance. The fact that they have not been, it is argued, is due to "mistaken" beliefs along the line of Bhaduri (1973) and the fact that subsidized state banks never made a serious effort to collect saving deposits, leading some to wrongly infer that the lack of savings is due to inability, not lack of opportunity (Adams, Graham, and von Pischke 1984). Moreover, Adams and von Pischke (1992) argue that very poor households can seldom produc-tively use loans. Exactly counter to Bhaduri, they argue that savings facilities (and not loans) are thus critical for the poorest. Only the "less poor" should thus be the target of microlending. The precepts that were the basis of the early microfinance movement have thus been turned on their head.

In chapter 6, we attempt to steer between these two poles of rheto-ric. Our view is that the very poor can profit from having better ways to both save and borrow—although the belief, for now, rests more on inference than on direct evidence. In chapter 6, we also consider new initiatives to provide "microinsurance." Like credit markets, insurance markets are plagued by information problems, high per-unit transac-tions costs, and a host of contract enforcement difficulties. These problems are magnified in rural areas (where the majority of the poor live) because of the high incidence of aggregate risk from floods, droughts, and infectious disease. This makes common types of losses particularly difficult to insure against through local measures, and the problems leave most poor households lagging far behind more afflu-ent individuals. But in chapter 6 we describe several innovations in insurance provision that attempt to match the successes of micro-finance to date.

Rethinking Subsidies

We began the chapter by describing two simple ideas that have inspired the microfinance movement and challenged decades of thinking: first, that poor households can profit from greater access to banks, and, second, that institutions can profit while serving poor customers. Microfinance presents itself as a new market-based strategy for poverty reduction, free of the heavy subsidies that brought down large state banks. In a world in search of easy answers, this "win-win" combina-tion has been a true winner itself. The international Microcredit Summit held in 1997 and its follow-up in 2002 have been graced by heads of state and royalty, and Bill Clinton, former president of the United States, made numerous official visits to microfinance programs while traveling overseas. As foreign aid budgets have been slashed, microfi-nance so far remains a relatively protected initiative.

Somewhat paradoxically, though, the movement continues to be driven by hundreds of millions of dollars of subsidies, and those sub-sidies beget many questions. The hope for many is that microfinance programs will use the subsidies in their early start-up phases only, and, as scale economies and experience drive costs down, programs will eventually be able to operate without subsidy. Once free of subsidy, it is argued, the programs can grow without the tether of donor support (be it from governments or donors). To do this, sustainability-minded advocates argue that programs will need to mobilize capital by taking savings deposits or by issuing bonds, or institutions must become so profitable that they can obtain funds from commercial sources, com-peting in the marketplace with computer makers, auto manufacturers, and large, established banks.

In the latter regard, Latin America's largest microlender, *Financiera Compartamos*, an affiliate of Boston-based ACCION International, has led the way by issuing a 100-million-peso bond (approximately $10 million) in July 2002. The three-year bond pays purchasers 2.5 percentage points above the Mexican Government ninety-one-day treasury-bill rate (which was 11.17 percent at the time of issue). A second 100-million-peso bond was planned for the end of 2002. ACCION's president, María Otero remarked at the time, "This sale is an exciting first for an ACCION partner and an important benchmark in microfinance. ACCION is committed to the growth of financially self-sufficient microlenders who need not depend on donor funding to fight poverty." Compartamos has grown quickly, serving over 100,000 clients in fifteen Mexican states by 2002, aiding clients in informal businesses like "making tortillas, selling fruit and vegetables, raising chickens." But its legacy is mixed. To win the (Mexico) A+ rating that it was granted by Standard and Poor's rating agency, Compartamos had to cover a relatively inefficient administra-tive structure by charging borrowers an effective interest rate above 110 percent per year, putting its charges well into the range of those of the moneylenders upon which microfinance was meant to improve.

If, as we saw in figure 1.1, the returns to capital function is steeply concave, typical poor borrowers may be able to routinely pay interest rates above 100 percent and still have surplus left over. The fact that Compartamos does not suffer from a lack of clients suggests that there are low-income customers in Mexico willing and able to pay high fees.

Microlenders elsewhere, though, have balked at charging high rates; in Bangladesh and Indonesia the main institutions keep interest rates below 50 percent per year, and typically around 30 percent (in economies with inflation at about 10 percent).

Why balk at high rates? Let us return to the principle of diminishing marginal returns to capital. Can all poorer borrowers really pay higher interest rates than richer households? An unspoken assumption made in figure 1.1 is that everything but capital is held constant; the analy-sis implicitly assumed that education levels, business savvy, commer-cial contacts, and access to other inputs are the same for rich and poor. If this is untrue (and it is hard to imagine it would be true), it is easy to see that entrepreneurs with less capital could have lower marginal returns than richer households. In this case, a poor individual would not be able to routinely pay very high interest rates. Some might, of course, but a considerable group would plausibly be screened out by high rates.

Even if we imagine, though, for the moment that both rich and poor were alike in these noncapital characteristics, the principle of diminish-ing marginal returns to capital may still not hold; this is because the pro-duction function may not be so "conveniently" concave. Figure 1.4, for example, shows a scenario where the production technology exhibits increasing returns to scale over a relevant range. Here, there may be larger profits per dollar invested by the larger-scale entrepreneur rela-tive to the returns generated by the entrepreneur with less capital.

Here, again, poorer households cannot pay for credit at high prices. This case has the feature that, without adequate financing, poorer entrepreneurs may never be able to achieve the required scale to compete with better-endowed entrepreneurs, yielding a credit-related poverty trap. The challenge taken up in Bangladesh and Indonesia has been to charge relatively low rates of interest (around 15-25 percent per year after inflation adjustments), while continuing to serve very poor clients and covering costs.

The programs in Bangladesh and Indonesia have also been strategic in their use of subsidies. Like other microfinance lenders, Compartamos received large start-up subsidies, as have most of the major microfinance institutions. Typical arguments for early subsidization echo "infant industry" arguments for protection found in the international trade literature. And, as found in such writings, there is fear that some of the "infants" will soon be getting a little long in the tooth. The Grameen Bank, for example, still takes advantages of subsidies twenty-five years after its start.

A different question is whether the anti-subsidy position is the right one—or, more precisely, whether it is the right position for all programs. Again, there is a parallel with trade theory. The strongly anti-protectionist sentiments that had characterized trade theory for decades (Bhagwati 1988) are now giving way to more nuanced approaches to globalization, with mainstream economists identifying cases that justify extended protection in the name of economic and social development (e.g., Krugman 1994; Rodrik 1997). So, too, with microfinance: Serious arguments are accumulating that suggest a role for ongoing subsidies if thoughtfully deployed. Of course, that is a big "if," and chapter 9 provides a guide through the thicket.

Sorting out the stories requires taking apart the "win-win" vision put forward by advocates within the donor community, and recognizing the great diversity of programs jostling under the microfinance tent. ASA's story, with which we started with the chapter, provides a pointed contrast to many other programs. In 1978 Shafiqual Choudhury started ASA as a small grassroots organization to provide legal aid and train-ing in villages, with the hope of raising the social consciousness of rural households. But in 1991, Choudhury and ASA took a very different turn. Instead of placing hope in consciousness-raising, the leaders of ASA decided that the way to most quickly raise the well-being of the rural poor was by providing banking services, and banking services only. ASA's stripped-down banking model makes profits in large part because of its self-imposed narrow mandate.

But other institutions started where ASA did and took a broader approach to microfinance. They can also count successes, but their bottom lines include improvements in health and education outcomes in addition to financial metrics. Like ASA, charitable organizations like BRAC, Catholic Relief Services, CARE, and Freedom from Hunger have become major microlenders, with missions that also include working to improve health conditions and to empower women. Latin America's *Pro Mujer* is a case in point. Pro Mujer adds education ses-sions on health topics to weekly bank meetings for customers. Freedom from Hunger's affiliates do so as well, and their evaluations show pos-itive impacts (relative to control groups) on breastfeeding practices, treatment of diarrhea in children, and rates of completed immuniza-tions (Dunford 2001). Bangladesh's BRAC is perhaps the most fully realized "integrated" provider, offering financial services along with schools, legal training, productive inputs, and help with marketing and business planning. If you are in Dhaka these days, for example, you can buy Aarong brand chocolate milk, which is produced by a BRAC dairy marketing affiliate. A different BRAC subsidiary produces Aarong brand textiles made by poor weavers, and still another sub-sidiary runs craft shops that sell the goods of microfinance clients.

The microfinance movement is thus populated by diverse institu-tions, some large and many small, some urban and some rural, some more focused on social change and others more focused on financial development. If the programs that are focusing on social change are cost-effectively achieving their goals, should we be concerned that part of their operation is subsidized? Should we be concerned that, to achieve financial success, Compartamos has had to charge very high interest rates—and that, while roughly 20 percent of its borrowers are poorer on average then their neighbors, most of its clients are less poor than their neighbors (Zeller, Wollni, and Shaman 2002)? It is not clear that there is only one correct answer to each of these questions—and, as we show, answers posed as simple, "universal" truths turn out to rest on strings of assumptions that need disentangling.

We focus on one important strand of these entangled assumptions in chapter 9. There, we describe the possibility for designing "smart sub-sidies." Doing so will mean making sure that institutions offer quality services that are better than those already available, while also paying close attention to the complicated incentives and constraints of insti-tutions and their staffs. The debate continues as to whether this is pos-sible and, if so, even desirable. Introducing a stronger economic frame will sharpen understandings, and in chapter 9 we analyze concepts behind the trade-offs between lending practices that maximize the depth of outreach (i.e., that serve a greater number of poorer clients) and those that aim to maximize the extent of outreach (those that serve more—but less poor—clients). The book closes by turning to a critical practical issue for microlenders: how to give staff members the appro-priate incentives to carry out their economic and social missions. In chapter 10 we draw lessons from agency theory and behavioral eco-nomics to describe and challenge conventional wisdom on good man-agement practices.

SUMMARY AND CONCLUSIONS

This chapter has set the scene for considering microfinance. We began by asking why "microfinance" is needed in the first place. Why don't existing markets take care of the problems already? Why doesn't capital today flow naturally from richer to poorer countries, and from more affluent individuals to poorer individuals? As described in greater detail in chapter 2, the problems largely hinge on market failures that stem from poor information, high transactions costs, and difficulties enforcing contracts.

Microfinance presents itself as an answer to these problems. It chal-lenges long-held assumptions about what poor households can and cannot achieve and, more broadly, shows the potential for innovative contracts and institutions to improve conditions in low-income com-munities. Microfinance is a clear improvement over the development banks that emerged in the 1960s, but the implicit "promise" to achieve complete financial self-reliance in short order has been far from ful-filled. And we question whether it should have been a promise in the first place. We have described institutions like Mexico's Compartamos that have pioneered the path toward commercialization by charging very high interest rates. We have described Bangladesh's ASA, which has kept a close eye on cost efficiency (and thus has managed to keep interest rates relatively low) and has approached financial self-sufficiency while keeping social objectives in clear view. And we have also described institutions like Bangladesh's BRAC that work with expanded mandates to provide schools, clinics, and marketing services along with financial services. They too may have a role. Can poverty be most effectively reduced by providing financial services alone? Or can the integrated provision of "complementary" services deliver important added benefits at reasonable costs?

Bold visions have taken the movement this far, and strong, clear ideas are needed to carry the movement forward. Reaching 100 million people (as practitioners hope to do by the time this book is first pub-lished) is impressive, but as the leaders of the movement are quick to point out, this is just a minority of those who lack access to efficient and reliable financial services at affordable interest rates.

In looking to the future, we will try to dispel microfinance "myths" and revisit ongoing debates in microfinance (particularly about how it works, which customers can be profitably served, and what is the appropriate role for subsidies). In the next chapters we set out ideas that will help evaluate experiences to date, frame debates, and point to new directions and challenges.

2

Why Intervene in Credit Markets?

INTRODUCTION

Policymakers throughout the world have actively tried to improve financial markets in poor regions, but often with disappointing results. As highlighted, good intentions repeatedly went awry as state-owned development banks mismanaged resources and interest rate restrictions prevented banks from operating viably in poor areas. Against this background, microfinance emerged as an especially prom-ising way to rethink banking for the poor.

Assessing the successes and failures of the early experiences—and, more important, thinking about newer ideas and innovations— requires clear understandings of the aims for intervening. Policymak-ers and practitioners often skip this beginning step in the hurry to get new programs started. But, as we show, the result is that debates remain unresolved about issues as basic as whether existing credit markets deserve any interventions at all. We believe that appropriately designed interventions can often help, and this chapter describes why. More generally, we aim to clarify principles to use when considering why and when microfinance works—and why and when it fails to achieve its promise. To help answer the questions, sections 2.3 and 2.4 describe common sources of financial market failure.

When markets fail, hardworking entrepreneurs cannot obtain all of the capital needed to run their businesses. As a result, they may turn to wage labor, stay in traditional farming, or take other paths that are less desirable and less profitable. Paulson and Townsend (2001) seek to understand who becomes an entrepreneur and why. Using a survey of 2,880 rural and semi-urban households in central and northeastern Thailand, Paulson and Townsend (2001, 2) find strong interests in entrepreneurship:

> One-third of households report that they would like to change occupations. Of the households who would like to change occupations, most would like to open a business. Many of these households report that they do not start businesses because they do not have the necessary funds. Among entrepreneurial house-holds, 54 percent report that their business would be more profitable if they could expand it. When asked why they do not undertake this profitable oppor-tunity, 56 percent of households report that they do not have enough money to do so. Both the formation of new businesses and the way that existing busi-nesses are run appears to be affected by financial constraints.

The costs of those financial constraints are suggested by the finding that the average annual income of business owners in the sample is three times higher than that of non–business owners. Business owners may, of course, also have more relevant skills than non–business owners. If that is so, the comparison overstates the advantage that an average person would gain by switching from farming to business. But the Thai data set is rich with measures for talent, and Paulson and Townsend find that, even after accounting for entrepreneurial ability, poorer households are less likely to start new businesses. They thus argue that the income difference is not explained away by a talent dif-ference, leaving credit rationing as the chief candidate. In principle, microlenders like Thailand's Bank of Agriculture and Agricultural Cooperatives (BAAC) can, as a result, play a pivotal role in expanding opportunities for poor but talented households.

Studies that directly measure financial constraints thus give one impetus for the microfinance movement. For others, merely knowing the high interest rates charged by moneylenders is enough to bring calls that "something must be done!" We argue, though, that just seeing high informal-sector interest rates is insufficient. Instead, determining whether there is an important niche for microfinance requires under-standing how markets work and how the informal sector fills gaps— and how and where markets and the informal sector come up short. This chapter describes rationales for interevention, common sources of market failure, and some simple possibilities (short of microfinance) to improve matters.

Section 2.2 considers economies without microfinance. In particular, we describe evidence on moneylenders and what they do. Since an important rationale for microfinance is that it improves on the status quo, we first assess the existing landscape of informal credit. Are mon-eylenders really exploitative? Will squeezing them out make matters better or worse? Why might it seem that microfinance can do better?

We focus both on the efficiency of outcomes and on their implications for the fair distribution of resources. Sections 2.3 and 2.4 turn to prob-lems faced by commercial banks that hope to lend in low-income communities. This is the other part of the existing financial landscape, although the scene is notable often for the absence of commercial banking rather than its presence. In providing the basic analytics of adverse selection (section 2.3) and moral hazard (section 2.4), we provide two important reasons why formal-sector commercial lenders have such a low profile in low-income communities. We employ both algebra and numerical examples to make the points, and we return to the same analytical structures in chapter 4 to explain why microfinance can help. Some of the arguments should be clear without the math, but we use the analytics to make several points that we don't think are so obvious. The most important is that raising interest rates is not always profitable for banks working in poor communities—and this can impose a major bind on commercial banks trying to expand access. We show that profitability can be undermined because raising interest rates can exacerbate incentive problems in lending. Without added measures to retain good incentives—such as those provided by microfinance con-tracts—commercial banks will understandably avoid places where col-lateral is scarce and operating costs are high.

RATIONALES FOR INTERVENTION

It is easy to see why moneylenders are viewed as being exploitative: Borrowers are typically poor and have few other options to get capital, while interest rates are typically well above those found in the formal banking sector. Moneylenders are routinely characterized as exploita-tive monopolists who systematically squeeze the poor. The poor, for their part, are seen as vulnerable, driven to pay usurious rates out of desperation. The enmity is long-standing. In ancient Babylon, Hammurabi's Code tolerated moneylenders and allowed interest charges, but ancient Greeks and Romans—including Plato and Aris-totle—inveighed against moneylenders and the very act of charging interest on loans (Vermeersch 1912). The Qur'an carries clear injunctions against charging interest, while the Old Testament is ambivalent. The New Testament is generally mute on the topic, although canonical laws in the Middle Ages took strong stands against moneylending (with an exception made for Jews). In ancient India, moneylenders were tolerated, but the early Hindu scriptures prescribe set interest rates that should be charged according to a borrower's caste, ranging from 2 percent per year for Brahmins to 60 percent for traders (Reddy 1999).

High interest rates continue to worry observers today. Singh (1968), for example, surveys seven moneylenders in a village close to Amritsar in the Punjab region of India, finding annualized interest rates from 134 to 159 percent—rates that were far higher than commercial bank interest rates. In Thailand, Siamwalla et al. (1990) find typical informal sector annualized rates of 60 percent (compared to 12–14 percent from BAAC). Siamwalla et al. also report rates that are as high as 120 percent in Thailand's remote areas. In the market town of Chambar in Pakistan, Aleem (1990) finds interest rates varying from 18 to 200 percent, with an average of just under 70 percent per year; in contrast, local banks in the region charged 12 percent per year. In Ghana, Malawi, Nigeria, and Tanzania, Steel et al. (1997) find moneylender interest rates at least 50 percentage points higher than formal sector rates.

In present-day low-income communities, moneylenders remain an important part of the financial landscape, with just as much debate about their roles. One of the hopes for microfinance is that it will facil-itate the start of new businesses and the adoption of new practices. Moneylenders, though, have been accused of doing the opposite. For example, Bhaduri (1973) pins India's technological stagnation in agri-culture at the feet of moneylenders who double as landlords. He argues that, in the latter role, moneylender-landlords discourage the adoption of new agricultural technologies that would improve the lot of poor farmers since, ultimately, it would make farmers richer and reduce the demand for loans. By keeping farmers perpetually in debt, Bhaduri argues, moneylenders strengthen their bargaining power in order to tighten the squeeze. According to this view, exploitation is possible since moneylenders have local monopoly power; that power is "pro-tected" because potential competitors lack the necessary information and connections to break into local markets. This kind of argument is commonly heard, and undermining the "exploitative moneylender" became a central goal of credit market strategies in India and other developing countries (e.g., RBI, cited in Bell 1990).

But things are not so simple. Getting rid of moneylenders could actu-ally make matters worse for villagers if the moneylenders provide valuable and unique services. After all, moneylenders can charge high interest rates because at least some villagers are willing to pay them. Moreover, the high interest rates may largely reflect the high costs of doing business (i.e., the costs associated with screening the borrow-ers, monitoring the use of loans, and enforcing repayments). Those costs may not be small, particularly when potential borrowers do not offer seizable collateral, and when legal enforcement mechanisms are weak. Braverman and Guasch (1989), for example, estimate that the administrative costs of handling small loans range from 15 to 40 percent of loan size.

So how and when can credit market interventions be justified? Econ-omists focus on two features of markets above all else—their efficiency and their effects on the distribution of resources. The first issue relates to "how large the pie is" and the second to "how the pie is sliced." Understanding both and making judgments about interventions requires a clear reckoning of cost structures and the nature of markets; the mere presence of moneylenders is not evidence enough.

Efficiency

Let's consider production loans; villagers, say, want to borrow to buy sewing machines to start small tailoring businesses. Maximizing effi-ciency does not imply that everyone in a village should have access to credit. Instead, only the most productive villagers should get access; those with mediocre prospects should be excluded (at least if efficiency is the sole criterion). Specifically, all villagers should be given the chance to buy sewing machines if (and only if) their expected returns are greater than the cost of capital.

Imagine that it costs 20 cents per year for a bank to acquire each dollar of capital (say, the bank has to pay 10 cents per dollar per year in interest to depositors and then cover 10 cents per dollar per year in administrative costs); then loans should be given to all borrowers who can take the capital and earn more than 20 cents per dollar. In this way, the total amount of funds generated in the economy expands; the size of the pie increases. In contrast, lending the money to someone who can only generate a return of 15 percent makes the pie smaller.

The ideas can be extended easily to accommodate risk. So far we have assumed that borrowers' returns to investing are given with cer-tainty. But more typically returns may be sometimes high, sometimes low, and most often somewhere in between. In the preceding scenario, we would want to lend only to those individuals with *expected* returns greater than 20 cents per dollar. If, for example, prospective borrowers earn 40 cents per dollar 75 percent percent of the time and zero the remaining 25 percent of the time, their expected returns are 30 cents per dollar (75% · $0.40 + 25% · $0), and they should be funded since capital costs are just 20 cents per dollar. This is ex ante efficiency, cap-turing the fact that judgments are made before knowing the actual out-comes of investments. If the individual only made positive profits half the time, it would still be ex ante efficient to lend to them (50% · $0.40 + 50% · $0 = $0.20). But if hypothetical success rates were any lower than 50 percent, it is no longer ex ante efficient to lend to them since capital costs are higher than expected returns.

No matter whether monopolists are exploitative or not, it can be inef-ficient to have them around. In the case of credit markets, monopolists can charge interest rates well above their marginal cost of capital (which we will assume is still 20 cents per dollar per year). So rather than charging an interest rate of 20 percent (as a competitive bank would charge), moneylenders might restrict the quantity lent and charge all borrowers, say, one dollar for each dollar that is lent (a 100 percent annual interest rate); the remaining 80 cents per dollar goes into the moneylender's pocket. When this is the case, only the exceedingly productive villagers can afford to borrow to finance their investments;

a wide range of otherwise worthy investment projects will go unfunded. The pie shrinks relative to how large it could potentially be in the absence of monopolistic practices.

Do high interest rates imply monopoly and inefficiency? Merely seeing interest rates of 100 percent does not imply that moneylenders are monopolists; the rates may instead genuinely reflect how costly it is for moneylenders to acquire capital, to transact business, monitor clients, and accommodate risk. When default rates are high, money-lenders may have to charge a lot merely to stay afloat. If this is the case, and if the moneylender is the only possible source of capital, the cause of efficiency will be furthered by only lending to the most productive villagers.

Adams (1984) argues that this is indeed the case: Rural credit markets are far more competitive than typically imagined, and he cites studies that show that moneylenders are charging rates in accord with their transactions costs and risks. If Adams is right and the market is truly competitive, microfinance providers will do little to improve access to credit, unless they can figure out a way to cut costs relative to moneylenders. Even worse, if microfinance providers are inappropriately subsidized, they may squeeze out moneylenders, worsening overall access to financial services for poor households: Good intentions will have had perverse consequences (Adams and von Pischke 1992). So sorting out the debate about moneylenders and market structure matters to whether supporting microfinance improves efficiency.

Bottomley (1975) uses a much-cited hypothetical example to argue that moneylender rates are plausibly competitive, and Basu (1997, 268) gives a comparison of two moneylenders in this spirit. Imagine one moneylender in the city and one in the countryside. Assuming away transactions costs and capital costs for now, the forces of competition will push the expected returns of the two moneylenders to be equal in a competitive setting. The first moneylender charges 10 percent per year to her urban customers who are so reliable that the chance of default is nil; the moneylender's expected net return is thus 10 percent. The second moneylender expects that half of his customers will default. His expected net return is [(1 + interest rate) · (1 - probability of default) - 1]. In order to do as well as the first moneylender, the second must charge at least 120 percent per year since (1 + 120%) · (1 - 50%) - 1 = 10%. Thus, if default rates are high, moneylender interest rates don't look usurious after all. (Looked at a different way, the example shows that default rates have to be 50 percent in order to explain interest rates of 120 percent in this setting.)

This stylized example relies on the assumption that moneylenders can recover nothing at all from those who default, and it ignores oppor-tunity costs and transactions costs. To resolve debates, we need data. A broad range of careful case studies show that typical default rates are nowhere close to 50 percent, but transactions costs and opportunity costs are high. Singh's (1968) study found, for example, that in 1 of 45 transactions, a moneylender lost the full principle, but in every other case it was recovered. In 29 of the cases some part of the interest was not recovered, but this could explain only 23–43 percentage points of the overall interest rates charged. In Pakistan, Aleem (1990) similarly finds that loans and interest are not always paid on time, but the cost is typically a matter of several months of delay in retrieving funds rather than a full loss. Similarly, a survey in Ghana showed that 70 to 80 percent of informal lenders had perfect loan recovery rates in 1990 and 1991, and in Nigeria, although moneylenders had delinquency rates of 14 percent, all were confident that loans would be fully paid within three months of the due date (Steel et al. 1997).

Singh argues that the high interest rates are mainly due to high opportunity costs, not to monopoly profits. With capital so scarce, he argues, if moneylenders invested their money directly in farm enter-prises they would earn net returns that average 77 percent per year. Once the costs of loan distribution are added in (14–31 percentage points), the residual left over for "monopoly profit" averages just 9 per-centage points. This is far from exploitation, but much hinges on how "opportunity costs" are interpreted. The high (77 percent) annual returns that the moneylenders can expect on their own farm invest-ments may themselves be partly due to monopoly profits (since capital is scarce in general). Moreover, if borrowers use the funds for farm investments, they must be able to earn returns that are roughly twice as high as the moneylender just to be able to pay back loans with inter-est rates that average 143 percent per year. It should not be surprising then that all of the borrowers in Singh's sample are borrowing to finance consumption needs (often at desperate times), not to finance production.

A larger issue concerns the structure of the market. Adams (1984) argues that markets are competitive since there is relatively free entry by locals (if not by outside banks). A simple test of this assertion is to check whether the introduction of new funds into an area drives down interest rates (as it should if markets are truly competitive). Siamwalla et al. (1990) do this and find no evidence of falling informal-sector rates in their sample from Thailand.

Aleem (1990) suggests that the apparent confusion may derive from a conflation of "free entry" and "competition." In Chambar market in Pakistan, for example, he too finds free entry, but the market structure better resembles "monopolistic competition" rather than perfect competition. In monopolistic competition, lenders segment markets, each handling a small share of the overall market. Specialization by geog-raphy or other characteristics give lenders local monopolies that allow them to make profits in the short term. At the same time, there may be free entry into the market, so lenders may have difficulty maintaining profits over the long run. To pursue this line, Aleem argues that only considering average costs misses the story. If markets are truly com-petitive, interest rates should be driven down to the marginal cost of lending—that is, the cost of lending an extra 100 rupees, which is typ-ically below the average cost.

In Aleem's sample, interest rates average 79 percent and average costs (after taking into account risk, opportunity costs, and transactions costs) also average 79 percent. Aleem estimates that the cost of lending an extra 100 rupees, though, is about 48 percent, which is considerably lower than the average cost. Steel et al. (1997) also provide evidence that average costs are much higher than marginal costs in surveys of moneylenders in Ghana, Malawi, Nigeria, and Tanzania. Most of the costs incurred by the moneylenders surveyed in Africa involve the pre-screening of clients. Once that is taken care of, administrative costs of handling loans—the largest element of the marginal cost of lending—is small (equal to only 0.6%–3.2% of loan amounts). In perfectly com-petitive markets, interest rates should be driven down to the marginal cost, but clearly this has not happened in these cases.

The fact that marginal costs are below average costs is a hallmark of monopolistic competition, as is the fact that average costs match inter-est rates and that entry into the market is relatively free for insiders. In Chambar market, Aleem describes a situation in which there are too many moneylenders serving too few clients. As a result, moneylend-ers have difficulty covering the fixed costs of lending, and interest rates stay high because returns to scale cannot be reaped. Although there is no evidence of exploitation of a kind stressed by Bhaduri (1977), the market is inefficient and, in principle at least, interventions could yield a larger pie. Robinson (2001, 170–171) concludes that "if much of informal moneylending can be explained by a form of monopolistic competition, then it can be argued that banks can cost-effectively gain reliable infor-mation about borrowers that is far broader in scope than the informa-tion to which informal lenders have access." The reason, she suggests, is that moneylenders only really get to know their own small segments of the market (in contrast to the claim that moneylenders have easy access to local information generally). Microfinance institutions, on the other hand, aim to serve many clients on a large scale, pushing exist-ing barriers out of the way as they proceed.

Before leaving these issues, we offer one more comment on Adams (1984). Let's accept—for the sake of argument—that it really does cost the moneylender one dollar to lend an additional dollar; the money-lender then just breaks even when charging 100 percent interest rates. He's not a greedy monopolist after all; he's merely a hardworking entrepreneur just scraping by. But readers would be too quick if they then concluded that interventions will not improve efficiency:

Efficiency must also be judged relative to what *could be*, not just by the current state of affairs. If a microfinance institution could find new ways to lend to those same villagers and charge 25, 50, or 75 percent, efficiency is improved: More projects get funded and the hardworking moneylender goes out of business in the name of progress. The promise is that microfinance can indeed do better than what exists.

Distribution

Considering distribution is another matter. Economists have histori-cally assumed that there is a trade-off between reaching distributional goals and efficiently allocating resources—the steady economic decline of the socialist economies is just the most dramatic recent example of the trade-off. But in a world with limited financial markets, there will not necessarily be a trade-off: Spreading access to financial services can both open opportunities for the poor and increase aggregate produc-tive efficiency.

One source of inequity is discrimination on the basis of race, gender, ethnicity, social class, or religion. Such discrimination manifests itself in credit markets, just as it does in labor markets. And when markets are characterized by monopoly, the "disciplining" nature of the market, imperfect as it may be, is even more restricted. Overcoming discrimi-nation will yield a more just society—and possibly a richer one if excluded individuals have worthy investment projects that are going unfunded.

In principle, then, taking resources from privileged households and using them to subsidize the financial access of excluded households can improve both equality and efficiency. As described earlier, policy-makers need to be careful, though, since as the experience of large, sub-sidized state banks showed, some ostensibly pro-poor credit market interventions can be so inefficient that, in the end, everyone might lose.

There may also be contexts in which concerns with efficiency and distribution run in opposite directions. To see this, let's return to the monopolist moneylender. We have assumed previously (implicitly) that moneylenders charge all borrowers the same rate of interest. Moneylenders will hold back loans in order to maximize revenues, pushing up average interest rates in the local market. The outcome is inefficient since the quantity of capital is restricted. But consider the case in which a savvy moneylender is able to perfectly adjust interest rates to each client's demand patterns. In this case, the moneylender will not restrict quantities in order to prop up prices. Instead, the moneylender will lend "efficient" quantities but charge rates that extract all of the "consumer surplus" from the clients. The savvy lender will raise interest rates just to the point at which each client is indifferent between borrowing or not, and the moneylender will then reduce the price by a small notch to convince clients to borrow.

The strategy maximizes the moneylender's potential for exploita-tion, since all of the borrower's benefits are siphoned off. But notice that it's not "inefficient" in the strict sense. Indeed, the moneylender is most successful if all productive borrowers get ample credit—as long as the moneylender can then grab the benefits. The pie grows, but the borrowers' slices shrink. The moral is that even fully efficient informal markets can be improved by pro-poor interventions.

The emerging evidence suggests important pro-poor impacts of microfinance, and in chapter 6 we return to issues of equity and dis-tribution in the context of subsidies. The rest of this chapter focuses on the problems that formal sector banks traditionally have when lending in poor regions, and it is efficiency that will be our first con-cern for now.

AGENCY PROBLEMS

Modern economics has made great strides in understanding the so-called agency problems that are ubiquitous in economic life. Consider a borrower and a lender. The borrower has a project, but no money to finance it; she must then turn to the lender. Here, the agency problem refers to the lender's inability to observe the borrower's characteristics (e.g., project riskiness), to observe the borrower's effort, or to observe her profits. These information problems create inefficiencies, and microfinance can be seen as one attempt to overcome them. In this case, the tension involves a "principal" (the lender) trying to do business with an "agent" (the borrower).

The information problems arise at three distinct stages. First, prior to extending a loan, the lender may have little if any reliable informa-tion about the quality of the borrower. Sometimes a bit of quick scout-ing around by a loan officer can yield the required information, but too often the necessary background research on borrowers is prohibitively costly. Better information can prevent the lender from mistakenly extending a loan to a "low quality" borrower without adequately accounting for the risk involved. Second, once the loan has been granted, the lender does not entirely know how the borrower will use the resources. Will the borrower work hard to ensure that the invest-ments are successful? Or might the borrower work less hard than he or she would if the project was entirely self-financed? Third, once investment returns have been realized, the lender may not be able to verify the magnitude of the returns. It is tempting then for the borrower to claim to have had bad luck (and to ask for a reprieve in paying the loan) when in fact the investment was highly profitable. Having infor-mation about the borrower's true profits would allow the lender to be able to claim full repayment and impose sanctions that could poten-tially prevent future misconduct by the borrower.

The absence of formal credit institutions in village economies is often attributed to these kinds of agency problems. They are accentuated when individuals cannot offer seizable collateral, and when legal enforcement mechanisms are weak. In what follows we describe the problems faced by a typical commercial bank, and in chapters 4 and 5 we describe microfinance solutions.

Limited Liability

Traditional banks face a series of problems because they come from outside the communities in which they seek to work. Clients have no inherent loyalty to outside banks, and lenders have little information about potential clients. Traditional banks thus tend to require collat-eral: "no collateral, no business." Before microfinance came along, this usually just meant "no business." The problem faced by traditional banks is that, on the one hand, they lack good mechanisms to disburse and collect funds profitably in poor areas; on the other hand, they often have abundant resources to lend.

De Soto (2000) has argued that the solution is to tackle the root of the problem by establishing formal titles to land and clear property rights over assets that make it easier for the poor to offer collateral. But even with clearer property rights, lenders may have difficulty seizing assets from the very poor for social and legal reasons. Steel et al. (1997, 822), for example, find that in their African surveys "it is much easier for a landlord-lender to make productive use of pledged farmland indefi-nitely than for a bank to seize it." Seizing assets from the poor can be particularly difficult since taking resources away from households that are already poor runs against the anti-poverty missions of many micro-finance banks. It also may run into stiff community opposition.

It is thus possible for very poor households to have adequate collateral—and to be willing to use it to secure loans—but for banks to neverthe-less to be wary of the offer.

In the analysis that follows, we assume that liability is limited: Bor-rowers cannot repay more than their current income. The task of micro-finance is thus to solve the information problems or to find mechanisms that compensate for borrowers' lack of collateral—or both.

Adverse Selection

We first analyze the agency problem that arises before the contractual arrangements actually take place. This is the "adverse selection" problem. Stiglitz and Weiss (1981) pioneered a family of adverse selec-tion models in which banks lack good information about the riskiness of the borrowers' projects. Banks, the argument goes, are therefore unable to discriminate against risky borrowers and interest rates become exceedingly high. Such rates in turn drive worthy borrowers out of the credit market. This is a market "imperfection" since worthy borrowers do not participate in the credit market when efficiency would suggest that they should. The extent of the imperfection is mag-nified by the extent of limited liability. Note that the concern here is with the *inherent* riskiness of borrowers. Some may simply be more prudent, more conservative, better insured. Others may be risk-loving, may be poorly disciplined, or may face competing claims on their funds.

We illustrate the mechanism with a simple example. Consider an economy populated by individuals who seek to maximize profits. Each individual can invest $1 in a one-period project. Individuals do not have wealth of their own, so they need to borrow to carry out their investment projects. Potential borrowers are heterogeneous: They can either be inherently "safe" or "risky." A safe borrower invests $1 and obtains revenue y with certainty. A risky borrower invests $1 and obtains revenue y with probability p, where $0 < p < 1$. When they are lucky, risky borrowers earn higher profits than safe borrowers. But when risky borrowers are not successful (which happens with com-plementary probability $1 - p$), they earn zero and cannot repay the loan. For simplicity we assume that both types have identical *expected* returns; that is, we suppose that riskier borrowers do better than safe borrowers when lucky *(y > y)* but that they do equivalently when returns are adjusted for risk *(py > y)*.

Assume that the lender is a competitive bank committed to breaking even. The assumption allows us to focus on problems raised by the lack of information and collateral without having to worry about prob-lems created by monopoly as well. Under competition, at minimum the bank tries to cover its gross cost, *k*, per unit lent. This gross cost includes the full cost of raising money from depositors or donor agencies: for every dollar lent, *k* > $1 since the bank must account for the loan principal itself as well as bearing transactions costs and paying interest to depositors, donors, or whoever supplied the capital. Suppose that even the low-revenue gross outcome exceeds the gross cost of capital (i.e., *y*>*k* and *p y* > *k)*, so that investment by either bor-rower is efficient in expectation. We can then see that if the population was made up of *only* safe borrowers, the competitive bank will set the gross interest rate (i.e., interest plus principal) exactly equal to *k* because safe borrowers always repay; there is no risk, and competitive pressures drive the bank's interest rate down to its marginal costs. At this rate, the bank just breaks even and the borrower keeps a net profit of *(y - k)*.

Things get more complicated when we consider the risky population too. When risky borrowers also apply for loans, the bank will want to charge them interest rates higher than *k* in order to compensate for the added risk. The complication arises when the bank cannot ade-quately distinguish between safe and risky borrowers beforehand. If the lender only knows that a portion *q* of the loan applications come from safe borrowers and that a portion 1 - *q* comes from risky bor-rowers, the break-even gross interest rate of the lender will increase from *k to Rb.*

Now we have to figure out what that rate *Rb* is—and what it means for the economy. The starting point is that for a lender hoping to just cover costs, the gross interest rate R_b must be set so that the *expected* return from lending to a borrower of an unknown type is exactly equal to *k*, the bank's gross cost of funds: $[\,q + (1 - q)\,p]\,Rb = k$. Flipping the equation around, we find that the gross interest rate charged by the bank in order to just break even will be

$$R_b = k/[q + (1 - q)p]. \qquad (2.1)$$

A bit of algebra shows that the new break-even rate Rb will exceed k by an amount $A = [k\ (1 - q)(1 - p)] / [q + (1 - q)\ p]$, so we can simply write $Rb = k + A$. Now, all borrowers, whether safe or risky, must pay this higher rate since the bank is unable to tell who is who.

It's not surprising that adding risky borrowers into the mix will cause the bank to raise interest rates. The problem is that R_b may rise so high that safe borrowers are discouraged from applying for loans. That would be inefficient since, by assumption, both the risky and the safe borrowers have worthy projects and, in the best of all worlds, they should both be funded. The bottom line is that the lender's lack of information on who is safe and who is risky leads to a situation where the lender may not be able to find an interest rate that both (a) appeals to all creditworthy customers and (b) allows the bank to cover its expected costs.

A Numerical Example

Let's take another look at adverse selection, this time using hypothet-ical data. Again, we assume that there are two types of borrowers, safe and risky, and the lender can't tell who is who. The lender, however, knows the fraction of safe types in the population. Again, all borrow-ers are risk neutral and neither has collateral to secure their loans.

And, again, the lender is in a competitive environment, so it simply tries to break even. The lender's net cost of capital is 40 cents per dollar lent, so it needs to get back at least that much from borrowers on average (after accounting for the probability of default). A project requires $100 of investment and takes one month to complete. If the prospective borrower chooses not to borrow, he can earn a wage of $45 for the month (his "reservation wage"). In the first scenario, let's assume that safe borrowers succeed all of the time and earn gross revenues of $2 for each dollar borrowed (i.e., before paying back the loan with interest). Their expected gross revenues are thus $200, and efficiency is achieved if $200 is greater than the value of the loan to be repaid ($100) plus the net cost of capital ($40) plus the opportunity cost of the borrower's labor ($45). It is: A $15 expected social surplus is gen-erated. The borrower can generate enough income to pay back the bank and still have more left over than he would make working for a wage.

Table 2.1: Numerical example: Base data

The economic environment			
Lender's cost of capital		*$40 per month per $100 loan*	
Borrowers'		*opportunity cost (wage)*	
$45 per		*month*	
Fraction of safe borrowers in the population		*50%*	
	Gross revenue if successful	**Probability of success**	**Expected gross revenue**
Scenario 1			
Safe type	$200	100%	$200
Risky type	$222	90%	$200
Scenario 2			
Safe type	$200	100%	$200
Risky type	$267	75%	$200

Risky borrowers invest in riskier projects. When they do well, they earn revenues of $222, but when they do badly (which is 10 percent of the time) they earn zero. Their expected gross return is thus also $200 (0.90·$222), and the expected social surplus is again $15.

Clearly, efficiency is enhanced if both safe and risky types are given loans—since both have projects that will earn more by investing than could be earned working for a wage. Will the bank offer them loans? If half the population is safe and the other half is risky, the average probability of success in the population is 0.95 (= 0.5 0.90 + 0.5 1.00), and the interest rate charged by the bank has to be at least 47.4 percent to cover capital costs and principal (0.95 · 147.4% ~ 140%). At a net inter-est rate of 47.4 percent both types will indeed borrow, since the expected net returns are better than what can be earned from working for a wage. For the safe borrower, ($200 - $147.4) ~ $52.6 > $45, and for the risky borrower, 0.90·($222 - $147.4) ~ $67.4 > $45. The calculation reflects that neither borrower repays interest or principal when he fails. Risky borrowers clearly do better here (at least in expectation), but safe borrowers at least do better than they would working in the wage job. In effect, the safe borrowers are cross-subsidizing their risky neighbors. Still, it beats working for a wage.

The example so far shows that the mere fact that the lender is poorly informed does not necessarily create an inefficiency. Asymmetric infor-mation does have distributional consequences (the safer borrowers are the worse for it), but there is no credit rationing and thus no pre-sumption that interventions will automatically make the pie bigger.

Now let's see what happens if we keep everything exactly the same, except we make the risky borrowers even more risky. In this second scenario, we'll assume that risky borrowers succeed only 75 percent of the time, but they earn revenues of $267 when they do well. As a result, the risky individuals again expect to gross $200 (= 0.75·$267) if they borrow. Since everything else has been kept the same, a $15 social surplus is again generated when either safe or risky individuals borrow.

But the lender's situation is now very different—it faces more risk. The average probability of success in the population is now just 0.875 (= 0.5 · 0.75 + 0.5 1.00), and the interest rate charged by the lender has to rise to at least 60 percent to cover expected capital costs and princi-pal (0.875·$160% ~ $140). At an interest rate of 60 percent, the risky individual will still want to borrow since 0.75 · ($267 - $160) ~ $80 > $45. But the safe individual will depart for a wage job; for him, ($200 - $160) = $40 < $45.

The situation is no longer efficient, since both safe and risky individuals should still borrow, but the bank cannot charge an interest rate that works for both. If the lender could charge different types of borrowers different interest rates, the situation might improve, but the lender lacks the information with which to tell who is who.

Once the safe individuals depart, the risky individuals are the only ones left as borrowers. The lender sees what has happened and is forced to raise interest rates even further in order to cover costs (since there is no longer any cross-subsidization by the safe individuals). Interest rates rise to 86.7 percent, which allows the lender to just break even and still gives the risky individuals reason to borrow (0.75[$267 - $187]) = $60 > $45, but they don't do quite as well as before.

The simple example shows that when a bank lacks information, the market may cease to be efficient. Microfinance presents itself as one way to address the inefficiencies, broaden access to markets, and improve distribution as well.

MORAL HAZARD

Moral hazard in lending refers to situations where lenders cannot observe either the effort made or action taken by the borrower, or the realization of project returns. As in the previous example, we assume that borrowers are protected by limited liability so they are prevented from repaying more than their current cash flows. In short, borrowers have no collateral.

Ex Ante Moral Hazard

Ex ante moral hazard relates to the idea that unobservable actions or efforts are taken by borrowers after the loan has been disbursed but *before* project returns are realized. In fact, these actions affect the probability of a good realization of returns.

In this section we show why the combination of limited liability and moral hazard can lead to inefficient outcomes. As in section 2.3, each individual can invest $1 in a one-period project. Individuals do not have wealth of their own, so they need to borrow to carry out their investment projects. Suppose that once a particular borrower has obtained a loan, she can either expend effort and thereby make posi-tive profits y with certainty, or not work at all, in which case she makes positive profits with probability $p < 1$ only.

We denote by c the cost of effort for the borrower (think of a nonmonetary cost, e.g., an opportu-nity cost of not earning a wage on a landlord's property). Suppose also that the required gross repayment (again, principal plus interest) to be made to the lender is equal to R, where $R > k$. Again, k is the cost of a unit of capital. Because of limited liability, the amount R will only be paid by the borrower if the borrower earns profits.

Now consider the borrower's decision about whether or not to expend effort on the project. Her net return if she expends effort is

$(y - R) - c$. If she doesn't work hard, the expected net return (accounting for uncertainty about the likelihood of succeeding) is $p(y - R)$. In this second case, she does not have to bear the cost c, but she only succeeds p percent of the time.

Comparing the two scenarios, the borrower is likely to expend effort only if $(y - R) - c > p\ (y - R)$. Solving the equa-tion yields a relationship in terms of the gross interest rate: $R < y - [c/(1-p)]$. That is, if the gross interest rate is raised above $y - [c/(1 - p)]$, the borrower will no longer have an incentive to expend effort. Instead she will take her chances and simply hope for a good outcome. If she's unlucky, it is the bank that will suffer the consequences of the default. So, if the bank wants to reduce its risk, it will have to cap gross inter-est rates. Just as we saw in the case of adverse selection in section 2.3, raising interest rates does not necessarily increase profits.

Imagine now that the bank's costs of funds k are such that $y - c > k$. In other words, when the borrower expends effort (and thus bears cost c), there is still a net return that is higher than the bank's cost of capital. In the perfect world, the borrower should then be given a loan, and the borrower will expend the effort necessary for success. Borrowing is ex ante efficient, tc use the economics terminology.

The problem, of course, is that the bank has no way to force the borrower to take the required effort. And it may be that the bank's cost of capital k, while smaller than $(y - c)$, is at the same time greater than $[y - c/(1 - p)]$. Since the bank needs to charge a gross interest rate at least as large as k in order to break even, it will have to set $R > [y - c/(1 - p)]$, and, as we saw previously, at that level the borrower will decide to take no effort. The bank thus knows that if it sets the interest rate at a level high enough to cover capital costs, it would lose money since the borrower would shirk. The bank in this situation thus decides not to lend money at all. If only the borrower could somehow commit not to shirk, the bank would make the loan. But the commitment would not be credi-ble without collateral or some other added incentive device. This is one sense in which poverty begets poverty.

If the borrower had private wealth to use as collateral, the preceding "credit rationing" problem might be avoided since the existence of collateral would relax the "limited liability constraint". Threatened with the possible loss of collateral, the borrower finds it more "costly" to shirk. For example, let w denote the borrower's collateral and suppose that w is less than k; then if the project fails (which happens with probability $1 - p$), the borrower loses w.

The bank gets w, which is not enough to fully cover the loan loss, but which can still help with the incentive problem. The borrower's incentive constraint now becomes $(y - R) - c > p\,(y - R) + (1 - p)(-w)$.

This says that her net return when expending effort should be greater than her expected return when shirking—which now takes into account that collateral is for-feited $(1 - p)$ percent of the time. Rearranging gives a ceiling for the largest feasible gross interest rate that the bank would charge: $R < y + w - c/(1 - p)$.

Thanks to the collateral, this interest rate is higher than the previous ceiling (derived previously). If the collateral were valu-able enough—namely, if $k < w$—the bank would be able to set interest rates at levels that always allow borrowing. One challenge of microfinance is to remedy the absence of collateral and use innovative mech-anisms as a substitute.

Ex Post Moral Hazard

Another source of credit market imperfection is often referred to as "ex post moral hazard" or the "enforcement problem." The term *ex post* refers to difficulties that emerge after the loan is made and the borrower has invested.

Even if those steps proceed well, the borrower may decide to "take the money and run" once project returns are realized. This kind of situation arises either when the lender does not fully observe the borrowers' profits (so the borrower can falsely claim a loss and default), or, when having observed returns, the lender cannot enforce repayment by the borrower.

In the extreme case where no repayment can be legally enforced ex post (e.g., because project returns are not verifiable), there is no point in making any loan unless the lender can rely on some kind of threat not to refinance a defaulting bor-rower. However, the threat may not pack much power when poten-tial borrowers can easily migrate and change identity; this poses yet another challenge for microlenders.

To be more explicit about the notion of ex post moral hazard, let us suppose that $1 is invested and the project is always successful, yield-ing revenue y with certainty.

Let us also assume that (1) the borrower has private wealth w, which she can use as collateral for the loan and which the lender is allowed to confiscate in case of default, (2) the gross interest rate R to the lender is fixed so that the lender breaks even when financing the extra cost of the project (once again, the gross interest rate includes principal plus interest), and (3) default is "verified" with prob-ability s. The question then is: When will the borrower choose to repay her loan? Her ex post payoff if she repays is $y + w - R$. Her payoff if she does not repay is $(1 - s)(y + w) + sy$.

The first term captures what happens if she is able to "take the money and run"; in this case, which happens with probability $(1 - s)$, she keeps her net returns and her wealth without having to pay interest charges. The second term cap-tures what happens when the bank catches her and seizes the collat-eral; in this case, which happens with probability s, she gets away with her net returns but forfeits her collateral. Therefore, the borrower will take the money and run if and only if the following enforcement (incen-tive) constraint is satisfied: $y + w - R > (1 - s)(y + w) + sy$. A bit of algebra shows that the constraint is satisfied if $R < sw$. In other words, where ex post moral hazard is an issue, the gross interest rate cannot exceed the borrower's collateral multiplied by the probability that it will be seized. A borrower without collateral (i.e., with $w = 0$) cannot access outside finance at all, since $s \cdot 0 = 0$. Moreover, if the probability that the bank can seize the collateral is very low, the bank will also refuse to lend. As de Soto (2000) argues, improving property rights and the court systems that enforce those rights can thus be critical to the ability of poor borrowers to get loans.

LINKING TO LOCAL MARKETS: A POTENTIAL SOLUTION

Before getting to the next chapter, we consider one potential solution to some of the problems outlined so far. Agency theory explains a mis-match of resources and abilities. On one side, banks have funds to lend, but they lack adequate information and effective ways of enforcing contracts. On the other side, moneylenders, traders, and others who live and work in poor communities have the opposite problem: They have quite good information and enforcement mechanisms, but they l.ck adequate resources.

This section tackles the question, Why don't banks and moneylenders join forces? The prominent microfinance models involve wholly new institutions like Bangladesh's ASA or Bolivia's BancoSol that compete head-on with local lenders, but why go to all the trouble? Why don't banks simply hire moneylenders to be their agents? Why not just pay moneylenders (or other local actors) to disburse loans and collect payments for a fee?

Consider the *susu* collectors of West Africa described by Aryeetey and Steel (1995). In Ghana, *susu* collectors visit clients daily, collecting fixed installments ranging from 25¢ to $2.50. Most of the money they collect (on average $218 daily) is deposited in interest-bearing bank accounts, and a small amount is directly lent to clients as advances on savings. *Susu* collectors are thus already positioned between poor clients and commercial banks.

Although 60 percent of clients typically request advances, collectors say they can only give credit to 13 percent of their clients (Steel and Aryeetey 1994). Why not then employ *susu* collectors as loan officers for banks?

The idea has special appeal since *susu* collectors are trusted and knowledgeable about their clients' financial situations, while lacking the baggage of moneylenders. Moreover, Aryeetey and Steel estimate that *susu* collectors who are already engaged with the poten-tial borrowers would only face marginal costs of 3 percent of the loan amounts if they expanded lending. The idea has promise, but, as we show, the bank can end up circumventing one agency problem only to be faced with another even more difficult problem: how to get the col-lectors to honestly and reliably carry out the bank's wishes.

A simpler idea is to create a link to local lenders indirectly. The problem identified earlier is that local lenders lack resources. So, instead of directly hiring local agents, a bank could simply make funds available to moneylenders and other small-scale intermediaries with the expectation that the increase in supply leads to more lending to poor households and lower interest rates.

The aim is to relax the local lenders' resource constraints but to stop short of a formal contractual linkage. This "trickle-down" approach is also promising, but new work shows that increasing the supply of credit may do more than just increase available capital; it may also change the dynamics of the market in unintended ways, possibly *raising* interest rates and ulti-mately hurting poor borrowers.

Although the discussion here carries cautionary messages, the ideas will continue to prove seductive due to their simplicity. As described in what follows, policymakers in India, possibly the world's largest untapped market for microfinance, have put much of their hope in linking banks and local agents.

In an interesting twist, the links are being made with "self-help groups" of poor women, most often organ-ized by NGOs. The experience is too new to properly assess, but expan-sion plans are ambitious. By early 2001, there were already 260,000 self-help groups linked to banks (involving 4 million poor families), and the plan is to increase to one million groups by 2008.

EMPLOYING WELL-INFORMED LOCAL AGENTS

Consider a bank that hires a moneylender as an agent. When lending his own money, the moneylender has a strong reputation for getting loans repaid.

But will the moneylender be as vigilant when acting as the bank's agent? What is to keep the moneylender from colluding with borrowers, pocketing the loan, and falsely telling the bank that the borrowers had bad luck and cannot repay? Since the bank is hiring the moneylender because the bank lacks reliable infor-mation on local conditions, how can the bank then keep tabs on the moneylender?

The bank can do better than simply paying the moneylender a fixed wage. The moneylender's incentives can be aligned with those of the bank by paying moneylenders a bonus based on loan repayments. As

Fuentes (1996) shows, the bonus should be a smaller part of the money-lender's compensation when the probability that a borrower will repay is relatively sensitive to the moneylender's effort. Since the money-lender doesn't need to do so much to achieve repayments, there is less need to provide strong incentives. But when repayment probabilities are less sensitive to effort (i.e., when moneylenders have to work hard to achieve the desired outcome), bonuses should be a bigger part of the compensation package.

The plan is simple to implement if the bank knows how sensitive borrowers are to the efforts of moneylenders. If the bank has concerns beyond just getting its money back, things get more complicated. If, for example, the bank also cares about *who* is borrowing (perhaps there is a preference for lending to women or to the very poor), there will be need for additional monitoring of the moneylender.

A similar concern arises if the bank worries about the moneylender's tactics (e.g., it may be against extreme strong-arm strategies). *Quis custodiet ipsos custodes?* Who will guard the guards? If the bank has to closely monitor the agent, the advantages of linking with the moneylender are undermined.

This concern explains why moneylenders are not usually the target when creating linkages. In the example of the Indian self-help groups, linking to NGO-sponsored groups of women mitigated many fears of government planners. All the same, NGOs have their own agendas and costs, making them imperfect conduits when the goal is simply to expand basic financial services. We return to these issues in chapter 10, where we address managerial incentives in microfinance.

Indirect Links to Local Markets

A different way to expand financial services is by increasing supply. Basic microeconomic theory suggests that increasing the supply of capital will alleviate credit constraints and reduce interest rates for poor borrowers. Subsidizing the capital infusion should, in principle, create even stronger downward pressure on interest rates. But when local markets are imperfectly competitive and information is costly to acquire, the prediction is not so simple. Hoff and Stiglitz (1998) start with the observation that a massive and prolonged injection of funds in the Thai and Indian rural banking systems lowered the interest rates charged by neither commercial banks nor rural moneylenders.

Hoff and Stiglitz (1998) and Bose (1998) seek to explain the puzzle. They illustrate cases in which the entry of a subsidized program worsens the terms and availability of loans offered by moneylenders in the informal sector. The negative impacts occur because the subsi-dized funds can change borrowers' incentives, reduce optimal scale for moneylenders, and siphon off the best borrowers, leaving moneylend-ers with a riskier pool of clients and higher enforcement costs than before.

Hoff and Stiglitz tell three stories. In the first, the injection of new funds into the market increases the number of moneylenders in the market. The new moneylenders compete for clients with established moneylenders, and each lender ends up with a small number of clients. Marginal costs thus rise, raising interest rates for borrowers. In the second story, the incentives of borrowers are adversely affected by the new funds.

Borrowers know that if they fail to repay their given lender, there are now more alternative lenders to turn to; incentives to work hard to avoid difficulties are thus weakened. The third story involves inherent borrower quality. Consider a market with borrowers of varying reliability. In the benchmark case, borrowers who have established reputations for reliability are favored by moneylend-ers. As before, once the banks make more funds available, a larger number of potential moneylenders can enter the market. With more lenders in the market and less attachment of lenders and borrowers, the establishment of borrower reputations weakens.

With less reliance on reputation-building as an enforcement device, moneylenders must put more effort into other forms of enforcement; since that is costly, interest rates again rise. Hoff and Stiglitz (1998) conclude that the new entry increases excess capacity among moneylenders and raises unit costs. The subsidy is not passed onto the small farmer. Instead, the subsidy is swallowed up by the reduced efficiency of the informal sector.

Bose (1998) tells a related story with a similar bottom line. In his model, new entrants must lend to lower-than-average-quality borrow-ers, since the highest-quality borrowers are already in relationships with established moneylenders. Serving lower-quality borrowers increases the average default rate and raises the risk premium that must be charged. Floro and Ray (1997) provide another scenario drawing on experiences in the Philippines.

Their focus is on trader-lenders who, again, are in a monopolistically competitive market. In their model, the moneylenders in a region want to collude to keep inter-est rates high, and collusion is enhanced by the threat of a "credit war." When the credit war occurs, lenders rapidly expand credit, which drives down interest rates and undercuts the profitability of the devi-ating lenders. The scarcity of resources keeps this impulse in check, which in turn renders collusion more difficult. But with the injection of funds, the possibility of a viable credit war increases, and, with that threat, collusion gets easier. With stronger collusive possibilities, inter-est rates rise and poor borrowers are the worse for it.

SUMMARY AND CONCLUSIONS

There are good and bad reasons for intervening in financial markets. If the markets are already working relatively well, interventions won't make much of a dent—or, worse, they might undermine the quality and extent of services provided by the market. Merely seeing high interest rates charged by moneylenders is not sufficient grounds for intervention. Instead, interventions (like creating a microfinance insti-tution) should be based on clear understandings of how the efficiency and equity of outcomes will change. This requires evaluation of possi-ble market failures.

The analyses of moral hazard and adverse selection provide two tools for analyzing market imperfections. Both are based on problems posed by informational asymmetries—the borrowers have better infor-mation on their creditworthiness and risk taking than does the bank.

In the case of moral hazard, inefficiencies arise when the bank cannot deter borrowers from taking excessive risks that raise the probability of default. The problem is that by defaulting, borrowers avoid facing the full consequences of their actions. Inefficiencies due to adverse selection arise when banks cannot adequately distinguish safer bor-rowers from riskier borrowers.

When that happens, all borrowers are charged the same interest rates, and safer borrowers end up effectively cross-subsidizing riskier borrowers. If the problem is acute enough, safer borrowers will refuse to borrow at the going interest rate, leaving the bank saddled with a riskier-than-average pool of customers. Both adverse selection and moral hazard show serious constraints faced by banks in low-income communities—posed especially by the lack of col-lateral. In these cases, if the bank raises its interest rates as a response to perceived risks, it may end up exacerbating incentive problems to such a degree that profits fall rather than rise. Commercial banks will understandably be reluctant to enter markets where collateral is scarce and transactions costs are high.

Both adverse selection and moral hazard could be solved if borrow-ers could credibly offer collateral to secure their loans. But the starting point here is that borrowers don't have adequate collateral. As a result, it would seem that for the bank to do better, it would need a way to get more information—but an important assumption is that commer-cial lenders face high costs in getting more information.

One of the notable aspects of these microfinance approaches is that improvements are possible even when lenders do not actually acquire more information. Instead, the contracts harness local information and give borrowers incentives to use their own information on their peers to the advantage of the bank. It is not that the older analyses of information problems were incorrect, it is just that they failed to consider new ideas to circumvent informa-tion problems.

The discussion in the chapter also helps to explain why microfinance has mainly been carried out by new institutions, rather than by trying to engage, coopt, and otherwise influence existing local lenders. In large part, the logic follows that of the modern theory of the firm, which seeks to explain why firms exist, rather than using independent con-tractors—from accountants to secretaries—to make all transactions (e.g., Hart 1995). Even though, as Fuentes (1996) suggests, incentive contracts in principle can be devised to facilitate hiring local lenders as agents for banks, practical implementation is a challenge. The chosen task of most microlenders has thus been to find cheap, simple mecha-nisms that improve *on* the informal sector—rather than trying to improve the informal sector itself.

Finally, the discussion of moral hazard and adverse selection pro-vides important perspective on arguments about setting interest rates. In *Undermining Rural Development with Cheap Credit*, Adams, Graham, and von Pischke (1984) drive home the argument that interest rates that are *too low* can undermine microfinance. In a related argument, policy-makers often argue that interest rates should be raised as high as is needed to fully cover costs, otherwise programs will not be financially sustainable (e.g., Consultative Group to Assist the Poorest 1996). This has been a hard-fought argument, and we agree that prudently raising interest rates can be a key to microfinance success. But the analysis in this chapter warns us that there can also be problems posed by inter-est rates that are *too high.*

The previous analyses of moral hazard and adverse selection show how raising interest rates too high can under-mine the quality of an institution's loan portfolio and reduce prof-itability As with charging interest rates that are too low, good intentions can again go awry when *raising* interest rates. The challenge for micro-finance is to couple smart interest rate policies with new ways of doing business to ensure good incentives for customers.

3

Roots of Microfinance: Roscas and Credit Cooperatives

INTRODUCTION

Even without microfinance, poor households' lack of collateral does not mean a complete lack of access to financial intermediation. On the contrary, poor households typically have multiple credit sources in village economies, as well as informal ways to save and insure. In a 1990 survey carried out in rural Indonesia, for example, Mosley (1996a) reports that as many as 70 percent of the households interviewed bor-rowed from informal lenders, a figure in line with studies of informal economies elsewhere.

More recently, scholars affiliated with the Uni-versity of Manchester's Institute for Development Policy and Manage-ment (IDPM) have collected "financial diaries" from poor households in India and Bangladesh; the households were visited every two weeks over a year, and all financial transactions were recorded, whether infor-mal, semi-formal, or formal. Morduch and Rutherford (2003, 5) sum-marize the main findings: "On average the Bangladeshi households push or pull through financial services and devices each year a sum of money ($839) equivalent to two-thirds of their annual cash income. In the Bangladesh case, households enter a fresh financial arrangement— with a moneylender, money guard, savings club, or formal provider, among others—on average every two weeks. In Bangladesh, a sample of just forty-two households were found to have used, between them, thirty-three types of service or device during the year: no household used less than four, and a third of them used more than ten." The devices are typically diverse and overlapping. At one end of the cost spectrum are loans among family, relatives, and friends. Because these loans are often made reciprocally (you lend to me now and, in return, I'll lend to you at a time when you particularly need some cash), they often do not carry interest charges and are part of broader informal insurance relationships (Ray 1998). At the other end are mon-eylenders, with long-standing, if not always accurate, reputations as loan sharks. Rotating savings and credit associations (ROSCAs) and credit cooperatives are in the middle. The premise of microfinance is that these mechanisms are far from perfect, constrained by local resources, and, in the case of moneylenders, often very costly. Still, understanding informal mechanisms can provide guidance about how to design workable microfinance contracts.

Like many microfinance models, both ROSCAs and credit coopera-tives involve groups. But ROSCAs, which are simpler, are built on informal understandings among friends and acquaintances, while cooperatives typically have a formal constitution and a degree of legal status. Understanding the way these two institutions function thus paves the way for understanding group lending in microfinance (i.e., how groups can help to reduce costs, mobilize funds, improve moni-toring, and deploy informal community-based enforcement mecha-nisms). They also foreshadow limits to group lending in microfinance.

Understanding how ROSCAs hold together sheds light on savings constraints as well. While ROSCAs and credit cooperatives are com-monly seen as ways to compensate for the credit market problems described in the last chapter, newer work suggests that they are just as valuable in providing simple ways to save. Indeed, their internal logic may hinge critically on the fact that ROSCAs can provide more effec-tive ways to save than are typically available to low-income house-holds. We then explain why ROSCAs don't fall apart, and, in answering that, we confront savings constraints.

In turning to nineteenth-century European credit cooperatives in section 3.3, we turn to an early antecedent for microfinance—a con-certed attempt to attack poverty in the countryside by creating new financial institutions aimed at low-income families without collateral. The discussion of credit cooperatives shows how these formalized group-based mechanisms have helped overcome the troubles that tra-ditional banks face when lending to poor borrowers. In particular, cooperatives can induce helpful "peer monitoring" among members.

ROSCAS

One way to avoid the steep costs charged by moneylenders is to borrow from neighbors and friends, but while interest rates may be low (or even zero), social costs and obligations can be considerable. ROSCAs provide an alternative solution, based on pooling resources with a broad group of neighbors and friends. ROSCAs do this in a systematic way, and they can be found nearly universally, from the *tontines* of rural Cameroon to the *hui* organized in Taipei, and the *tanda* and the *polla* of Mexico and Chile, respectively. A few examples illustrate just how important they can be. In Indonesia, for example, a recent survey shows that even among households with steady access to microfinance services provided by Bank Rakyat Indonesia, roughly 40 percent also participate in ROSCAs. Bouman (1977) reports that ROSCAs in Ethiopia comprised 8–10 percent of GDP in the early 1970s, and 20 percent of all bank deposits in Kerala State, India. Bouman (1995) reports that at least half the rural residents in Cameroon, Côte d'Ivoire, the Congo, Libera, Togo, and Nigeria participated in ROSCAs. Leven-son and Besley (1996) find that between 1977 and 1991 roughly one-fifth of the Taiwanese population participated in ROSCAs in any given year, and, to their surprise, the data show robustly that participation increased with income.

ROSCAs tend to have simple structures. The basic element is a group of individuals who agree to regularly contribute money to a common "pot" that is allocated to one member of the group each period. Twenty people, say, may agree to contribute $15 each for twenty months, gen-erating a monthly pot of $300. At monthly intervals the group meets to collect dues and allocate the proceeds, with past recipients excluded from getting the pot again, until every member has had a turn with the $300 pot (unless it is a "bidding" ROSCA; more on that later). ROSCAs thus successfully take the bits of surplus funds that come into house-holds and translate those bits into a large chunk that can be used to fund a major purchase. The simplicity has advantages. The life of a ROSCA has a clear begin-ning and end, accounting is straightforward (one only has to keep track of who has received the pot already and who is in line to do so), and storage of funds is not required since money goes straight from one person's pocket into another's. ROSCAs come in a number of varia-tions, and each has implications for what the ROSCA offers, how it stays together, and who is attracted to join. The main variants involve the way groups determine who gets the pot. The order of receipt may be predetermined and unchanging from cycle to cycle, the order may be chosen randomly at the beginning of each cycle, or, in a third twist, members may be allowed to bid for a given pot, rather than simply waiting their turn (e.g., this is the main form found in Taiwan; see Levenson and Besley 1996, and Calomiris and Rajaraman 1998).

Like moneylenders, ROSCAs are very much local institutions. In Bangladesh, for example, ROSCAs are known as *loteri samities*, and among the ninety-five *samities* investigated by Rutherford (1997), 70 percent were made up of people in the same neighborhood, with the others based on a shared workplace. ROSCA memberships ranged from five members to over one hundred, and the pots ranged from about $25 to $400. The larger ROSCAs in Bangladesh provided enough capital for members to make investments like the purchase of a rick-shaw, freeing drivers from having to pay high rental rates. About two-thirds of the ROSCAs had daily collections in amounts as small as 5–25 cents (with less frequent disbursements), and about one-quarter col-lected payments monthly, which was especially popular with garment workers receiving monthly paychecks.

Gugerty (2003) reports on seventy ROSCAs in western Kenya, close to the Uganda border. Most of the ROSCAs formed as groups of friends and neighbors, and, on average, participants report that other members visit their homes fourteen times per month (for reasons other than a ROSCA meeting). The area is rural, mainly dependent on small-scale subsistence farming, some cash crops (cotton, tobacco, and sugarcane), and local market trade. The average daily agricultural wage is less than $1, so it is noteworthy that the average pot is about $25, usually dis-bursed monthly (with an average individual contribution of $2). The typical ROSCA cycle lasts for about one year. The pot is roughly one-quarter of average monthly household expenditures, which is adequate to pay primary school fees, or to buy two bags of maize, two iron roofing sheets, or a mattress or blanket (Gugerty 2003).

The survey covers over one thou-sand households from across the country, and nearly half of the house-holds turned out to include current ROSCA members (with another 7 percent including individuals previously in ROSCAs). As in Taiwan, the probability of having participated rises with income—although the median size of the pots fails to keep up with income so that ROSCAs become increasingly less important as households get richer. As in Bangladesh, richer households favor less frequent collections: The top two richest quintiles strongly favor monthly or quarterly pots, while poorer groups tend to favor daily, weekly, or biweekly pots.

Table 3.1: ROSCA Participation in Indonesia

Quintile	Ever a member (%)	Median income per capita per month of participants (rupiah)	Median size of pot (rupiah)	Ratio of median income to median pot (%)	Frequency (percentage): Daily, weekly, or biweekly pots	Monthly or quarterly pots	Ot
Bottom	33	40,260	3,000	7.5	38	49	12
Second	44	75,000	3,000	4.0	45	41	14
Third	60	134,150	3,500	2.6	45	52	3
Fourth	71	241,667	5,000	2.1	26	70	4
Fifth	63	600,000	10,000	1.7	24	71	5

Source: Survey of 1,066 households collected by BRI in fall 2000. Calculations are by Jonathan Morduch. The poverty line averaged 90,901 rupiah per capita per month, and at the end of 1999 the exchange rate was 7,855 rupiah per U.S. dollar.

THE SIMPLE ANALYTICS OF ROSCAS

To see how ROSCAs work, we give an example of a case where the order in which individuals obtain the pot is predetermined. We begin with a group of individuals who voluntarily commit to putting resources into a common pot at regular intervals. At each meeting, every participant adds her share to the pot. The order of who gets the pot is decided at the first meeting by picking names from a hat.

To see one appeal of ROSCAs (and continuing our previous example), suppose that there are twenty individuals who each wish to acquire a sewing machine that costs $300. (Instead of a sewing machine, the desired good may be a radio or a piece of farm equipment—what really matters is that it is *indivisible*; that is, there is no value in just half a radio or two-thirds of a sewing machine—you need to obtain the whole thing.) As a result, each individual has to wait until she has the $300 fully in hand before making the purchase, and the sooner she can buy it, the better off she is.

Each participant earns $50 each month, but once the sewing machine has been purchased the owner can earn extra income of $20 each month. Everyone needs at minimum $35 to meet basic subsistence needs, so that prior to the purchase of the sewing machine, there is at most only $15 per month left over for saving. If the individual does not join the ROSCA, she can save up the $15 per month and be able to buy the sewing machine after twenty months (assuming, for simplicity, that savings generate no interest.) Her pattern of consumption will thus be $35 per month for twenty months and then $50 + $20 = $70 per month thereafter. Owning the sewing machine allows her to double her consumption!

Now let us consider an individual who joins a ROSCA with twenty neighbors, each of whom is willing and able to contribute $15 each month; her order of receiving the pot is a number between 1 and 20. Before ranks are determined she can a priori end up with any rank with equal probability 1/20, but on average she will be the tenth recipient. If she is indeed the tenth recipient, she will consume $35 for nine periods and get the pot in the tenth. At that point, she can consume $35 + $20 = $55 for the remaining ten periods, at which time the ROSCA cycle has been completed and her obligations are over. From then on, she earns $50 + $20 = $70 each month. By speeding up the expected date of purchasing the sewing machine, the ROSCA is a better bet than saving on one's own. In fact, it's better for everyone except the last person to get the pot, and they are no worse off than they would have been when saving up on their own. One is the "household conflict motive" favored by Anderson, Baland, and Moene (2003); in this explanation, participants —who are often women—seek to get money out of the household and away from their husbands. The other is the "commitment to savings" motive argued by Gugerty (hinging on the fact that ROSCAs present a clear, public, disciplined way to accumulate funds).

ENFORCING AGREEMENTS AND FACILITATING SAVING

The existence of ROSCAs can make everyone better off in principle, but how do they work in practice? The ROSCA model that we have just described hinges on three crucial assumptions: first, that all individu-als wish to buy an indivisible durable good; second, that they are impa-tient to do so; and, third, that ROSCA participation is enforced in that all individuals who win the pot earlier keep on turning up and con-tributing to the pot until every participant has their chance to purchase the durable good.

If the good was not indivisible, participants could start buying pieces of it and reap the returns immediately. Instead, indivisibility means that without a ROSCA, individuals are forced to save until they have payment in full. The role of indivisibility is in line with evidence from two very different contexts. Besley and Levenson (1996), for example, use data for Taiwan to show that ROSCA participants are indeed more likely than others to buy durables like microwave ovens, videocassette recorders, and air conditioners, even after controlling for income and for the endogeneity of participation. In the slums of Nairobi, Anderson and Baland (2002) similarly find that ROSCA participation is associated with making lumpy purchases (in this case, school fees, clothing, rent, and medical costs).

These results are only suggestive. Gugerty (2003) counters that in western Kenya, it is not uncommon to use the pot for more than one item, the most expensive of which takes up no more than two-thirds of the pot on average. Moreover, the expenditures generally favored by ROSCA participants are often divisible. School fees, for example, can be paid in installments; food can be purchased in small quantities; and household items like cups or plates can be purchased individually. Of course, making bulk purchases may cut costs, and the early pot motive for ROSCAs then survives. But Gugerty also shows evidence that in fact most participants do not put an especially high value on getting an early pot; instead, for example, getting the pot during the harvest season is often a bigger prize.

The assumption of impatience also matters to the early pot story; oth-erwise, households would be content to save up on their own. Assum-ing impatience is common, economists routinely assume some degree of impatience (i.e., that a given amount of money today is valued by individuals more than the same amount tomorrow). In practice, though, we suggest that the constraint may not be impatience so much as the absence of an effective way to save, an argument in line with Gugerty's evidence from Kenya.

To see this, we need to first turn to enforcement issues. In our simple description of the model, we have emphasized the benefits of ROSCA participation versus those of going solo. But enforcement issues arise once the order of who gets the pot is determined. Consider the partic-ipant who is very last in line. Why should she stay in the agreement when, after all, she is at least as well off saving up on her own? The ROSCA will not help her get the durable good sooner than she could on her own. In fact, the ROSCA could impose costs since it forces her to save in fixed, regular increments each period when she might instead prefer flexibility in deciding how to accumulate. If the last person refuses to stay in, the whole arrangement unravels since someone always has to be last. One reason why this may work is that in fact ROSCA members do not have better ways to save. The absence of well-established savings institutions for small savings may thus be a key to making ROSCAs work.

The incentive problem with regard to the first participants who win the pot may be even worse. What prevents them from taking the pot and then refusing to make contributions in later periods? The participants that get the pot first are de facto borrowing from the other members of the ROSCA; and they therefore must turn up at sub-sequent meetings to repay their debt obligations, just like any borrower. Rutherford (2000, 34) notes that the risk of early absconders is the most commonly heard worry of people when presented with the idea of a ROSCA. To work,

ROSCAs must rely on potential penalties for not honoring one's obligations.

One possible sanction is to refuse the absconders access to future cycles of the ROSCA, but, as Anderson, Baland, and Moene (2003) argue, this is insufficient; the sanction will not work since the absconder could simply save up on his own and do just as well. Again con-sider the example of a twenty-member ROSCA with $15 contributions and a $300 pot. Also assume that the order of who gets the pot is unchanged from cycle to cycle—and that once one twenty-period cycle ends, another immediately starts up. Would exclusion from subsequent cycles help the enforcement problem? If the individual stays in the ROSCA, she would have to contribute $15 to the pot for the next nine-teen periods until the round ends. In the following period, a new round of the ROSCA commences. Since we have assumed that this individ-ual is again first in line to get the pot, she will make her $15 contribu-tion and again get the allotted $300. Then, again, she is obligated to pay $15 for another nineteen periods, and so forth.

The enforcement problem arises because the individual could do better by reneging. After the first period of the first round, she absconds with a "free" $300, and then, rather than making good on their obliga-tions, she could simply save $15 on her own each period for twenty periods. Twenty periods later, she would have another $300 in hand, just as she would if she had stayed true to the ROSCA rules. Not only that, but she would be able to save flexibly, freed from the rigidity of the ROSCA contribution schedule. The ROSCA will thus fall apart if it is true that, as a ROSCA member in Nairobi said: "You cannot trust people in matters of money. People tend to cheat" (Anderson, Baland, and Moene 2003).

Can the way that the ROSCA is designed affect the ease of enforce-ment? Specifically, what if we drop the assumption that the order of who gets the pot is unchanged from cycle to cycle? Imagine, instead, that the order was chosen by random lottery at the start of each twenty-period cycle. This would only make the incentive problem worse for the first in line. Rather than staying true and getting the second pot in twenty more periods under the fixed order, she would not expect to get the pot for another thirty periods (since the average lottery number in the next round would be 10). The advantages to reneging are then much greater.

Why then, do we often see assignment by random lottery? First, it seems fairer. Second, it provides the best incentives for the last person in line. She may be number 20 this time, but next time she can expect to be number 10 on average. There is thus a conflict between "fairness" and providing the right incentives for the first in line. One solution used in Kenya is to use a fixed order and to put people known as being most untrustworthy at the end of the line; this is perceived to be most fair (except by those deemed untrustworthy!) and helps address incen-tive problems (Anderson, Baland, and Moene 2003). To facilitate this, ROSCA managers devote considerable energy to ex ante screening of prospective members. Even if members are poorly acquainted before-hand, requiring recommendations from existing members helps, and reputations can be allowed to accumulate over time (such that one's order of getting the pot moves forward after maintaining a clean record).

Other ways to keep ROSCAs together include banning problem participants from access to other relationships like trade credit, credit cooperatives, or access to material inputs. ROSCA participants in Kenya also report sometimes using force to obtain goods to be resold from members who fall behind in their obligations (Anderson, Baland, and Moene 2003). Social sanctions may be employed as well, such that those who renege are ostracized within the village or excluded from social and religious events (e.g., Ardener 1964).

Imperfect alternative means to save can also explain why ROSCAs stay together. We have assumed up to this point that people who are not in ROSCAs have no constraints in saving; this is why it made sense to argue that absconders would be just as well off without the ROSCA (and often better off). But Rutherford (1997) finds that, when asked, the most commonly cited reason that slum dwellers in Dhaka joined a ROSCA was in fact to save, particularly given their difficulties in saving at home. Anderson and Baland (2002) find, similarly, that women favor ROSCAs since it helps them get money out of the house (and away from husbands). Nearly all ROSCA participants in their Nairobi sample are women, and this is common globally. Anderson and Baland find an interesting "inverted-U" shaped pattern in their data: Women who have little autonomy from their husbands are unlikely to join ROSCAs, as are women with great autonomy (since they do not need the protections that ROSCAs afford). Participation is greatest in the middle, by women who have some autonomy and are looking for addi-tional levers to facilitate household management. We will come back to this issue in chapter 7 on gender.

As far as saving goes, ROSCAs have an important advantage that is missing from other informal mechanisms: The beauty is that ROSCAS do not require a physical place to store money since on the same day that funds are collected, they are distributed again. The public nature and precommitment associated with ROSCA participation also serves as a device to foster discipline and encourage saving in ways that may be otherwise impossible. These advantages follow a logic given by new work in behavioral economics in which commitment devices are supe-rior when self-control is weak (e.g., Thaler 1994). Participating in a ROSCA thus provides a secure, structured way to save that would oth-erwise be missing. Even households that are not particularly impatient may join a ROSCA simply for the help it provides with saving.

Gugerty's (2003) analysis of a detailed survey of 1,066 ROSCA members in western Kenya pushes the commitment to saving argu-ment for why individuals form ROSCAs. As one ROSCA participant responded in her survey, "You can't save alone—it is easy to misuse money." Another remarked, "Saving money at home can make you extravagant in using it." And another said, "It is difficult to keep money at home as demands are high." Gugerty analyzes the responses of 308 ROSCA members to the question "What is the most important reason you joined this ROSCA?" She finds that 37 percent reported that it was "difficult to save at home because money got used up in small house-hold needs." Another 22 percent reported that it was "difficult to save alone, that they 'got the strength to save' by sitting with others." And just 10 percent reported that they joined "as a response to household conflict, fear of theft, or demands by kin."

ROSCAs are so widely observed, and seen in such varying circum-stances, that there cannot be one rationale for their existence that uni-versally trumps all others. We see truths in each of the explanations considered here: the early pot motive, the household conflict motive, and the commitment to saving motive. But we have highlighted the latter explanations because they remain underappreciated.

Limits to ROSCAs

The ubiquity of ROSCAs attests to their usefulness, but they have limits as well. First, neither the size of the pot nor the size of contributions is flexible within the life of a given ROSCA. Creating a bigger pot can be done by making the contributions larger (which may be difficult for some members) or by recruiting more members. Adding members, though, can lead to management problems and lengthens the life of the ROSCA (and thus lengthens the time that members must wait to get their next chance at the pot).

Second, and perhaps more important, ROSCAs put locally held funds to good use, but they do not provide a regular way to mobilize funds from outside a given group. So, from the point of view of microfinance, ROSCAs show an interesting precedent for using groups to allocate resources (foreshadowing the practice of group lending), but they fail to present an effective way to move resources across inde-pendent communities or to easily expand in size.

One partial way to address the first problem is through a "bidding ROSCA." Here, rather than allocating the pot by a predetermined order, the pot is allocated each period to whoever is willing to pay the most for it. The rest of the participants pocket the proceeds. For those who primarily wish to save, the bidding ROSCA provides a return to saving not available under the other forms—and members do not need to take the pot at a prescribed moment. For those bidding on the pot, the ROSCA provides access to money when it is needed, albeit at a cost. In this way, the bidding ROSCA can help mitigate risk in difficult times (for more on ROSCAs and risk, see Calomiris and Rajaraman 1998). One problem, of course, is that there may be multiple bidders seeking the pot during downturns. A bidding war ensues, leading to a result that may be economically efficient but not necessarily equitable since needy, poorer households will easily get outbid. In this light, credit cooperatives present themselves as a more flexible institutional solution—and we turn to this next.

CREDIT COOPERATIVES

ROSCAs show a way to formalize and systematize the use of groups to allocate resources in poor communities, but their simplicity can also be a disadvantage. As described earlier, many use ROSCAs largely as a way to save, rather than as a means to borrow. At the cost of a bit of complexity, the ROSCA structure can be modified to allow some participants to mainly save and others to mainly borrow—and for more than one person to borrow at a time. In this way, the ROSCA transforms into an ASCA (accumulating savings and credit association) as described by Bouman (1995) and Rutherford (2000). An ASCA in its most formalized mode is essentially a credit cooperative (or credit union as they are more often called in the Americas—we will use the terms interchangeably). A chief advantage is that savers are no longer required to borrow, and the size of loans can vary with need. A cost is that funds must now be stored, and bookkeeping and management become more complex.

In moving in this direction, we get a step closer to modern microfinance. Indeed, the cooperatives share some of the features of the "village banks" promoted by microfinance NGOs like FINCA, Pro Mujer, and Freedom from Hunger, and credit cooperatives are playing an increasing role in today's microfinance landscape. The roots of credit cooperatives, however, are much older. Not unlike the modern microfinance "revolution," a century before microfinance became a global movement, Friedrich Raiffeissen, a village mayor, had spearheaded a similar drive in the German countryside; his aim was to spread new group-based ways to provide financial services to the poor (Guinnane 2002; Ghatak and Guinnane 1999). Typical loans in Raiffeisen's coop-eratives had ten-year durations and were made for farm investments. Raiffeisen's credit cooperative movement built on a broader movement that started in the 1850s, and by the turn of the century it had spread to Ireland, Italy, and Japan (and later to Korea, Taiwan, Canada, the United States, and parts of Latin America; see Adams 1995). In Germany, there were over 15,000 institutions operating in 1910, serving 2.5 million people and accounting for 9 percent of the German banking market (Guinnane 2002, 89, table 3); by the early 1900s, nearly one-third of rural households were cooperative members (Adams 1995).

The British too were intrigued, and they fostered credit cooperatives in India, creating a precedent for modern microfinance in South Asia. In the 1890s the government of Madras in South India, then under British rule, looked to the German experiences for solutions in address-ing poverty in India, and in 1904 the Cooperative Credit Societies Act established cooperatives along Raiffeisen's basic model. By 1912, over four hundred thousand Indians belonged to the new credit coopera-tives, and by 1946 membership exceeded nine million (Bedi, cited in Woolcock 1998). The cooperatives took hold in the state of Bengal, the eastern part of which became East Pakistan at independence in 1947 and is now Bangladesh. The credit cooperatives eventually lost steam in Bangladesh, but the notion of group lending had established itself.

The credit cooperatives function like ROSCAs in that they gather funds from those in a community who are able to save, and those funds are allocated to those who want to invest (or consume) in a lump sum. Unlike ROSCAs, however, credit cooperatives share the following fea-tures: First, members do not have to wait their turn in order to borrow, nor do they need to bid for a loan. Second, participants, be they savers or borrowers, are all shareholders in the cooperative. Key decisions about the prevailing interest rates, the maximum loan size, and changes to the constitutional chart of the credit cooperative are taken demo-cratically by all members, on a one-share-one vote basis. Like ROSCA participants, they share a common bond—that is, they live in the same neighborhood, attend the same church, and/or work nearby—and thus social sanctions are available for enforcing contracts (on top of the possibility that a defaulting borrower loses her shares in the credit cooperative). In the subsections that follow we analyze how these various features contribute to the success of credit cooperatives and, in particular, to mobilizing savings, inducing peer monitoring, and addressing risk.

CREDIT COOPERATIVES AND SAVINGS

In a study of German rural cooperatives during the period 1850–1914, Prinz (2002) analyzes the emergence of credit associations on the Raiffeisen model. The main features of the Raiffeisen model were:

(a) members should belong to the same local parish;

(b) there was unlimited liability in that defaulting members would lose their current assets, as well as suffering social costs;

(c) low-income individuals could not be discriminated against and should be given the equal rights when becoming members of the cooperative;

(d) the cooperative was not merely a financial intermediary in that it performed other functions such as facilitating the purchase of inputs of production for its members; and,

(e) the cooperatives would extend both short-term and long-term loans.

Although Prinz does not have direct evidence on savings, he argues that such savings by participant members were most likely long-term savings since interest rates were stable, remaining fairly constant (at around 4 percent) for the entire period from 1897 to 1911. This interest rate stability is quite remarkable, the argument goes, especially for credit cooperatives operating in rural areas, and the natural explana-tion is that members' savings were stable too.

How were members' savings sustained and stable over time in these rural settings? Prinz emphasizes the importance of what he calls "face-to-face" relations and trust-building ties among villagers. Over time, such ties became so strong that even with the advent of strong com-petition at the turn of century, the Raiffeisen cooperatives continued to enjoy stable levels of savings. In Prinz's words: "Whereas villagers in the 1860s often had no choice but to deposit their saving in the Raif-feisen cooperatives, their grandsons and granddaughters definitely had. It appears that villagers, after leaving their initial suspicion behind, came to regard the Raiffeisen cooperative more and more as an extension of their own businesses" (2002, 15). We formalize this feature of the Raiffeisen cooperatives in appendix 3B. In particular, we show that members of a cooperative will be keen to invest all of their savings in the cooperative when social sanctions are sufficiently high and/or when the opportunity cost of investing elsewhere is high. The reason is that in those cases, the incidence of default falls sharply through the combination of social commitment, unlimited liability, and interest rate stability. And savings are in turn encouraged by a lower probability of default on loans.

Credit Cooperatives and Peer Monitoring

Also inspired by Raiffeisen's cooperatives experience, Banerjee, Besley, and Guinnane (1994) develop a model of credit cooperatives that emphasizes peer monitoring among members. The model yields insights into why a borrower's peers have incentives to monitor and enforce contracts. The insights have been applied to group lending in microfinance as well.

Consider a cooperative with only two members (it's not a realistic assumption but it allows us to show some critical features in a simple way). One of the two has a new investment opportunity and needs to finance it. The borrower's project is risky: The borrower achieves gross income y with probability p, and zero with probability $(1 - p)$, where p is the probability of success. Undertaking the opportunity requires a cost F that can be financed in part by borrowing from an outside lender. So the project will depend on securing funds from an outside lender and a lender inside the cooperative.

Suppose first that the two cooperative members have zero wealth. Then the loan contract between the borrower and outside lender is simply a standard debt contract that specifies an amount b lent and a gross interest rate R, with $R \cdot b < y$ whenever the project succeeds. This simply says that the outside lender cannot charge a gross interest rate that is greater than the borrower's income—in the case in which the borrower makes profits. When the project fails, the borrower is pro-tected by limited liability and does not repay.

Now consider how a well-designed credit cooperative can improve matters. Consider the case in which the borrower's fellow cooperative member (the "insider") has funds to lend the borrower, making up the difference between the full project cost F and b, the amount that the outsider is willing to lend. Thus one role of the insider is simply to lend an amount $F - b$ to the borrower. The second role of the insider is to act as a guarantor, possibly offering collateral that would secure the loan from the outsider. We'll show why offering the collateral might make sense here, even if the loan goes to the insider's partner. The third role that the insider plays is as a monitor, taking actions to encourage the borrower to work hard and increase the chances for success. A bor-rower who shirks suffers penalties or social sanctions imposed by their peers, and the chance of being caught shirking increases with moni-toring effort.

The questions are: What will determine how much the insider mon-itors her peer? What will be the effect of offering collateral? How high an interest rate will the insider charge the peer for the "inside loan"?

To simplify matters, we assume that effort by the borrower translates one-for-one into a higher chance of doing well—so we can use one symbol, p, to denote both effort and the probability of success. The question is: How is p determined? The probability that the borrower will succeed is a function of how hard the borrower works. That, in turn, is a function of how much the insider monitors. To capture these elements, the cost of effort is assumed to take the particular form $(1/2)(1/m)\, p^1$, where m denotes the monitoring intensity provided by the insider. The function shows that the cost of effort *decreases* with the extent of monitoring, m. One way to think about this is to consider the relationship the other way round: the cost of shirking *increases* with the extent of monitoring, since more monitoring means that the bor-rower is more likely to get caught and punished. The role of p^2 in the cost function means that the cost of effort rises less than proportionally with added effort (since p, which is a probability, must be less than one).

The timing of decisions is as follows. First, the borrower contracts loans with both the inside and the outside lenders. We assume perfect competition among potential outside lenders, so that the contract will guarantee that the outside lender expects to get back the market rate of interest r plus compensation for risk. Second, the inside lender chooses how much to monitor the borrower (picks m). Third, the bor-rower decides how much effort p to invest in her project. Fourth, project revenues are realized.

Given the sequencing, the borrower chooses effort conditional on knowing how much the insider is going to monitor her. So, for a given monitoring intensity m by the insider, the borrower chooses effort, p, to maximize her expected returns net of costs:

$p(y\text{-}Rb)\text{-}(12)(1m)p^2$. (3.1)

It turns out that the optimal level of effort, p, equals $m(y - Rb)$. We immediately see that a higher monitoring intensity m increases p, as described previously. This is because a higher monitoring intensity m lowers the borrower's marginal cost of effort, leading to higher bor-rower effort and a higher probability of success. We have taken the interest rate R as given, but we know that it must be higher than the market rate available on alternative, safe investments (like government bonds). This is because the outsider must bear some risk of default.

The problem is that the inside lender has no incentive to invest in peer monitoring. So, what guarantees that m will in fact be positive? To see, we have to modify our assumptions slightly. Suppose that the inside cooperative member has private wealth w that she can use as collateral for the loan contract between the borrower and the outside lender.

That is, the insider promises w to the outside lender in case the gross interest rate R is not repaid by the borrower. Furthermore, assume that w is sufficiently large so that the outside lender is always repaid in full. Now, the outside lender faces no risk in making this loan, so he no longer requires a risk premium. Given the assumption of perfect competition, R will then fall to equal r, the market return on safe invest-ments. The falling interest rate, in turn, implies that the borrower's effort rises, since p now equals $m(y - rb)$, which is larger than before.

Clearly, the willingness of the insider to put up collateral is helpful for the borrower. But why should the insider do so? If the project fails, the inside lender loses w.

The insider can be compensated by getting a return—effectively an interest rate—in the case that the project is suc-cessful. If the insider has strong bargaining power, she will be able to obtain most of the residual return $(y - rb)$, which remains after the bor-rower has repaid the outside lender. So, the insider under this scenario now has an incentive to put up collateral.

Moreover, the insider now also has an incentive to invest in moni-toring in order to increase the probability of success. The monitoring effort, m, that the insider applies in order to elicit higher repayments from the borrower should increase in the amount of collateral w—since more collateral means more to lose when the borrower shirks. Increases in the interest rate charged by the outside lender, however, is apt to have a negative effect on monitoring. This is because the outside lender is paid in priority, so when the interest rate that the outsider receives rises, any additional monitoring that the inside lender applies will increasingly accrue to the outsider.

The model shows ways in which groups can function to increase lending. Here, the insider acts as a guarantor and a monitor, with the incentive given by the fact that the insider is a lender too. In the case of microfinance, fellow group members also act as guarantors and monitors. But in that case, their motivation is fueled by the promise of future access to credit if all group members repay loans.

The Banerjee, Besley, and Guinnane (1994) model is important in demonstrating how monitoring can come about as a function of insti-tutional design.

The optimality of monitoring is another matter. We close by noting that it is entirely possible here that insiders will monitor too much and punish borrowers too often relative to outcomes that would emerge if a benevolent social planner were making decisions.

SUMMARY AND CONCLUSIONS

In this chapter we have analyzed ROSCAs and credit cooperatives, two precursors to modern microfinance institutions. Credit cooperatives (or credit unions) are also playing an increasingly active role in the micro-finance market today.

In the model we described, ROSCAs can help credit-constrained individuals purchase indivisible goods through a simple sharing arrangement. The idea is beautifully simple, but not very flexible. The approach can be made more complicated, but it will remain limited to intermediating local resources only.

While ROSCAs are commonly cited as indigenous ways that com-munities use to overcome credit constraints, the closer one looks, the more that ROSCAs seem notable as devices for saving. Indeed, we showed that in principle, one very common form of ROSCA will fall apart if it does not offer a way to save that is more attractive than alter-native mechanisms. Given the variety of ROSCAs observed in practice, one explanation of their use will not be universally valid, but recent evidence has stressed the savings side in particular.

Credit cooperatives are another way to mobilize local resources, and cited evidence from the German credit cooperatives of the nineteenth century that the cooperatives also functioned as impor-tant ways to save. The model of the German credit cooperatives in turned instead to the nature of the institutional design of cooperatives. The design of cooperatives encourages peer monitoring and guaranteeing the loans of one's neighbors.

The level of peer mon-itoring is not necessarily optimal from a social standpoint, however— which is a lesson that carries over to group lending in microfinance.

The analysis raises the question as to whether the 98 percent (plus) loan repayment rates boasted by microlenders might ever be too *high* from a social standpoint. Are too many resources being put into monitoring and enforcement? Are borrowers ever pressured to be too risk-averse rather than seeking the greater profits that can come with risk taking? These are questions that have so far received little attention from the microfinance community.

The discussion of credit cooperatives also introduces practical com-plications. While the cooperatives add flexibility to what can be achieved through ROSCAs, cooperatives are much more challenging to run. Indeed, in order to borrow, participants must commit to helping run the institution. This is surely appealing for some, but most micro-finance programs instead pursue a more traditional bank-client relationship. As Adams (1995, 11) concludes, based on his survey of the modern credit union experience in Latin America:

Most credit unions in low-income countries are fragile. They typically have thin capital bases, often lack access to funds to meet liquidity shortfalls, have diffi-culties diversifying their risks, are easily crippled by inflation, and are quickly damaged when their members have economic reverses. Credit unions also face dilemmas as they grow: they lose their informational advantages, they are forced to rely on paid rather than voluntary managers, and they must increas-ingly count on formal sanctions to enforce contracts... Principal-agent prob-lems, transaction costs, and prudential regulation also become increasingly important as credit unions grow.

What does modern microfinance add? As we will see in greater detail in the next chapter, microfinance not only is a device for pooling risk and cross-subsidizing borrowers in order to improve efficiency, it also increases their access to outside sources of finance and institutes a pro-fessional management structure from the start.

Microfinance institu-tions typically borrow (or otherwise obtain funds) from outside the locality (and often outside the country) to fund borrowers' needs, whereas both ROSCAs and credit unions rely mainly on local savings. A pressing question, taken up in the next chapter, is how to attract outside finance when lending to poor borrowers without collateral.

4

Group Lending

INTRODUCTION

Once every week in villages throughout Bangladesh, groups of forty villagers meet together for half an hour or so, joined by a loan officer from a microfinance organization. The loan officer sits in the front of the group (the "center") and begins his business. The large group of villagers is subdivided into eight five-person groups, each with its own chairperson, and the eight chairs, in turn, hand over their group's pass-books to the chairperson of the center, who then passes the books to the loan officer.

The loan officer duly records the individual transac-tions in his ledger, noting weekly installments on loans outstanding, savings deposits, and fees. Quick arithmetic on a calculator ensures that the totals add up correctly, and, if they do not, the loan officer sorts out discrepancies. Before leaving, he may dispense advice and make arrangements for customers to obtain new loans at the branch office. All of this is done in public, making the process more transparent and letting the villagers know who among them is moving forward and who may be running into difficulties.

This scene is repeated over 70,000 times each week in Bangladesh by members and staff of the Grameen Bank, and versions have been adapted around the world by Grameen-style replicators. Other insti-tutions instead base their methods on the "solidarity group" approach of Bolivia's BancoSol or the "village bank" approach operated by microlenders in seventy countries throughout Africa, Latin America, and Asia (including affiliates of FINCA, Pro Mujer, and Freedom from Hunger). For many, this kind of "group lending" has become syn-onymous with microfinance.

Group lending refers specifically to arrangements by individuals without collateral who get together and form groups with the aim of obtaining loans from a lender. The special feature is that the loans are made individually to group members, but all in the group face conse-quences if any member runs into serious repayment difficulties. In the Grameen Bank case, the groups are made up of five people. In the Ban-coSol case, groups can be as small as three people, and in the village banking system pioneered by FINCA groups can range from ten to fifty women. The fundamental idea of "group responsibility" (sometimes called "joint liability") coupled with regular group meetings is common across approaches.

Grameen Bank's weekly group meetings have some obvious and simple advantages for the lender and customers. Most immediately, they offer convenience to the villagers; the bank comes to them, and any problems (a missing document, being a few taka short) can be resolved on the spot. The bank thus offers the same convenience as a local ROSCA or moneylender. Meanwhile, transactions costs are greatly reduced for the loan officer since the multiple savings and loan transactions of forty people can take place in a short block of time.

Transacting through groups also has more subtle advantages (and some limitations). In particular, the group responsibility clause of con-tracts can mitigate the moral hazard, adverse selection, and enforce-ment problems that crippled previous attempts at lending to the poor by outside financial institutions. In chapter 2 we described how these problems are caused by information asymmetries, and one implication is that if the bank gets more information, it can always do better. A solu-tion to the resulting inefficiency is thus to create contracts that gener-ate better information.

But the contracts described in this chapter all improve matters *without* the bank necessarily learning anything new. Instead, the con-tracts take advantage of the fact that group members themselves may have good information about fellow members—and the contract gives the members incentives to use their information to the bank's advan-tage. This can occur in subtle ways, and we present different scenarios in turn.

While the advantages of group lending will be spelled out, there is another side to the coin. Might groups collude against the microlender by collectively deciding not to repay? If the group of borrowers is not willing to impose social sanctions upon itself, can the group nonethe-less provide advantages? Another set of questions relates to peer mon-itoring. What will happen if the population of potential borrowers is dispersed and local information is thus weak and costly to obtain? If group lending takes place in urban areas, where labor mobility is high and individuals also may not have much information about their potential partners, are there still any advantages for groups? And if bor-rowers cannot observe each other's effort levels (or are otherwise reluc-tant to punish shirkers) then group lending can undermine incentives by encouraging "free riding." Borrowers will ask themselves: Why should I work hard if I am liable for a penalty when my partner shirks—even when I cannot control their actions?

The Group-Lending Methodology

Access to finance via groups is not new. The example of ROSCAs in chapter 3 shows how groups function to give participants access to a pot of communal money, and credit cooperatives similarly function to allow members to obtain loans from their peers. The place of groups in microfinance, however, strengthens and extends earlier uses of groups (although not without some added costs).

To see this, we describe "Grameen-style" group lending. The model has been adapted in different contexts, but replicators have tried to stay true to the main features described in this section. The Grameen Bank itself has undergone changes in the twenty-five years since it started (most recently with a major overhaul dubbed "Grameen Bank II"), and we will describe elements of what is now called the Grameen "classic" system (Yunus 2002). This is the model that has figured most promi-nently in economic research.

When the Grameen Bank first got started as an experimental bank in the village of Jobra, near Chittagong University, the first loans were made to individuals without a group responsibility clause (Yunus 2001).

Instead, economies of scale motivated the first use of groups. But Yunus and his associates soon realized that requesting potential bor-rowers to organize themselves into groups had another advantage: The costs of screening and monitoring loans and the costs of enforcing debt repayments could be substantially reduced.

To institute this systematically, the bank developed a system in which two members of each five-person group receive their loans first. If all installments are paid on time, the initial loans are followed four to six weeks later by loans to two other members, and then, after another four to six weeks, by a loan to the group chairperson. (This pattern is known as 2:2:1 staggering.) At first, the groups were seen just as sources of sol-idarity, offering mutual assistance in times of need. For example, if a member of a group fails to attend a meeting, the group leader repays on her behalf, and thus the credit record of the absentee borrower remains clean, and so does the group's. The original premise was that perhaps someone might experience a delay in getting a loan if there were a problem within their group, but there would not be further sanctions.

Over time, though, formal sanctions became more common. In prin-ciple, if serious repayment problems emerge, all group members will be cut off from future borrowing. The original idea was not that group members would be forced to repay for others, rather it was that they would lose the privilege of borrowing. In practice, of course, a bor-rower who does not want to lose access to microcredit loans accepts the possibility of having to bail out her fellow group members in times of need. It is not unheard of that a loan officer will stay in a village until group members (or members of the forty-person center) are able to make good on all installments due that week (although the practice is not in keeping with the early vision of top Grameen managers).

In a typical situation, when all goes well with repayments, borrow-ers are offered a larger loan repayable in the next "loan cycle" (loan cycles—from initial disbursement to repayment of the final install-ment—were typically a year in the "classic" Grameen system). Thus, if the relationship between Grameen and the borrowers continues, loan sizes grow over the years and credit histories are built up. Eventually loans may be large enough to build or repair a house or to make lumpy investments like purchasing a rickshaw or, in a recent loan innovation, sending a child to university.

MITIGATING ADVERSE SELECTION

The adverse selection problem occurs when lenders cannot distinguish inherently risky borrowers from safer borrowers. If lenders could dis-tinguish by risk type, they could charge different interest rates to different types of borrowers. But with poor information, options are limited. As we saw adverse selection may lead to credit rationing because it induces lenders to charge everyone high interest rates to compensate for the possibility of having very risky borrowers in the customer population. The trouble (and source of inefficiency) arises when safe borrowers are thus deterred from applying for loans. In principle, group lending with joint responsibility can mitigate this inefficiency.

The most direct mechanism occurs when customers inform the bank about the reliability of potential joiners, allowing the bank to adjust terms accordingly. We describe a less direct mechanism that may also work, and that does not rely on revealing information to the bank. Because the result is somewhat surprising, we develop it in several steps.

Consider a microfinance institution or a bank committed to covering its costs so that it just breaks even. Assume that the bank introduces the group lending methodology described previously, and that it has no idea about the borrowers' characteristics. Borrowers, on the other hand, know each other's types, and, borrowers are either "risky" or "safe." As before, the problem is that the bank wants to charge lower interest rates to safe borrowers and higher rates to risky borrowers, but, since the bank cannot easily tell who is who, everyone has to pay the same rate. In practice, then, the safer borrowers—when they actually decide to apply for a loan at the prevailing interest rates— implicitly subsidize the risky borrowers (who are more costly for the bank to serve). The inefficiency arises when this implicit subsidy is so large that safe borrowers leave the market rather than shouldering the burden—namely, when the presence of risky borrowers raises the inter-est rate to levels that are simply unaffordable for safer borrowers. The question here is whether group lending can make it possible to *implic-itly* charge safe borrowers lower interest rates and thus keep them in the market.

The fact that groups are encouraged to form on their own is the key to the solution; potential borrowers can then use their information to find the best partners. How they sort themselves depends on the nature of the loan contract. Faced with the prospect of joint responsibility for loans, it is clearly better to be grouped with safe types than with risky types. So, given the choice, the safe types stick together. The risky bor-rowers thus have no alternative but to form groups with other risky types, leading to a segregated outcome often referred to in the labor economics literature as "assortative matching."

How does this help the bank charge lower prices to safe types? Because investment projects undertaken by risky borrowers fail more often than those of safe borrowers, risky borrowers have to repay for their defaulting peers more often under group lending with joint responsibility; otherwise, they will be denied future access to credit. Safe borrowers no longer have to shoulder the burden of default by the risky types. What this boils down to is a transfer of risk from the bank onto the risky borrowers themselves. It also means that, effectively, the safe types pay lower interest rates than the risky types—because they no longer have to cross-subsidize risky borrowers. Strikingly, the result is that the group lending methodology does the trick even though (1) the bank remains as ignorant as ever about who is safe and who is risky, and (2) all customers are offered exactly the same contract. All of the action occurs through the joint responsibility condition combined with the sorting mechanism.

Moreover, because banks are now better insured against defaults, average interest rates for both risky and safe types can be reduced while banks still make profits. The lower interest rates in turn bring a secondary positive effect. In the adverse selection problem analyzed, "safe" borrowers were inefficiently pushed out of the market by high interest rates; here, the reduction in interest charges faced by safe types further encourages them to reenter the market, mit-igating the market failure.

To see this formally, suppose that the bank requests that borrowers form two-person groups and that each individual in the pair holds herself responsible for her peer. The analysis is sim-plified by assuming that individuals try to maximize their expected income without concern for risk. As before, we first present the analy-sis using algebra and then provide a simple numerical example.

Again, each individual has a one-period project requiring \$1 of investment. The fraction of the population that is safe is $q < 1$, and the fraction of the population that is risky is $(1 - q)$. A dollar invested by safe borrowers yields a gross return $\underline{y}$ with certainty. A risky borrower who invests \$1, on the other hand, obtains a gross return $\bar{y} > \underline{y}$ i f suc-cessful, and this occurs with probability $p < 1$. If not successful, they earn 0, which happens with probability $(1 - p)$. Again, to simplify things we assume that both types have identical *expected* returns, so that $p\bar{y} = \underline{y}$. How do the types sort themselves into groups? Since bor-rowers know each other's types, safe borrowers pair with other safe types, and risky borrowers pair with other risky types (i.e., there will be assortative matching in equilibrium). Now consider more closely sit-uations where both types of borrowers participate in the credit market. Since the fraction of the population that is safe is $q < 1$, this will also be the fraction of groups made up of (safe, safe) types. If, say, a quarter of the population is "safe," then a quarter of the two-person groups will be made up of "safe" couples.

What is the gross interest rate Rb (principal plus interest) that the bank should charge in order to break even? To make the problem inter-esting, assume that $y > 2R_b$ so that, when lucky, a risky borrower can always repay for her peer. Then the expected revenue of the bank if it sets its break-even interest rate at Rb is straightforward to compute: With probability q the bank faces a (safe, safe) pair of borrowers and therefore gets repaid for sure; with probability $(1 - q)$, the bank faces a (risky, risky) pair, in which case it is always repaid unless both bor-rowers in that pair have a bad draw; we denote the probability that the bank is repaid in this case as g. Since the chance that *both* are simulta-neously unlucky is $(1 - p) \cdot (1 - p)$, the chance that one or both are lucky is $g = 1 - (1 - p)^2$. The expected payment to the bank is thus

$$[q + (1-q)g]Rb. \qquad (4.1)$$

The equation reflects that a fraction q of groups return R_b always (i.e., the safe groups) and a fraction $(1 - q)$ of groups return R_b just

g pro-portion of the time. This expected payment must be equal to the bank's cost of funds k in order for the bank to break even in expectation. Solving for R_b gives

$$R_b = k/[q + (1 - q)g] \quad (4.2)$$

which is smaller than the interest rate in the absence of group lending found in chapter 2 (there, without group lending, we found that $Rb = k/[q + (1 - q)p]$). The fact that the interest rate is smaller here arises because $g > p$; that is, the process of matching means that risky bor-rowers can pay back their loans more often (thanks to joint liability) than they could if just dealing with the bank as individuals. The risk is thus passed on from the bank to the risky borrowers. The bank can thus reduce the interest rate and lure deserving safe types back into the market.

The beauty of the arrangement is that all borrowers face the *same con-tract,* but, thanks to assortative matching, the risky types pay more on average. The bank thus effectively price discriminates—without needing to know who is safe and who is risky.

Group Lending beyond Villages

Not all microfinance programs start with close-knit borrowers with rich information on each other. Karlan (2003), for example, describes village banks in the Andes town of Ayacucho (with a population of 150,000). The FINCA affiliate spreads the word about the village banks, and interested borrowers are invited to come to FINCA's office to put their names on a list; once the list reaches thirty names (typically in less than two weeks), a group is formed. The process is easy and efficient, but a consequence is that few of the group members know each other before joining the village bank.

In contrast, showed how banks can circumvent credit rationing due to adverse selection through group lending when borrowers are perfectly informed about each other's types. The village banks of Ayachucho represent a different context, one more typical of urban areas such as Mexico City and Bogotá, where populations are highly mobile and often have little information about each other. Can group lending still help to overcome adverse selection? Can group lending carry benefits even if the "getting to know each other" process is slow or imperfect?

Consider the extreme scenario where potential borrowers remain completely anonymous; that is, they do not have any information about the characteristics of their peers. Group lending can no longer lead to assortative matching; instead, it will typically involve mixed pairs of safe and risky borrowers. Is this enough to discourage safe borrowers from applying for a loan? Can an appropriately structured group-lending contract improve on standard "individual-lending" contracts?

Risky borrowers will gain from the possibility of matching with a safe borrower who can always repay for them. But can safe borrowers gain too? Yes, if the contract takes advantage of the pos-sibility that when risky borrowers are lucky, they get higher returns than safe borrowers.

The optimal group lending contract will in prac-tice extract more from risky borrowers when they are lucky but paired with an unlucky risky borrower, while the contract will not extract as much from a safe borrower who is paired with an unlucky risky bor-rower. The reason is "limited liability" as described previously. Group lending here makes risky borrowers indirectly cross-subsidize safe bor-rowers, allowing the latter to access loans at a lower interest rate than without group lending. Once again, lower interest rates mitigate the credit rationing problem by increasing the participation of safe bor-rowers in the credit market.

We show the potential for the welfare-improving use of group lending here, using a stylized example based on the analysis of Armendáriz de Aghion and Gollier (2000). The example follows the spirit of the analysis at the start, and, as previously, our goal is to show the potential for gains, rather than to claim that there will *always* be gains. More formally, again let R_b denote the gross inter-est rate set by the bank (set so that the bank just breaks even), and again suppose that returns are set such that $\underline{y} < 2R_b < \bar{y}$. In this case, $\underline{y} < 2R_b$ means that the safe borrowers are unable to fully pay for an unlucky partner's failure. Groups are now matched randomly. Since a fraction q of the population is made up of safe types, the chance that a (safe, safe) pair emerges through random matching is q^2. Similarly, the chance that a (risky, risky) pair emerges is $(1 - q)^2$. And the chance that a (safe, risky) pair emerges is accordingly $1 - q^2 - (1 - q)^2$, or, after sim-plifying, $2q(1 - q)$.

The bank's expected gross revenues are then $2R_b$ from (safe, safe) pairs. This is because both repay the interest rate with certainty. Since the expected fraction of matches that are (safe, safe) is q^2, the bank expects to get $2R_b$ in a fraction q^2 *of* cases. With probability $(1 - q)^2$ the pair is (risky, risky), and the bank gets $2R_b$ if both are lucky. The chance that both are lucky is p^2 since p is the probability that either independ-ently succeeds (again as in chapter 2). The probability that both risky borrowers fail is correspondingly $(1 - p)^2$; in this case, the bank gets nothing back. And the chance that one is lucky while the other is not is $2p(1 - p)$; in that case, the lucky partner can pay for both, so the bank gets $2R_b$ once more. Finally, with probability $2q(1 - q)$, the bank faces a mixed (safe, risky) pair. We know that the safe partner always does well, so the question is: What happens to the risky partner? If the risky partner is lucky (which happens p percent of the time), the bank again gets $2R_b$. But $(1 - p)$ of the time the risky partner has bad luck. Note that here the safe partner cannot fully pay for the risky partner (by the assumption that $y < 2R_b$). Instead, the bank can only extract the amount y from the the safe partner by the assumption of limited liability (i.e., the bank cannot extract more than the safe borrower's current revenue).

In equilibrium, the gross interest rate R_b must be set so that the expected repayment per borrower is equal to the bank's full cost of funds k. Since we are analyzing loans to each member in a two-person group, the expected gross repayment must be at least $2k$. Now we can put all of this information together to yield

$$q^2 2R_b + (1 - q)^2\{p^2 + 2p(1 - p)) 2R_b + 2q(1 - q)[p^2R_b + (1 - p)y] = 2k \tag{4.3}$$

or, simplifying by dividing by two:

$$q^2R_b + (1 - q)^2\{p^2 + 2p(1 - p)) R_b + 2q(1 - q)[pR_b + (1 - p) y/2] = k \tag{4.4}$$

The next step is to solve for the equilibrium gross interest rate R_b that makes the equation hold. The question is whether the R_b that emerges is lower than $k/[q + (1 - q) p]$, which is the gross interest rate in the absence of group lending. After a bit more algebra (which we leave to readers as an exercise), we see that the break-even gross interest rate will indeed be lower than before. The bottom line is quite surprising: in principle, the group-lending contract can help lenders reduce interest rates—even where neither the bank nor the clients have information about who is safe or risky! In the process, adverse selection can be mitigated and a greater number of worthy bor-rowers can get access to credit.

The intuition is that risky borrowers, if lucky, can always repay their defaulting partners—whether safe or risky. But safe borrowers cannot repay for others due to the fact that their returns are lower and that all borrowers are protected by limited liability. Thus, defaults are de facto shouldered by risky borrowers only. Since risks are thereby passed on to risky borrowers specifically (rather than the average borrower), the bank is able to set interest rates that are low enough to win back the business of the safe borrowers. We end this section where we started, by reminding readers that the analysis only shows the *potential* for gains, and it draws on specific assumptions about the nature of risks and the role of limited liability. All the same, it is a striking example of the potential for group-lending contracts to make improvements— even in situations where it had been thought impossible.

OVERCOMING MORAL HAZARD

In this section we show how group lending with joint responsibility may circumvent moral hazard problems in lending, thereby further relaxing credit constraints. Here, we draw on the possibility that group members, who often live and work closely together, can impose social or economic sanctions on each other, possibilities that are impossible for an outside bank to impose.

Ex Ante Moral Hazard and the Role of Joint Responsibility

In important early work on the theory of group lending, Stiglitz (1990) set out an ex ante moral hazard approach to group lending. In a widely cited article in the *World Bank Economic Review*, Stiglitz argues that the group-lending contract circumvents ex ante moral hazard by inducing borrowers to monitor each others' choice of projects and to inflict penalties upon borrowers who have chosen excessively risky projects. As Laffont and Rey (2003) argue, the fact that group members are affected by the actions—and inactions!—of other members means that they will take steps to punish anyone who puts in little effort and thus burdens the group with excessive risk.

A nonshirk-ing borrower generates gross revenue y with certainty, whereas a shirk-ing borrower generates gross revenue y with probability p and zero with probability $(1 - p)$. Consider again a borrower's decision whether or not to put effort into her project. If R denotes the gross interest rate (interest plus principal) to be paid to the lender and c is the cost of effort, then a borrower's expected return if she puts in effort equals $(y-R) - c$, as before. Members of the group act to maximize group income, and anyone who deviates is punished with serious social sanctions.

The borrower had the option to put in the requisite effort and get net revenues of $(y - R) - c$. Or, alternatively, the borrower had the option to take a gamble by shirking; in this second case, the borrower only succeeds p percent of the time but does not have to bear the cost of effort. So, effort is only forthcoming if $(y - R) - c > p\,(y - R)$, which implies that the gross interest rate must be set so that $R < y - [c/(1 - p)]$. Interest rates higher than this level will encourage shirking. These inequalities are termed incentive compatibility constraints (or, simply, IC constraints), and they play a key role in understanding the function of contracts.

The group-lending contract allows the lender to do better than this: Interest rates can be raised higher without undermining good incen-tives. To see this, we consider a "group IC constraint." We show that the maximum feasible interest rate that the bank can elicit from the group of borrowers without inducing default is higher because the IC constraint is "more relaxed" (i.e., easier to satisfy) than the individual IC constraint described in the previous paragraph.

We again consider a two-person group. If both put in effort, they both pay back loans and incur the costs of effort. Together, the return is $(2y - 2R) - 2c$. On the other hand, if they both shirk, they expect to be able to pay their full joint obligation $(2y - 2R)$ only p^2 fraction of the time. If the borrowers both shirk and one is lucky but not the other, the lucky one is responsible for the full repayment of both, leaving no surplus left over.

Thus, the group IC constraint under joint responsibility reflects the fact that positive rewards are only received when both projects succeeed:

$$(2y\text{-}2R)\text{-}2c>p^2\ (2y\text{-}2R), \tag{4.5}$$

or equivalently $R < y - c/(1 - p^2)$. Since $p < 1$, it must be that $p^2 < p$, which means that $(1 - p^2) > (1 - p)$. Accordingly, the maximum achiev-able gross interest rate R under group lending with joint responsibil-ity—namely, $y - [c/(1 - p^2)]$—is strictly larger than the maximum achievable interest rate in the absence of joint responsibility—namely, $y - [c/(1 - p)]$.

The joint liability contract relies on the group's ability to sanction individuals who try to shirk. In Stiglitz's model, the sanctions are cost-less, but in subsequent work by others, monitoring and enforcement costs are derived as part of the decision framework. Given the contract, in principle both group members will never shirk, so it turns that out the sanctions are never actually used. In principle, all that is needed is the *threat* of their use.

Ex Post Moral Hazard and the Role of Peer Monitoring

Now suppose that everybody works hard, so the kinds of concerns are allayed. But now consider a problem that can occur after production has been completed and profits have been real-ized. The new concern is that borrowers may now be tempted to pocket the revenues without repaying the lender (i.e, to "take the money and run"). The problem then is that the bank cannot tell which borrowers truthfully cannot repay—versus those borrowers who are seeking to run away with their earnings.

To sharpen the tension, assume that, in the absence of peer monitoring, a borrower will default with certainty on her loan (whether or not she in fact has the resources to repay). Everything else equal, we saw earlier that this sort of ex post moral hazard eliminates the scope for lending as no bank will extend credit if it anticipates that the borrower will escape repayment. Group lending with peer monitoring can, however, induce each group member to incur a monitoring cost k ex post to check the actual revenue realization of her peer. We assume that with this information, the partner can force the peer to repay. Let us assume that by incurring a cost k, a borrower can observe the actual revenue of her peer with probability q, and let d denote a social sanction that can be applied to a borrower who tries to divert due repayments. Then, if R denotes the gross interest rate set by the bank, a borrower will choose to repay if and only if

$$y\text{-}R>y\text{-}q(d + R), \quad (4.6)$$

or equivalently

$$R<[q/(1\text{-}q)]d. \quad (4.7)$$

This in turn means that borrowers can contract any loans of size less than or equal to $[q / (1 - q)] d$. In the absence of peer monitoring, we had $q = 0$ (zero chance of observing the borrower's actual revenue) and therefore no lending at all in equilibrium. Now, why do we have mon-itoring (implied by $q > 0$) in equilibrium?

The answer to this question is somewhat similar to that developed by Banerjee, Besley and Guin-nane (1994). In their analysis of credit cooperatives, it was the insider's fear of losing her collateral w, which induced her to monitor her peer borrower.

Here, it is the borrower's incentive to minimize the probability of suffering from joint responsibility that induces monitoring (provided the monitoring cost k is sufficiently small). Specifically, a borrower will choose to monitor her peer when-ever the monitoring cost k is less than her expected gain qy from avoid-ing the need to assume responsibility for her peer's repayment. Thus, joint responsibility makes lending sustainable by inducing peer moni-toring and overcoming enforcement problems associated with ex post moral hazard.

So, the group lending contract again does better than the traditional individual lending contract. But can the microlender do even better than that? Rai and Sjöström (2004) argue in an important theoretical contribution that the answer is yes—and we return to the issue at the end of this chapter.

EVIDENCE ON GROUPS AND CONTRACTS

While the theories of group lending work on paper, how do they work in practice? Is the group lending mechanism in fact the key to the high loan repayment rates boasted by microlenders? Over the past few years empirical researchers have studied these questions, and they have arrived at a series of competing results. Some results support the the-ories presented here, while others point to tensions and constraints in the group-lending approach.

Richard Montgomery turns a critical eye to BRAC in Bangladesh, a Grameen Bank replicator (at least as far as its credit operations go). Montgomery (1996, 289) argues that BRAC's implementation of group lending "can lead to forms of borrower discipline which are unneces-sarily exclusionary, and which can contradict the broader (social) aims of solidarity group lending." This is an important reminder: The dis-cussion so far has focused on ways that group lending can improve the bank's performance. We have focused little on how the practice affects borrowers' lives, other than by assuming that improvements are made when group lending improves access to credit for individuals lacking collateral. Montgomery's main concern is that group lending can create peer pressure that works against the poorest and most vulnerable members of the community. In attempting to keep repayment rates up, Montgomery contends, loan officers put sharp pressure on borrowers to repay, even when the borrowers faced difficulties beyond their control.

He mentions stories of the "forced" acquisition of household utensils, livestock, and other assets of defaulting members. In one case, a woman's house was pulled down for failure to pay a housing loan (Montgomery 1996, 297). One response raised in chapter 6 involves providing insurance alongside credit, so that borrowers have a way to cope with major risks. Without such insurance, there is a legitimate question as to whether microfinance (whether implemented via group lending or via other methods) can make some borrowers more vul-nerable than they had been. There may be other ways to get the benefits of group lending without all of the drawbacks.

Montgomery also suggests that the "reality" of group lending in Bangladesh is that the traditional five-person group ultimately plays a small role in ensuring repayment discipline. Instead it is the larger, village-level group that plays the key role. Montgomery (1996, 296–297) writes the following with regard to this "village organization" (VO):

The VO leaders commonly treat overdue installments as a VO issue. If the indi-vidual continues to default on their installments, and the outstanding amount grows or the loan term expires, the VO leader and the group (VO) as a whole comes under pressure from the field staff. Rather than invoking the idea that four other members are jointly liable for the outstanding loan, field staff threaten to withdraw access to loans for VO members in general. The use of this sanction was freely admitted by the program staff in several of the five area offices in which field work was carried out; and it is because of the wide-spread use of this sanction that it is the VO, not the formal sub-groups within a VO, which becomes the joint-liability group in practice. In reality the 5–6 member joint-liability groups rarely exist, and especially in older VOs ordinary members cannot name the sub-group leaders stipulated in BRAC's formal blueprint of VO structure.

Similar stories have been told about Grameen Bank practices, and it happens often enough that one observer has called it "meeting day joint-liability." The idea is that the loan officer is keenly aware of which borrowers in the larger, village-level group are finishing up their current loans and are about to request a next (often larger) loan. Those individuals are particularly susceptible to pressure to help with problem clients. Loan officers will thus be tempted to tell these soon-to-borrow-again customers that if help in dealing with the problem is not forthcoming, the anticipated loans may be delayed. To make the point sharper, it is not unheard of for the loan officer to refuse to leave the village until the books are completely squared. As Matin (1997) has written, the staggered disbursal of loans helps to ensure that there is often someone in the larger group that is close to qualifying for a next loan—and thus particularly open to suasion.

The practice of "meeting day joint-liability" is not universal, and it is not necessarily a bad thing. Indeed, there is nothing sacred about the number five as the perfect group size. Elsewhere, solidarity groups stretch from three to nine borrowers. And the village banking model used by FINCA, Freedom from Hunger, Pro Mujer, and others encom-passes a single village-level group. While the adverse selection story of Ghatak (1999) hinges on the functioning of multiple groups within a village (so that borrowers can freely sort themselves into groups on the basis of risk), the preceding moral hazard stories do not depend criti-cally on whether there is one group or more. Indeed, larger groups may be better able to deal with risks and less vulnerable to collusion.

Empirical researchers have tried to shine a bit of light on questions around the roles of groups, but getting clean results has not been easy. In the perfect world, empirical researchers would be able to directly compare situations under group-lending contracts with comparable situations under traditional banking contracts. The best test would involve a single lender who employs a range of contracts. But in prac-tice most microlenders use just one main type of contract, leaving little variation with which to identify impacts. Where several different con-tracts are used, a different problem then emerges: Why do some cus-tomers voluntarily choose one contract over another? Or why does a lender offer one version to some borrowers and a different version to others? Making comparisons thus opens up questions of whether "self-selection" or other aspects of the programs (e.g., management style, training policies, and loan officer behavior) are driving results. The best evidence would come from well-designed, deliberate experiments in which loan contracts are varied but everything else is kept the same. This can be achieved in a lab setting (see, e.g., Abbink, Irlenbusch, and Renner 2002), but it has not yet been done in the field.

The lab experiment of Abbink, Irlenbusch, and Renner (2002) involves a game played in ten rounds. Participants are invited to the lab as part of a research experiment. In one case, the participants must register in groups of four, so that participants presumably sign up along with their friends. This case reflects the self-selection into groups at the heart of the Grameen Bank model. In the other cases, individu-als register independently and are then placed into groups by the researchers, akin to the practice of the FINCA village bank in Ayachu-cho, Peru, studied by Karlan (2003) in which FINCA forms groups from people who have independently come into the FINCA offices to join a list. The researchers aim to test the role of social ties by comparing out-comes of the self-selected groups relative to those of the groups put together by the researchers. The hypothesis is that stronger social ties should increase repayments.

The advantage of doing research in the lab is that the context can be kept exactly the same: the rules of the experiment, the way the partic-ipants are treated, and the eventual rewards received by the partici-pants. Experimenters can then change just one aspect (the way groups are formed) and see what happens holding all else constant. The dis-advantage, of course, is that the experiment proceeds in a deliberately artificial setting; for example, no mention was even made of "microfinance" for fear that it would trigger associations with certain kinds of behavior, actual loans are not made, and actual businesses are not oper-ated. Moreover, the participants here were students at the University of Erfurt, Germany, not actual microfinance customers. And, on top of it, we have some reservations about how this particular experiment was designed. All the same, experiments like this can help researchers understand the basic logic of contracts and develop hypotheses that can be pursued later in the field.

Each round of the Erfurt experiment begins with participants being given a "loan" that they must pay back. They are then told that either they have been lucky and their income is high, or else they are unlucky (less than 20 percent of the time) and their income is zero. With zero income, debts cannot be repaid by the unlucky individuals, so it falls to their group to repay all debts. If the group fails to fully repay for all, no one in the group can move forward to the next round of loans. The question is whether the lucky participants are willing to pitch in to help the unlucky members—and if those who are lucky will cheat and pretend that they have been unlucky (in order to avoid repaying). Groups that trust more and cheat less will do better, and the experi-ment is structured so that cooperation is unlikely without some basic trust between members—which suggests that the self-selected groups with preexisting social ties should do better than the groups put together by the researchers. The researchers find, though, that, to the contrary, there is little difference in outcomes between the two groups; in fact, in some cases the self-selected groups do *worse* in terms of repayment rates, perhaps because shirking among friends is tolerated less than shirking among unconnected participants who can be expected to behave in a more self-centered way (the lower level of tolerance among friends destroys trust and, with it, reduces average repayment rates).

Both types of groups, though, have slightly higher overall repayment rates than would be expected under traditional individual contracts. The experiment also reveals that women appear to be more reliable, that larger groups do worse, and that "dynamic incentives" play a major role in determining repayments.

The finding that groups of strangers do as well as (and, in some cases, better than) groups of friends conflicts with arguments about the role of social capital and social sanctions in microfinance. But the finding has some support in theory, and it is given support in the field by Wydick (1999) whose study of group lending in Guatemala leads him to conclude that social ties per se have little impact on repayment rates: Friends do not make more reliable group members than others. In fact, the participants he studies are sometimes softer on their friends, wors-ening average repayment rates (an interesting contrast to the experi-mental results in which friends appear to be tougher on each other, at least when dishonesty is perceived). Ahlin and Townsend (2003a) also find that proxies for strong social ties are associated with weaker repay-ment performance in evidence on group lending in Thailand. Karlan (2003), though, argues that social capital helps in Peru, and Wenner (1995) finds that social cohesion is a positive force in groups in Costa Rica. Wydick too finds that social cohesion helps (as proxied by living close together or knowing each other prior to joining the microfinance group), even if *friendship* specifically creates tensions. Gómez and Santor (2003) find that default is less likely if there is greater trust and, social capital, and if members have known each other before joining the groups.

In sum, the five empirical studies discussed here give a mixed picture. In thinking about the way forward, we pause here to take a more detailed look at the last of the studies. In any study based on survey data (based on actual borrowers and actual loans), the job for researchers is to convince readers that the comparisons of situations under different contracts are meaningful—that apples are not being compared to oranges. Gómez and Santor (2003) wrestle with compa-rability in their study of contracts used by two Canadian microlenders, Calmeadow Metrofund of Toronto and Calmeadow Nova Scotia of Halifax. Both programs make loans using individual-lending and group-lending methods. The individual loans tend to be larger (the median size is $2,700 versus $1,000 for group loans), but interest rates are identical at 12 percent per year plus a 6.5 percent upfront adminis-tration fee. As suspected, quite different types of people opt for group lending over individual lending. Group members are more likely to be female, Hispanic, and immigrant. Individual borrowers are more likely to be male, Canada-born, and of African descent; they are also more likely to have higher income and larger, older businesses, and to rely more on self-employment income. A simple comparison of perform-ance across groups shows that group loans are more likely to be repaid (just over 20 percent of group loan customers have defaulted on their loans versus just over 40 percent of individual loan customers), but the comparison does not take into account other social and economic differences.

The approach taken by Gomez and Santor is to follow the "match-ing method" approach of Rosenbaum and Rubin (1983). Using a sample of almost 1,400 borrowers, the method involves first pooling all of the data and estimating the likelihood that a borrower will have a group loan (rather than a standard individual loan). Determinants include age, income, neighborhood, education level, and ethnicity. The estimates yield an index of the probability of taking a group loan, with the important feature that borrowers within the same level of the index also have similar observed characteristics. Reliable comparisons are thus achieved by comparing only borrowers within similar levels of the index. In principle, apples are compared to apples, and oranges to oranges. Using this method, Gómez and Santor find that borrowers under group contracts repay more often. The result, they argue, arises both because more reliable borrowers are more likely to choose group contracts and because, once in the group contracts, the borrowers work harder.

The estimation approach is simple and intuitive, but it rests on one vital assumption: that the choice of contract can be explained entirely by the variables in their equation (age, income, neighborhood, etc.). If there are important variables omitted from the equation (say, entre-preneurial ability or inherent riskiness), the method ceases to guaran-tee consistent estimates: riskier borrowers may more likely end up in individual contracts, for example, and they may also be more likely to default. In this hypothetical case, the correlation between being in an individual-lending contract and having a worse outcome is not a product of behavior induced by the contract. Ideally, we would like to be able to investigate situations in which borrowers are sorted into con-tracts with some element of randomness—but such situations are rare.

Karlan's (2003) study of the FINCA village bank in Ayacucho, Peru, cleverly takes advantage of a quirk in the way that groups are formed that introduces some randomness into the process. There is only one main kind of contract (FINCA's village banking contract), but there is randomness in which group a borrower is placed. The FINCA contract involves groups of thirty women who meet weekly; each week, they receive new loans, pay installments on existing loans, and/or contribute to savings accounts. Unlike other models, the meeting is not held in the local neighborhood or village; instead meetings are held at the FINCA office in the town center. And, again unlike other models, it is FINCA that forms the groups in Ayacucho. FINCA broadcasts its intention to start village banks and invites prospective borrowers to sign up. A list is posted on a wall, and once thirty names are listed, a group is formed.

The next thirty people make up another group, and so forth. The staff find this the quickest way to form groups, and they hope to build social ties between strangers that will deliver independent benefits. In general, clients do not sign up as preformed groups, and most people do not know each other before FINCA puts them together. From an econometric standpoint, the fact that FINCA selects the groups in this somewhat arbitrary way minimizes biases due to unobserved characeristics. Specifically, when researchers compare why one group had higher repayments than another, concerns are alleviated that results will be biased due to peer selection based on unobserved strengths. Karlan's tests show that the composition of groups indeed looks similar to the general characteristics of the broader population—groups look like what you would expect from a random draw.

Karlan is most interested in the role of social capital—the links between clients that are foundations of trust and cooperation. Unlike real capital (cash, machines, and equipment), "social" capital cannot be observed and simply counted. To proxy for social capital, Karlan thus considers cultural similarity as indicated by language (Spanish only or Quechua—the most common indigenous language—only?), hair (braided, long, or short?), dress (indigenous *pollera* skirt or Western-style clothes?), and hat (indigenous-style hat or not?), as well as con-sidering geographic proximity (percentage of group members living within a 10-minute walk of each other). These "social capital" mea-sures correlate well with the level of social and business interactions and with who sits next to whom at group meetings.

Do these measures of social capital make a difference to loan repay-ment rates? There are in fact two types of loan repayment rates. The first pertains to loans made by the central FINCA organization to the local group; these loans were all repaid on time during the period in question (1998–2000). The second pertains to loans made to group members from a pool of savings that was generated by the members themselves; here, repayment rates are much lower: around 20 percent. Karlan finds that larger scores on the measures of geographic proxim-ity and cultural similarity predict lower default rates, a finding in line with the theory we sketched earlier in the chapter in which the threat of social sanctions aids repayment rates (and in line with, e.g., Stiglitz 1990). Interestingly, while Karlan finds that default leads to dropout from the program, the effect is attenuated for clients with more social capital. The finding suggests the possibility of beneficial risk sharing: namely, that clients who are forced to default due to circumstances beyond their control (as opposed to exhibiting moral hazard) are less likely to be forced to leave the program when the clients have strong social ties to the rest of the group.

Karlan's results thus show that the group contract can harness local ties in ways that traditional lending contracts cannot. The limit of the results is that they can not nail down whether the improvements occur because of greater trust (and more effective use of social sanctions) as the stress on "social capital" in the paper's title suggests—or, on the other hand, whether the improvements flow simply from the fact that people who are more similar and who live more closely may have an easier time monitoring each other (or perhaps both) than those who are/do not.

The latter interpretation is consistent with Wydick (1999), who finds little support that stronger social ties help in group lending in Guatemala, but finds that repayment rates rise with variables that proxy for group members' ability to monitor and enforce group rela-tionships (e.g., repayments rise with knowledge of the weekly sales of fellow group members). The distinction between the two interpreta-tions may not matter in practice (institutions may just be happy that the contracts help), but the unanswered questions point to future steps for research on contracts.

A different perspective on contracts is provided by the ambitious studies of Ahlin and Townsend (2003a, 2003b). They start with the theoretical models of group lending developed by Besley and Coate (1995), Banerjee, Besley, and Guinnane (1994), Ghatak (1999), and Stiglitz (1990). After putting the models into a comparable theoretical framework, Ahlin and Townsend take them to data, trying to deter-mine which does a better job of explaining patterns in practice. Their data come from 262 joint liability groups of the Bank for Agriculture and Agricultural Cooperatives (BAAC) in Thailand in addition to data on 2,880 households from the same villages.

Ahlin and Townsend do not seek to judge group lending versus alternative contracts. Rather, as with some of the other papers described here, their aim is to see what makes group lending work. Their answer is that there is no single uni-versal answer. In the poorer regions of northeast Thailand, expected repayment rates increase when village social sanctions rise. But in the wealthier, central region, the extent of joint liability matters, and the higher joint liability payments are, the higher default rates are. Also, the greater the extent of cooperation among group members (e.g., the more family members are in a group), the higher the default. These latter results suggest that too much social capital can be a bad thing when it fosters collusion against the bank.

Theory predicts that a borrower's alternative options will influence outcomes as well. The more other good ways to borrow exist, the less a microfinance client will feel compelled to minimize chances of default—since defaulters can always fall back on their other options. Unlike the findings on social capital, there is fairly broad agreement here. Ahlin and Townsend (2003a), for example, find that everywhere in their sample, the better a borrower's alternative options for bor-rowing, the worse her repayment rates. Wenner's (1995) investigation of repayment rates in twenty-five village banks in Costa Rica affiliated with FINCA shows that delinquency rates are higher in wealthier towns where, presumably, clients have more abundant outside options.

The result is echoed by Sharma and Zeller (1996) in their study of three programs in Bangladesh (but not Grameen). An exception to these findings is found by Khandker, Khalily, and Kahn in investigating the Grameen Bank and other Bangladesh banks. They find that both dropout rates and repayment rates increase in better-developed villages (which tend to have better business opportunities).

A final empirical issue involves the role of diversity in groups. The theories that stress the positive roles of social capital and social sanc-tions suggest that less diverse groups will do better. Where collusion is a possibility, on the other hand, the opposite may hold: Greater diversity may aid repayments by diminishing the chance for collusion.

Sadoulet (2003) provides another reason that diversity can help: Greater diversity means that group members' incomes are less likely to vary together, and thus group members' ability to insure each other increases (i.e., there's a greater chance to provide mutual aid in times of need). Since insurance should help repayment rates, diversity helps. And, if diversity helps, borrowers should try to form groups that are broad, which is exactly what Sadoulet and Carpenter (2001) find in a study of groups in Guatemala. Ahlin and Townsend (2003a, 2003b), though, find that in Thailand it is positive correlations of income that, holding all else constant, appear to predict entry into group contracts.

Results from different parts of the world thus reveal different (some-times opposing) relationships. Advancing understanding of group lending will thus entail better understanding of the kinds of positive outcomes described in the first part of this chapter—along with under-standing of potentially negative scenarios as well.

LIMITS TO GROUP LENDING: HIDDEN COSTS, COLLUSION, AND EMERGING TENSIONS

We started this chapter by reviewing the standard features of the group-lending methodology introduced by the Grameen Bank in the

1970s. Theorists have been particularly interested in the ways that the model takes advantage of existing local information and social ties. But models that succeed in rural Bangladesh have not succeeded everywhere else.

Using social sanctions, in particular, has limitations. Typically, social sanctions involve excluding "problem" borrowers from privileged access to input supplies, from further trade credit, from social and reli-gious events, or from day-to-day courtesies. Commercial banks hoping to move into the "microfinance niche" have particular difficulties invoking these kinds of mechanisms among their clients, but so do NGOs. For example, will the threat of social sanctions be credible in small village communities among very close friends and relatives? Or, at the other extreme, can social sanctions have teeth in urban environ-ments where borrowers come and go and remain fairly anonymous to one another? Practitioners have thus had to tinker with contracts and redesign according to their contexts.

The tinkering and redesigning has had to address the costs inherent in group-lending contracts, as well as the many advantages described previously. The essence of group lending is to transfer responsibilities from bank staff to borrowers. Traditionally, loan officers select clients, monitor performance, and enforce contracts. Under group lending, borrowers share part of these burdens too. The gain for clients is that they obtain loans (and other financial services) at reasonable prices. But, given the choice, most clients would not opt to help start a bank and run it just in order to get loans. Ladman and Afcha (1990), for example, argue that in the case of the Small Farmer Credit Program (PCPA) in Bolivia, it was difficult to find potential borrowers to volunteer to lead their groups, and group leaders had to spend a great deal of time persuading borrowers to accept the group-lending con-tract. In one village, group leaders had to put in four times as many hours in preparation before initial loan disbursal relative to the time needed under traditional individual lending procedures.

Other concerns hinge on the group meetings that are at the core of group lending models. Attitudes are mixed. One complaint is that attending group meetings and monitoring group members can be costly, especially where houses are not close together. In two of the three

Chinese programs studied by Albert Park and Changqing Ren, for example, 8 percent of clients had to walk more than an hour to get to meetings. Overall, attending meetings and travel time took just over one hundred minutes on average. In a survey of dropouts from group lending programs in Uganda and Bangladesh, a Women's World Banking (2003) study found that 28 percent of dropouts in Bangladesh left in part because of the frequency of meetings; this was so for 11 percent of former clients surveyed in Uganda. On the other hand, nearly all current clients of Women's World Banking affiliates in Uganda and Bangladesh report that they enjoy coming to meetings (Women's World Banking 2003, 5). In Uganda, the most-cited reason (65 percent) was that they liked the chance to share ideas and learn from each other; in Bangladesh, the most-cited reason (43 percent) was the social aspect of meetings.

A second issue relates to the fact that group lending works by trans-ferring what are typically the bank's responsibilities to the customers themselves. As we noted, these responsibilities can carry hidden costs. Some borrowers may be tempted to think: I simply want a loan, why am I asked to help run the bank in return? But there is another aspect that goes beyond these kinds of costs. Group lending can bring added risks for borrowers, and if borrowers are risk averse, those risks can weigh heavily. The risk is embedded in the contract: A borrower is now not just at risk of defaulting on her own, but she also faces the risk that her partners will default also. If monitoring and enforcing contracts is costless—as assumed in Stiglitz's (1990) treatment—borrowers can address moral hazard effectively and the risks are minimized. This is the great hope of the group lending contract. But, as noted previously, monitoring is not costless, even for individuals living in close proxim-ity. Typically, then, monitoring will be imperfect, opening the way for moral hazard to enter back into the picture. But under the group lending contract, it is now the group that is exposed to the risk, not the bank. The threat of social sanctions can help, as we described earlier, but in practice they are applied only imperfectly too. The sum, as argued by Madajewicz (2003a) in an important theoret-ical analysis, is that the benefits of group lending—which have been detailed in the first part of this chapter—are counterbalanced by costs. Those costs emerge when borrowers are risk averse and monitoring is costly. Moreover, the costs grow as the scale of lending grows, since the financial implications of default rise with the size of loans. Madajewicz argues that loan sizes are limited by what the group can jointly guarantee, so clients with growing businesses or those who get well ahead of their peers in scale may find that the group contract bogs everyone down. Below a certain scale, group lending dominates individual lending. But her analysis shows that at a certain size of busi-ness, individual lending will be preferred by customers. In an investi-gation of data from Bangladesh, Madajewicz (2003b) estimates that the switch toward the greater net benefits of individual loans already happens for households holding 1.25 acres. Such households would not be considered to be "functionally landless," but they are mainly poor nonetheless.

One implication is that wealthier clients tend to seek individual loans as they move forward, pushing Bolivia's BancoSol and the Grameen Bank, both group-lending pioneers, to introduce new individual-lending contracts for successful clients. A related issue is that some clients simply prefer not having to be obligated to others. As the Women's World Banking (2003, 3) study reports:

This issue was tested further through the question: "Which do you prefer, to have the security that the group will help you out when you are not able to pay back each week, or to assume complete responsibility for your own loan and not having to pay for someone else's loan?" Most customers of both insti-tutions indicated a desire to be independent and to forsake the security of the group. In Bangladesh, 76% of the affiliate's current borrowers and 82% of dropouts answered that they would want to assume total responsibility for their own loan. In Uganda, 87% of the affiliate's current borrowers and 84% of dropouts expressed a similar desire for independence.

A third issue is that under some conditions, borrowers in group-lending contracts may collude against the bank and undermine the bank's ability to harness "social collateral." Stronger social ties within a group can push up repayment rates in some places, while, in others, social ties increase the likelihood of default. Laffont and Rey (2003) take up these tensions from a theoretical per-spective and come to a somewhat optimistic conclusion. In their inves-tigation of moral hazard and group lending, close ties and information sharing among borrowers open the way for contracts that improve on traditional individual-lending contracts. But, on the other hand, the scope for collusion against the lender increases when borrowers share knowledge and social ties. If borrowers do *not* collude, Laffont and Rey show (in a stylized model) that group-lending contracts are superior to individual-lending contracts (because the contracts take advantage of borrowers' knowledge and social ties—as described at the start of the chapter). But even better contracts exist in principle. These include using yardstick competition (judging one member's performance according to the performances of others) and information revelation mechanisms (such as cross-reporting arrangements).

But what if borrowers collude? In that case, Laffont and Rey show that group lending is superior to these alternative mechanisms. The contract delivers outcomes that are not as good as could be obtained if the lender had full information on borrowers, but it beats any alterna-tives. Their bottom line is that having more information (either on the part of borrowers or on the part of the lender directly) leads to con-tracts that improve on standard individual-lending contracts, even when borrowers collude against the lender.

A final issue is whether the group-lending contract is more efficient than alternatives *even when it is successful on its own terms*. We raised this question: Even if the group-lending con-tract does better than the traditional individual-lending contract, can the microlender do even better than that? Rai and Sjöström (2004) argue that the answer is yes (as do, in somewhat different contexts, Laffont and Rey [2003]). The criticism of the group-lending contract as we see it on paper (and as we have described it above) is that punishments are too harsh. For example, in the widely replicated original Grameen Bank contract with five-person groups, when one borrower defaults, all four others are cut off from future lending, too. It is that threat that drives the "peer monitoring," "peer selection," and "peer enforcement" mechanisms. But what if the defaulter got into trouble because her husband fell ill? Or her cow died? Or prices dropped for the goods she sells? What if the problem occurred despite good monitoring, selection, and enforcement?

Rai and Sjöström's particular criticism does not hinge on the moral-ity of the situation, but rather on its efficiency (in the sense used in chapter 2); in the dispassionate language of economics, the punishment implies a "deadweight" loss. They argue that by using a system of cross-reports (see the end of chapter 5 for more), punishments need not be levied so bluntly. Rai and Sjöström argue that rather than writing a contract and passively following the rules, the bank (and borrowers) can take active steps to gather more information when crises emerge. Their idea of cross-reports is to elicit truthful information about what has happened (e.g., was default due to shirking or to a deeper problem?). This information can be elicited by the microlender by solic-iting reports from the problem borrower and her neighbors and showing leniency when all of the independent reports agree with each other.

Some overly harsh punishments can thus be avoided. The pro-posed system of cross-reports is just one way to improve on contracts, and it works well on paper in a specific theoretical context. With modification it might work in practice too, but, even without cross-reports, microlenders are taking steps to address the inefficiencies.

We take the Rai and Sjöström criticism seriously, and microlenders act as if they do as well. Our firsthand observations in Latin America and Asia indicate that group contracts are seldom enforced exactly as they should be on paper. When asked, loan officers respond that they see no reason to automatically punish everyone for the problem of a single person. Instead, loan officers typically spend a great deal of time investigating and managing "problem" cases.

In doing so, staff call on defaulters' neighbors for advice and information (in the spirit, loosely, of cross-reporting). And, once the problem has been investigated (and if the defaulter's peers are found to be relatively blameless), microlen-ders' staff try to get as much of the problem loan repaid as possible and then (if called for) drop just the one defaulter from the group and replace her with an alternative borrower. This is a natural route to improving efficiency (and equity), even as it undermines the strict reading of group-lending contracts.

In a notable break, Grameen Bank's "Grameen Bank II" proposal rec-ognizes the tension between what works on paper and what happens in practice by formally introducing mechanisms through which loan officers can address the problems of individual borrowers without invoking punishments for the entire group (Yunus 2002). The heart of Grameen Bank II is comprised of two types of loans. Borrowers first start with a Basic Loan (in Bangla, this is an "Easy Loan"). The new system allows loans of any duration—from three months to three years—and allows for installments to be smaller in some seasons and larger in others. The weekly repayment practice remains, however. Then, if borrowers get into trouble, they will be offered a Flexible Loan (with the penalty of a sharp drop in their loan size limit). The Flexible Loan has easier terms spread over a longer period, and it allows the borrower to get back on track, eventually returning to Basic Loan status. Half of the loan is provisioned for at the time of switching status to the Flexible Loan. Only when the customer fails to repay the Flexible Loans are they expelled, and the loan is fully written off as bad debt. Some see this proposal as a major departure from group lending by the pioneer of the group-lending contract.

SUMMARY AND CONCLUSIONS

This chapter took up one of the major innovations of the microfinance movement—group lending. From the lender's perspective, the beauty of the contract is that it's a way to transfer (in whole or part) onto customers the responsibility for jobs usually undertaken by lenders. These jobs include screening potential customers, monitoring their efforts, and enforcing contracts. In return, customers get loans that would otherwise be inaccessible or at least that would not be available at such low interest rates.

From the standpoint of economic theory, the group-lending contract addresses the problems raised in chapter 2, notably information imper-fections that cause moral hazard and adverse selection. In principle, the group-lending contract provides a way to achieve efficient outcomes even when the lender remains ignorant or unable to effectively enforce contracts. Moreover, in principle, the group lending methodology can potentially promote social capital, and thus further enhance efficiency.

But if the *borrowers* also lack good information on each other—as may be the case in sparsely populated areas of Latin America and

Africa, for example—a bank employing group-lending contracts may end up worse off than it would if other types of contracts are used. In the next chapter we describe alternative lending mechanisms, all of which can be used with or without group lending. Our belief is that the future of microfinance rests in understanding these alternative mechanisms, taking them apart, reconfiguring them, and, possibly, combining them with new, emerging ideas.

Our stress on alternative contracts stems in large part from the mixed results from the empirical work that we surveyed in section 4.5, as well as from anecdotal evidence and theoretical insight in section 4.6. Emerging tensions include borrowers growing frustrated at the cost of attending regular meetings, loan officers refusing to sanction good borrowers who happen to be in "bad" groups, and constraints imposed by the diverging ambitions of group members. In a telling step, the Grameen Bank has proposed a major overhaul to its lending practices, opening the way for greater flexibility. Empirical research on group lending lags behind theory, but the data so far suggest impor-tant challenges to the generally optimistic tenor of the theoretical research.

5

Beyond Group Lending

INTRODUCTION

The "discovery" of group lending opened up possibilities for microfinance. It is by far the most celebrated microfinance innovation, and with good reason. Group lending showed how unconventional con-tracts can work where tried-and-true banking practices failed again and again, and the shift in understandings led to other new ideas that borrowed as much from traditional moneylenders as from modern banking practices. Today, group lending is just one element that makes microfinance different from conventional banking.

Many of these other new ideas are also used by institutions practic-ing group lending. But the mechanisms are not intrinsically linked, and institutions are increasingly finding that they can pick and choose dif-ferent elements. A case in point is "progressive lending," which is a staple of the "classic" Grameen Bank model but which does not hinge on group lending per se. Progressive lending refers to the practice of promising larger and larger loans for groups and individuals in good standing. Other innovations already present in the classic Grameen model include repayment schedules with weekly or monthly install-ments, public repayments, and the targeting of women. In addition, microlenders have adopted more flexible attitudes to collateral. The emerging new contracts do not necessarily involve groups, and they have been especially helpful in areas with low population densities or highly diverse populations—and in situations where more established clients seek greater flexibility.

Bangladesh's ASA, with its obsession with maximal efficiency, has weakened joint liability in its lending approach, for example, and even the Grameen Bank has proposed to soften joint liability in "Grameen Bank II," which (on paper at least) allows problem loans to be routinely renegotiated without invoking group pressure. In Bolivia, BancoSol has moved a large share of its portfolio out of "solidarity group" con-tracts into individual contracts. "Solidarity group" contracts are still used for small loans (from $50 to $2,000) that are offered to less-established clients, but individual contracts (up to $30,000 but averag-ing $1,000) are the norm for established clients. Bank Rakyat Indone-sia, another microfinance leader, eschewed group loans from the start, and it is joined on that path by urban microlenders in Latin America and Eastern Europe.

Table 5.1 provides comparative data for the 147 programs surveyed in the *Microbanking Bulletin*. Of these "top performers," 73 are individ-ual lenders and the rest either lend through Grameen-type groups of from three to nine borrowers, or through the larger groups associated with the village banking approach. Relative to lenders using group-lending methodologies, microlenders focusing on individuals tend to (a) be smaller and serve better-off clients, as reflected by average loan size; (b) be more self-reliant as proxied by the percentage of their finan-cial costs covered—102 percent relative to just 89 for group-lending microentrepreneurs; (c) serve a smaller population of women clients—on average 46 percent of the clients of individual microlenders are women versus 73 percent for group lenders and 89 percent for village banks; and (d) charge lower interest rates and fees as reflected in the real portfolio yield: 49 percent for village banks, 30 percent for group lenders, and 21 percent for individual lenders. On this latter point, however, it should be noted that village banks and group lenders also have considerably higher expenses relative to loan size. While individ-ual lenders devote 20 cents of each dollar lent to operational costs, group lenders must devote 37 cents, and village banks 61 cents.

The bottom line is that the group lenders and village banks tend to serve poorer clients and have higher costs relative to loan size. As microlenders have matured and diversified, their push to serve better-off clients and reduce costs has opened the door to individual-lending approaches. But individual-lending approaches also have appeal in sparsely populated regions, areas with heterogenous populations, and areas marked by social divisions, where peer monitoring costs are high and social punishments for noncompliance more difficult to imple-ment. Individual-lending approaches may thus be critical in serving some very poor areas as well.

We first discuss the recent trend toward bilateral con-tracting and its emphasis on dynamic incentives via progressive lending techniques. By isolating these lending methods, we aim to shed light on alternative variants of the classic group-lending model as described in chapter 4. This in turn can open the door for microfinance to expand to areas where barriers were thought to be too high.

We also discuss the use of collateral requirements and the replacement of joint liability clauses with public repayments as a simpler way of maintaining peer pressure, and how these innovations are reshaping the microfinance landscape. At the chapter's end, we revisit the group-lending methodology and the challenges it faces as the microfinance industry moves forward.

CREATING DYNAMIC INCENTIVES

Even without recourse to peer monitoring, collateral, or social sanc-tions, microlenders can give incentives to borrowers by threatening to exclude defaulting borrowers from future access to loans. In this way, microlenders have a weapon that was unavailable to failed state-run banks of the past. Those banks were often pressured to extend loans based on political exigencies and could not be counted on to supply a steady flow of financing to small entrepreneurs.

One striking finding about India's troubled Integrated Rural Development Program, for example, was that only 11 percent of all IRDP borrowers borrowed more than once (Pulley 1989). If you suspect that you'll only ever take one loan from an institution, the chance that you'll go to great lengths to repay it falls sharply, and it is not surprising that IRDP's repayment rates fell below 50 percent over time. Microlenders ratchet up incen-tives even further by giving borrowers in goodstanding access to ever-larger loans, creating the promise of turning startup businesses into steady enterprises.

Table 5.1: Financial performance comparisons by lending methodology

Definition	**Individual 1 borrower**	**Solidarity groups Groups of 3–9 borrowers**	**Village banks 10 or more borrowers per group**
Observations	73	47	27
Scale			
Number of borrowers	9,610	47,884	16,163
Average loan size	$973	$371	$136
Outreach			
Average loan size/GNP per capita (%)	88	46	20
Fraction female (%)	46	73	89
Financial performance			
Return on assets (%)	-1.2	-4.1	-7.2
Return on equity (%)	0.6	-12.5	-10.7
Operational self-sufficiency ratio (%)	121	102	107
Financial self-sufficiency ratio (%)	102	89	89
Portfolio yield (real, %)	21	30	49
Portfolio at risk > 90 days	3.7	3.6	3.5
Efficiency			
Operating expense/loan portfolio (%)	20	37	61
Cost per borrower (US$)	155	93	62
Number of borrowers/ total staff	147	155	160
Number of borrowers/ loan officer	508	356	309

Source: The Microbanking Bulletin 2002, Table aA.

In this section we present a simple model of debt without collateral to analyze how bilateral contracts work. We then explore the role of "pro-gressive lending" as an additional tool. While a thick, competitive microfinance market ought to be a microfinance dream, we describe cases in which competition has undermined dynamic incentives in microfinance (and led to microfinance crises in Bolivia and Bangladesh). And we describe why credit bureaus are needed to improve matters.

Threatening to Stop Lending

Nearly all moneylenders surveyed by Aleem (1990) rely principally on two devices for eliciting debt repayments from their clients: develop-ing repeated relationships with the borrowers and making sure that existing borrowers do not contract new loans with other lenders. The two devices make the threat of not refinancing a customer a powerful weapon. We begin by analyzing the theory of these "non-refinancing threats."

Suppose that monitoring costs are very high so that lenders cannot induce repayments via peer groups. As before, we maintain the assumption that borrowers do not have collateral. Moreover, we assume for the moment that social sanctions cannot be used as a way of putting pressure on borrowers to fulfill their contractual obligations. Starting from these basic assumptions, we present a stripped-down version of a model by Bolton and Scharfstein (1990). The model is inspired by the "sovereign debt" problem of the 1980s, which involved lending relationships between "foreign" commercial banks and sover-eign nations.

Assume that there are two periods of production and an investment project that requires \$1. At the end of each period the borrower can generate a gross return $y > \$1$, calculated before repayment of the loan with interest, provided that her current project is financed by the bank. At the repayment stage, however, the borrower may decide to default strategically by simply not repaying the loan. In order to deter the bor-rower from "taking the money and running," the bank can extend a second-period loan contingent upon full repayment of the first-period obligations. The borrower's penalty for defaulting after the first period is thus that she will not be able to invest in the second period. Is this threat enough to elicit payment from the borrower?

Suppose that the borrower decides to default. Her expected payoff in this case will be $y + dvy$, where d is the borrower's discount factor, and v is the probability of being refinanced by the bank despite having defaulted. The discount factor captures the fact that most people weigh payoffs in the future less than payoffs today. To fix ideas, we assume for simplicity that the borrower needs the bank in order to finance a second-period investment, even in the case where he pockets the entire first-period return realization.

Now suppose that, having done well with her investment, the bor-rower decides to repay. In this case, her payoff will be $y - R + dy$, where R is the gross interest rate payable to the bank (principal plus interest). Here, the bank refinances the borrower's second-period investment for sure, setting $v = 1$. As we argue here, this is an equilibrium strategy.

Clearly, because of the *finite* number of periods (two in this case), the borrower has no incentive to repay at the end of the second period.

So if she repaid in period 1 and is refinanced with certainty, her net expected payoff in period 2—evaluated in period 1—is equal to dy. Similarly, if she defaulted in period 1 and is consequently refinanced with probability $v < 1$, her expected payoff in period 2 (evaluated as of period 1), is equal to vdy.

Now moving back to period 1, it is easy to see that the borrower will decide to meet her first-period debt obligation if and only if $y + vdy$ £ $y - R + dy$. This is an "incentive compatibility" (IC) constraint in the jargon of contract theory. As we saw in chapter 4, the constraint determines the largest feasible interest rate that the bank can elicit from the group of borrowers without inducing default. The constraint says that the bank should make sure that the borrower's net present payoff is at least as large when she does not default as when she does. And the obvious way that the bank can do this is by setting an interest rate that is not "too high."

From this, we use the incentive compatibility constraint to derive the maximum gross interest rate R that the bank can elicit from the borrower at the end of the first period is equal to $dy(1 - v)$. The expression is maximized by setting $v = 0$ for defaulters, that is, by fully denying access to future refinancing. Thus, the maximum repayment that the bank can request after the first period is simply R = d*y*, which is the borrower's opportunity cost of defaulting strategically. It will never pay for the borrower to repay more than d*y* in this setup. If, say, the borrower's discount factor is 0.90 and the borrower's gross return is 160 percent, the maximum feasible gross interest rate is 144 percent (or a maximum net interest rate of 44 percent). When operating costs are high, the constraint may well bind. And banks will be even more constrained when borrowers have low discount factors or perceive a relatively high chance of getting refinanced despite default. As described in section 5.2.3, competition without coordination—say, without a credit bureau that keeps tabs on defaulters from other banks—may serve in effect to push the effective refinancing probabil-ity v above zero.

This simple framework also suggests why maintaining the appear-ance of stability is important for lenders. If borrowers begin to think that the bank could go under in future periods, they are more likely to default now, since it is not clear whether there will be a future flow of loans. Whether based in fact or not, such speculation can trigger a "debtor run" that becomes a self-fulfilling prophecy. Bond and Rai (2002), for example, describe a ballooning of defaults faced by Childreach, a microlender in Ecuador, in response to rumors that the organization faced a looming financial crisis.

Progressive Lending

Table 5.2 shows that the Grameen Bank not only provides a continu-ing series of loans but that the loans quickly increase in size. The table shows data for three borrowers randomly chosen from a 1991–1992 sample of thirty Grameen Bank borrowers who each had had six loans to date. The first borrower doubled the value of her loan by the fifth loan; the second borrower had doubled the size by the fourth loan. The final column shows average loan sizes for the entire sample, growing from 2,124 taka for first loans ($57 in 1991) to 4,983 taka ($135) for sixth loans. For the lender, progressive lending cuts average costs since serv-icing a taka. 2,000 loan is not twice as expensive as servicing a 4,000 taka loan. Progressive lending also enables the lender to "test" bor-rowers with small loans at the start in order to screen out the worst prospects before expanding the loan scale (see Ghosh and Ray 1997). From the previous analysis, progressive lending has a third, impor-tant role with regard to incentives. Microlenders can elicit even larger repayments by offering loans of larger size to borrowers that repay their debts. Specifically, progressive lending schemes increase the opportu-nity cost of non-repayment and thereby discourage strategic default even further. To see this, suppose that the bank decides to increase the size of its short-period loans by a factor l > 1 between period 1 and period 2, and that the production technology has constant returns to scale. The opportunity cost of strategic default will then increase by the same factor between the two periods. In particular, by not repaying the gross interest rate R, the borrower now suffers a loss ldy' > dy. This in turn relaxes the incentive compatibility constraint, and the bank can now achieve a maximum interest rate equal to R¢ = ldy > R = dy. Inter-est rates can be raised while keeping the borrowers happy.

Table 5.2: Loan size increases (taka), Grameen Bank, Bangladesh

Borrower A	Borrower B	Borrower C	Full sample average
2000	2000	3500	2124
2500	2500	4000	2897
3000	3000	3000	3656
3500	4000	4000	4182
4000	4000	5000	4736
4000	5000	4000	4983

Source: Authors' calculations from the World Bank–Bangladesh Institute of Development Studies 1991–1992 Survey. Data are in current taka (in 1991, \$1 = Tk. 37; in 1986, \$1 = Tk. 30). The final column averages loan sizes over the full sample of Grameen Bank bor-rowers in the data set (excluding loans used for land/building), and sample sizes dimin-ish with loan number; starting from the first row downward, there are 319, 286, 250, 168, 89, and 30 observations.

Note though that, as before, the analysis rests on an assumption that may not be fully tenable—that if a borrower defaults in the first period, she nonetheless needs a loan to be able to invest in the second period. In principle, borrowers may be able to keep at least part of the princi-pal from the first period and use that to invest in the second. If so, dynamic incentives are harder to maintain; in this case, borrowers can expect a return of y - $R¢$ + ldy if they pay their first-period debt. If they do not, their return is y (1 - j) + jd$y$, where j < 1 is the fraction of the first-period gross return that is invested in the second period. Suppose that, if the borrower defaults, her choice is to hold back a fraction j = R/y. That is, from first-period gross returns, she saves for the next period exactly the amount that she would have paid to the bank (had she chosen to repay the loan with interest). In this case, the household will not default if l > j. Since loan sizes are growing (l > 1) and since not all of the loan is retained (j < 1), this inequality must hold: the bor-rower will not default. But incentives will erode if loans shrink in size, or if the borrower can scale up their own resources faster than the bank can (for more on this, see Bond and Krishnamurty 2001).

This leads to another observation. A borrower who is disposed to strategically default will wait until loan sizes have grown substantially before ultimately choosing to renege on the loan contract. The lender (if also acting strategically) will in turn carefully determine loan sched-ules in order to minimize default. More specifically, consider a multi-period debt relationship between the lender and the borrower. If the growth factor l is large at first (i.e., initial loans increase in size very quickly and then growth slows), the borrower has incentives to default earlier than they would when compared to a steadier path of loan size increases. The incentive problem imposes an upper bound on the desir-able growth rate of loan size over time. On the other hand, reputation considerations on the borrower's side (which are absent from the preceding simple model) should mitigate this effect by reducing the borrower's incentive to default (see, e.g., Sobel 2002).

Competition and Incentives

Economists usually view competition as a good thing, and most theo-retical models assume that there is perfect competition. So far, we have assumed in fact that microlenders are either perfectly competitive or that they simply wish to break even. But in this section we argue that strong competition can undermine dynamic incentives. If a microlender is a monopolist, its threat to cut access to defaulters has greatest bite since they are the only source of credit. Dynamic incentives can weaken when alternative lenders enter the market (assuming that the defaulter has a chance to borrow from them instead). Not only that, but competition can weaken reputation effects.

Problems with competition have emerged most notably in two coun-tries where microfinance was first to take hold: Bolivia and Bangladesh. McIntosh and Wydick (2002) also report on problems of competition in Uganda, Kenya, Guatemala, El Salvador, and Nicaragua. The Bolivian crisis took root when aggressive providers of consumer credit entered the market. In this case, the new entrants were outsiders, notably Acceso FFP, a large Chilean finance company.

Acceso came in with streamlined operations and over one thousand highly motivated employees (most of whose pay came in the form of incentives rather than base salary). Within three years, Acceso had ninety thousand loans outstanding, a level that BancoSol had not reached in its twelve-year history. In 1999, the worst year of the crisis, BancoSol lost 11 percent of its clients, and loan overdue rates for regulated microlenders fell from 2.4 percent at the end of 1997 to 8.4 percent by mid-1999. BancoSol saw its return on equity fall from 29 percent in 1998 to 9 percent in 1999.

The immediate problem with competition in Bolivia was borrowers taking multiple loans simultaneously from different lenders. The bor-rowers then became overindebted, paying one lender's installments by taking a loan from another, leading to a spiral of debt and, too often, financial peril. Carmen Velasco, co-executive director of Pro Mujer, tells of visiting a client in Cochabamba who had loans from two different institutions and was sinking under the weight.

The client's husband reported a proposed solution—the next day they planned to seek a loan from BancoSol to help pay off the first two loans! While our discus-sion here concerns problems that occur when borrowers can turn from one lender to another in sequence (rather than simultaneously), the root of the problem is similar. As long as borrowers believe that they have multiple options, no single lender will have the power to clamp down and maintain full discipline.

Pro Mujer declared that clients holding loans from other banks were henceforth ineligible to borrow, but following up on all financial activ-ities of clients and their families is costly in practice. The general situ-ation in Bolivia improved, though, as regulators tightened rules, the Chilean financiers retreated, and the early microfinance providers like BancoSol and Pro Mujer took extra steps to keep their clients satisfied. Looking forward, the most effective solution would be a credit bureau that keeps track of the credit histories of all borrowers across the nation.

The Bolivian crisis occurred around the same time as the crisis in Bangladesh. The middle and late 1990s saw the explosive growth of the Grameen Bank, ASA, BRAC, and Proshika. While it is impossible to accurately count (because borrowers from a given institution also borrowed from others), around ten million new microfinance clients signed on over the decade. The main microfinance providers had agree-ments not to work with the same clients, but that did not prevent a crisis of simultaneous borrowing along the lines of what occurred in Bolivia. In Bangladesh the problem has been dubbed "overlapping," and Matin and Chaudhury (2001) report that by the end of the decade, there was more than one microlender operating in 95 percent of eighty villages surveyed by researchers at the Bangladesh Institute of Devel-opment Studies (BIDS). Matin (n.d.) reports on a BIDS study that esti-mates that 15 percent of all borrowers took loans from more than one institution. The result, coupled with a broader pattern of lending more than clients could fully absorb, was a repayment crisis that took Grameen Bank's reported repayment rates from above 98 percent to below 90 percent, with greater difficulties in densely served areas like Tangail district.

The lesson from these experiences is not that monopolies should be protected. In both Bangladesh and Bolivia, competition has brought a healthy round of general rethinking that would have not otherwise happened so soon. The chief lesson is instead that cooperative behav-ior among microlenders can help to mitigate the problem. Programs would be aided by the creation of credit bureaus to better share infor-mation on credit access and performance history of borrowers. Having credit bureaus enables lenders to address overindebtedness and to make borrowers face the consequences of strategic defaults (which is not to say that it would be simple to set up credit bureaus in countries like Bangladesh, where there is no system of social security numbers or national ID numbers). No one can force microlenders to join a credit bureau, but the argument in favor of fierce competition cannot be defended without the presence of an adequate regulatory framework.

In Bolivia, regulated financial intermediaries like BancoSol are required by law to report both names and national identification card numbers of delinquent borrowers to the Superintendency of Banks and Financial Institutions (Gonzalez-Vega et al. 1997). In return, all regu-lated financial intermediaries are allowed to view the information pro-vided by the others, and informal arrangements are used to share information with nonregulated microlenders. These measures strengthen dynamic incentives, but lenders must fend for themselves in dealing with "overlapping" clients.

FREQUENT REPAYMENT INSTALLMENTS

One important issue that has so far been mainly overlooked by aca-demics is a curious (or at least nonstandard) aspect of microfinance contracts. This is that lenders often expect loans to be paid in small installments, starting soon after the initial disbursement. In the Grameen Bank model, the installments are weekly. Similarly, in Bolivia between 1987 and 1995 the microlenders Caja Los Andes demanded weekly repayments from about half of its clients. Another 42 percent made repayments every other week (i.e., biweekly), and the remaining 6 percent made monthly installments. For its competitor, BancoSol, over one-third of clients were asked to repay weekly, about one-quarter paid biweekly, and the rest paid monthly.

While having several installments is not unusual for consumer loans made by commercial banks, it is atypical for loans made (at least on paper) for investing in businesses. In "standard" business loans made by traditional commercial banks, the process is just as you would think: entrepreneurs borrow, invest and grow their businesses, and then—once sufficient profits have been earned—repay the loan with interest. Here, it is quite common to expect repayment to start the next month or week!

Table 5.3 provides more data from Bolivia collected by a research team from the Ohio State University. For both Caja Los Andes and BancoSol, the weekly repayment schedules were demanded on smaller-sized loans, while the larger loans carried biweekly or monthly installments. On average, it is poorer households that are being asked to repay in more frequent installments, since it is poorer households that tend to take smaller loans.

Table 5.3: Loan terms and conditions in Bolivia, BancoSol, and Caja Los Andes, 1995

Repayment frequency	**Median amount initially disbursed ($)**	**Median term to maturity (months)**	**Effective annual real interest rate (percent per year)**
Caja Los Andes			
Monthly	37	1	35
Weekly	62	3	35
Weekly	106	5	34
Bi-weekly	309	5	33
Monthly	309	6	26
Monthly	309	6	23
BancoSol			
Weekly	62	3	59
Biweekly	72	4	53
Monthly	82	6	48

Source: Gonzalez-Vega et al. 1997, Table 15, 49–50. Amounts are in U.S. dollars at the exchange rate of 4.93 bolivianos per dollar. The effective annual real interest rate is cal-culated as twelve times the internal monthly rate of return of the contract (in real terms) for loans with median size and median term to maturity. The data reflect loans denom-inated in bolivianos only; both lenders also provided dollar-denominated loans—in much larger sizes (e.g., the median size for Caja Los Andes was about $2,500) with monthly or biweekly installments, lower real interest rates (30 percent per year or below), and yearlong terms to maturity.

The puzzle is why repayments should be scheduled this way. One explanation is that it creates an early warning system. By meeting weekly, credit officers get to know their clients well by seeing them face-to-face on a regular basis. This information can provide loan offi-cers with early warnings about emerging problems and offer bank staff a protocol by which to get to know borrowers more effectively—and clamp down more quickly when needed. Personalized relationships and regular opportunities for monitoring are thus established, just as with local moneylenders. Drawing on their research in Bolivia, Gonzalez-Vega et al. (1997, 74) stress the value of the early warning feature, asserting that "the most important tool for the monitoring of borrowers in these lending technologies is requiring frequent repay-ments followed by immediate reaction in the case of arrears." The observation is reinforced through an example: "After the creation of BancoSol, the proportion of its clients making monthly repayments increased. A couple of years later, BancoSol revised this policy, most likely in response to higher arrears in 1992–93. Thus, the proportion of loans with weekly repayments increased from 27 percent in 1993 to 47 percent in 1995" (Gonzalez-Vega et al. 1997, 74).

Silwal (2003) also notes the correlation between repayment troubles and the frequency of required installments. He compares repayment performance in nine "village banks" in Nepal and finds that 11 percent of loans were not repaid by the end of the loan period when install-ments were weekly, while twice that rate (19.8 percent) were delinquent when loans were paid in a single lump-sum payment at the end of the loan's maturity (which was generally 3–4 months). Similarly, when BRAC in Bangladesh experimented with moving from weekly repayments to twice-per-month repayments, delinquencies soon rose, and BRAC—just like BancoSol—quickly retreated to its weekly scheme.

But puzzles remain. After all, the "early warning system" explana-tion does not answer why it could make sense to demand repayments *before* investments are likely to have borne fruit. Moreover, as Gonzalez-Vega et al. (1997, 74) argue: "While frequent repayments are critical in keeping the probability of default low, they increase the transaction costs incurred by borrowers and thereby reduce the quality of service to the client." On the face of it, having to pay more frequently does seem to impose an added constraint on borrowers. But we suggest in what follows that this is too simple. For borrowers that have diffi-culty saving, the frequent repayment schedules can *increase* the quality of service to the client.

Before we get to that, we suggest why it could make sense for the bank to demand initial installments to be repaid so soon after loans are disbursed. One answer is that it helps the bank select less risky clients. The frequent repayment schedule reduces the bank's risk by selecting borrowers that are more likely to be able to repay loans even if their investments fail. This is because households must have some *other* stream of income on which to draw in order to repay the early install-ments. So, requiring frequent and early installments means that the bank is effectively lending partly against that stream of outside income, not just the proceeds from the project. The bank is therefore taking advantage of the borrower's ability to obtain funds from family members or from household activities apart from the given investment project.

For example, if before borrowing the household has a net income flow of $10 per week after expenses from the husband's wage job, the microfinance institution can fairly safely lend the wife an amount under $520 (52 weeks times $10) to be repaid in a year with the confi-dence that the household in principle has resources to repay even if the project fails. The example assumes that the husband is happy to help pay off the loan, and to the extent that's not so, the bank would have to reduce its calculations of maximum feasible loan size for the wife. But the example captures the flavor of the way that loan officers assess the repayment ability of their clients. Strikingly, in most of the pro-grams surveyed by Churchill (1999), lenders estimate repayment capacity *without* taking into account expected revenues from the loan in question, and they take into account income flows provided by all household members.

We have to push a bit further, though, to more satisfactorily explain the requirement of frequent installments. One question is: Why not do as before and estimate repayment capacity based on household income (rather than expected investment income) but not require frequent installments? An answer is that the repayment schedule is the easiest way for the microlender to "capture" those other household income flows (which are earned throughout the year) and guarantee that they are put toward paying off the bank loan.

A related part of the story is that frequent installments will be par-ticularly valuable for households that have difficulty holding onto income. This takes us back to issues of savings constraints addressed in the context of ROSCA enforcement in chapter 3—and about which we will say more in chapter 6. If borrowers must wait months before they repay loan installments, part of their earnings may be dissipated as neighbors and relatives come by for handouts, spouses dip into the household kitty, and discretionary purchases command attention. Months later, funds may no longer be there to pay the bank. A repayment schedule with frequent installments instead takes the money out of the house soon after it is earned. The essential insight is that everyone gains by matching repayment schedules as closely as feasible to the cash flowing into borrowers' households. In this way, loan products become like saving products, and the result is the ini-tially puzzling hybrids that we see in practice. It is also why we asserted previously that for borrowers who have difficulty saving, the frequent repayment schedules can *increase* the quality of service received.

The calculation of optimal repayment schedules will then involve the timing and amount of the income that is earned by the household, the difficulty that households have holding onto that income, the bank's desire for early warnings of troubles, and both the bank's and customers' transactions costs associated with collecting repayments. All else the same, if households can save without difficulty and trans-actions costs are high, the optimal number of installments falls. PRODEM, a rural lender in Bolivia, for example, requires monthly installments because it finds that weekly installments are too costly in the low population density areas in which they work (Gonzalez-Vega et al. 1997). But where saving is hard and transactions costs are rela-tively low, weekly repayments are more likely to appeal. The latter sce-nario will hold with poorer households, where the opportunity cost of time is relatively low, and where the mechanisms to enforce financial discipline are relatively limited. These tendencies are reinforced by the fact that small-scale business like petty trading tend to generate a flow of revenue on a daily or weekly basis, making frequent collections especially desirable in the absence of satisfactory savings facilities. In wealthier households, however, opportunity costs are likely to be higher and revenue costs less frequent, militating toward less frequent loan installments. These arguments are in line with the pattern of weekly versus monthly installment schedules seen in table 5.3, in which bigger loans, which tend to go to wealthier clients, are more likely to be repaid in larger but less frequent installments.

One notable problem is that these regular repayment schedules are difficult to impose in areas focused on highly seasonal occupations like agricultural cultivation. Indeed, seasonality poses one of the largest challenges to the spread of microfinance in areas centered on rain-fed agriculture, areas that include some of the poorest regions of South Asia and Africa. (Another major challenge in lending in agriculture is covariant risk, where a bad drought, a pest infestation, or the like can devastate an entire region, debilitating the microlender too.)

The Grameen Bank's proposed "Grameen Bank II" attempts to address this issue in part by maintaining weekly repayment schedules (for all of the reasons discussed earlier) but allowing loan officers to vary the size of weekly installments according to season (Yunus 2002). In low seasons borrowers can ask to pay less in return for paying more during high seasons.

We close this section with a question: Since many lenders appear to judge repayment capacity without taking into account expected rev-enues from the investment that the loan is intended for, why don't the borrowers simply save up the money needed, rather than taking out a loan with interest? The answer must partly hinge on discount rates (borrowers would rather have assets sooner if possible) and partly on savings constraints (saving up is not so easy). We suspect that if more households did have better ways to save, the demand for loans would fall considerably. Which takes us to a provocative thought. As Rutherford (2000) notes, the requirement of frequent installments not only builds recognition of saving difficulties into loan products, but also means that some customers with particular problems saving may logically look to the new microfinance loan products as an alternative way to "save"—namely, as a useful mechanism to help convert the small, frequent bits of money that enter the household into a big lump that can be used for a major purchase or investment. For these cus-tomers, that the particular financial product is structured and labeled as a "loan product" may be of secondary concern.

COMPLEMENTARY INCENTIVE MECHANISMS

In the rest of the chapter we describe additional means used by microlenders to secure repayments. We describe important mecha-nisms now in use and one interesting proposal (on "cross-reporting" strategies) that could, in theory, improve on or supplement existing schemes.

Flexible Approaches to Collateral

One premise of microfinance is that most clients are too poor to be able to offer collateral. Loans are thus "secured" through nontraditional means like group lending. But in practice some microfinance lenders do require collateral, the best-known being Indonesia's BRI. In rural Albania, for example, microlenders require tangible assets such as live-stock, land, and housing to be put up (in addition to any assets pur-chased with loans), and the programs have been vigilant in enforcing agreements if clients fail to repay. In urban Albania, a borrower's home or business is typically required as collateral (Benjamin and Ledgerwood 1999).

Table 5.4: Collateral value (rupiah ¥ 10,000,000)

	25th percentile	Median	75th percentile
Value ¥ *10,000,000*			
BRI borrower	1.1	2.3	4.1
BRI saver only	0.9	1.9	3.8
Noncustomer	0.4	0.91	2.1

Source: BRI survey, 2000. Calculations by Morduch.

Note: cell size for BRI borrowers, n = 175; for BRI saver only, n = 170; and for noncus-tomers, n = 741. On June 1, 2000, 10 million rupiah were equivalent to $1,160.

Microlenders like BRI take a nontraditional view of collateral. While BRI requires collateral in general, the bank is flexible in the assets that it will accept, and in practice collateral is not a major constraint when seeking poor clients. A survey completed in 2000, for example, shows that 88 percent of noncustomers had acceptable collateral of some sort. All the same, the survey shows that non-customers have much less in the way of assets to use as collateral. Table 5.4 shows that the median value of collateralizable assets held by BRI borrowers is roughly 2.5 times the median value of those held by a random sample of noncustomers drawn from the same area. In order to reach poorer customers, BRI has introduced products that require no collateral at all for loans up to Rp. 2 million ($225 in 2003), offered at the discretion of the unit manager.

BRI's view is that the resale value of collateral is far less important than the judgment that the pledged items should be particularly prob-lematic for households to give up. Thus, household items may be con-sidered collateral if they have sufficient personal value for borrowers, even if they are worth relatively little in the hands of BRI. The idea breaks with the traditional banker's view that collateral should be valu-able enough so that banks can sell the collateral to cover the costs of problem loans.

In other words, for BRI the value of collateral is deter-mined by the *notional* value of the asset, not the expected sale value. Land without a certificate of title, for example, may be nearly impos-sible to sell without the cooperation of the borrower and the local community. It thus has very little value to BRI if the client is hostile. But BRI still sees such collateral as potentially valuable. In part, it is an indicator of borrower intent and a guarantee that borrowers have resources to use if they should get into repayment difficulty.

More formally, we extend this framework to show how collateral requirements discourage borrowers from defaulting on debt obliga-tions. Let w be the collateral that the bank confiscates at the contract-ing stage. Returning to the setup in section 5.2, take $v = 0$ which, again, is the optimal refinancing strategy from the bank's standpoint. Then, the borrower's incentive compatibility constraint becomes $y - w$ £ $y - R + dy$, or, equivalently, $- w$ £ $- R + dy$.

This, in turn, implies that the bank's maximum gross interest rate can be as large as $R = vdy + w$. Thus, with collateral requirements the bank is now able to charge a higher interest rate while not fearing a greater probability of default. But note that the bank does not need to take possession of and *sell* the collateral for this constraint to bind; it only needs to deny the borrower access to the collateral. The result also says that at a given interest rate, average default rates will fall, reducing losses for the bank. In this way, adding a collateral requirement can help the bank improve profitability without raising interest rates—or even while reducing charges.

Financial Collateral

The flexible approach to collateral described is one solution when bor-rowers lack assets. Another solution is to address the problem straight on—to provide ways for borrowers to build up financial assets and then to base lending on those assets. Many microlenders, for example, require that borrowers show that they can save regularly for a period before they become eligible to borrow. Demonstrating the ability to save demonstrates characteristics like discipline and money manage-ment skills that correlate with being a good borrower. But saving also leads to deposits in the bank, and that can help directly by providing security for loans.

At *Safe*Save in the Dhaka slums, the first loan product developed required that borrowers hold a savings account for three months before borrowing was allowed. The maximum size of the loan was deter-mined as (current savings balance) + (10 times the smallest monthly net inflow of savings over the previous three months). While loans are outstanding, savings withdrawals are restricted in some *Safe*Save loan products.

At Grameen Bank, the policy at the end of 2003 was that borrowers holding loans must deposit between 5 and 50 taka per week into oblig-atory personal savings accounts (between about 10 cents and one dollar in December 2003), with the amount depending on their loan size. For most loans, an obligatory deposit equal to 2.5 percent of the loan value is also deducted off the top of the loan and placed into the borrowers' personal savings accounts. Another 2.5 percent is put into a "special savings" account. On top of this, borrowers taking loans larger than 8,000 taka (about $145) are required to open a Grameen Pension Scheme (GPS) account with a monthly deposit of at least 50 taka. The GPS requires monthly deposits for a term of from five to ten years. Borrowers in good standing can withdraw from their personal savings accounts at any time, provided they visit the branch with their passbook. The "special savings" accounts, though, have heavier restrictions—for example, withdrawals are not allowed for the first three years. And the GPS is a fixed term account that, if it goes into arrears, is closed and the funds are returned with reduced interest. Loan ceil-ings are predicated in part on the size of these various loan balances.

How well can these kinds of deposits function as collateral? On the one hand, if borrowers get into repayment trouble, the microlender can, in principle, hold onto the deposits to minimize their exposure to the full extent of the default. Saving up is not easy, so borrowers will surely be careful when their nest egg is at risk. On the other hand, if the out-standing loan is larger than the funds on deposit, the lender remains exposed to the possibility of default on the difference. From this vantage, the use of financial collateral does little more than effectively reduce the capital that borrowers have available to them, since the bor-rower's savings are tied up with the lender and not available to be invested by the borrower. Since borrowers have to pay higher interest rates on the money that they borrow than on the money they receive as interest on their deposits, the scheme can also add substantial, "hidden" costs to borrowing.

This discussion assumes, though, that borrowers see a dollar as a dollar, a peso as a peso, and a taka as a taka. In other words, it assumes that money saved is "counted" the same as money borrowed. But if borrowers attach special worth to money saved over time, the microlender might be able to capitalize on financial collateral and its "special" place in the borrower's heart and mind—and in the process to provide larger loans with lower risk. It is often noted, for example, that individuals will prefer to borrow—even at relatively high interest rates—than to draw down the savings that they have diligently built up over years. The bottom line is that using financial collateral can be an effective way to facilitate lending, but it hinges on special assump-tions about borrower psychology and constraints that are unlikely to hold for everyone or at all times.

Making Repayments Public

In an important break from its original model, ASA of Bangladesh ulti-mately weakened its insistence on the group lending mechanism in its credit practices. Customers often still meet as groups, though, making public repayments. Similarly in "Grameen Bank II" the focus shifts from the group to individual relations between borrowers and loan officers. Still, though, customers meet as groups and make public repayments.

A telling story on the importance of public repayments comes from a Grameen Bank replication in Kenya that ran into trouble before insti-tuting monthly public meetings with borrowers. Originally, the lender had instructed borrowers to deposit their installments directly into a bank account, but the incidence of default soared. Repayment rates come under control only after bank officials started meeting in villages with borrowers each month, collecting installments face-to-face.

Public repayment schemes have several advantages for the lender. First, without the ability to secure collateral, microlenders can use the avoidance of social stigma as an inducement for individual borrowers to promptly repay loans (Rahman 1999). Public repayments heighten the ability to generate stigma—or, more powerfully, the *threat* of stigma. Second, by meeting as a cluster of borrowers in scheduled locations, and at scheduled times, some transactions for bank staff might be reduced, even if it adds to clients' costs. Third, the group is often a useful resource through which staff can directly elicit information about errant borrowers and create pressure as needed (i.e., "cross-reports"). Fourth, group meetings can facili-tate education and training, which may be particularly helpful for clients with little business experience and/or low literacy levels. The education might aid financial performance or it might be valued intrin-sically as a way to improve levels of health and knowledge. Fifth, it is often said that the comfort of clients (many of whom have had no prior experience with commercial banks) is enhanced by encouraging them to approach the bank with their neighbors. And, sixth, by keeping transactions in the open, public repayments can help enhance internal control for the bank and reduce opportunities for fraud.

Targeting Women

The Grameen Bank has bound microfinance to creating opportunities for poor women. Much that is written on Grameen focuses on gender issues, and we devote chapter 7 to this topic. But

Grameen did not start with such a strong focus on women. The bank lent originally to large numbers of men, in addition to women, keeping both groups and centers segregated by sex. When the focus shifted, in the early 1980s, the move was mainly a response to growing repayment problems in male centers, and by the end of that decade well over 90 percent of clients were women. At the end of 2002, 95 percent of clients were women.

Women seem to be more reliable than men when it comes to repaying their loans (before conditioning on other variables like social status and education). Hossain (1988), for example, argues that women in Bangladesh are more reliable cus-tomers, citing evidence that 81 percent of women had no repayment problems versus 74 percent of men. Similarly, Khandker, Khalily, and Kahn (1995) find that 15.3 percent of male borrowers were "struggling" in 1991 (i.e., missing some payments before the final due date), while only 1.3 percent of women were having difficulties. In Malawi, Hulme (1991) finds on-time repayments for women customers to be 92 percent versus 83 percent for men, and Gibbons and Kasim (1991) find that in Malaysia the repayment comparison is 95 percent for women versus 72 percent for men.

The evidence suggests that it may thus be profit-maximizing for banks to lend to women, independent of other concerns about gender. Why women often seem to be more reliable customers is up for debate. Todd's (1996, 182) time in two Grameen villages in Tangail leads her to argue that it has to do with women being "more cautious" than men, who are more likely to have trouble sustaining membership over the long term. Based on a later village study, Rahman (2001) finds that women instead tend to be much more sensitive to the verbal hostility of fellow members and bank employees when repayment difficulties arise, while men are more likely to be argumentative and noncompliant. In Indonesia, a manager of a Grameen Bank replicator argued that women were better customers because they tended to stay close by the home rather than going out to work. This makes women, on average, easier to find when troubles arise and gives them little way to escape pressures; men, on the other hand, more easily remove themselves (physically) from difficult situations.

In terms of the dynamic incentives, women will be more likely to repay (than men) if they have fewer alternative sources of credit. Since men may have greater access to formal credit and to informal credit from traders and moneylenders, men may have weaker repayment histories than their wives and sisters.

These observations are surely not universal and are apt to change over time. And not all successful microlenders focus on women. BRI, for example, does not especially target women, but they still boast near-perfect repayment rates. Concerns with gender should thus be seen within the broader context of a lender's approach and objectives, as well as wider social, cultural, and economic constraints.

INFORMATION GATHERING BY BANK STAFF

In the nineteenth-century German credit cooperatives, borrowers were asked to obtain a loan guarantee from a neighbor. By inducing joint liability, the loan guarantee was a precursor to group lending. More recent experience shows that even without a formal loan guarantee, incorporating neighbors in credit decisions can improve bank performance.

In another step away from traditional bank practices, many microlenders spend considerable time talking with prospective bor-rowers' neighbors and friends when making lending decisions. One microlender in Russia, for example, relies heavily on staff visits to applicants' businesses and homes, rather than just on business docu-ments (Zeitinger 1996). In rural Albania, applicants must often obtain a loan guarantee and character reference from a member of the local "village credit committee." Similarly, Churchill (1999, 55) describes practices at BRI in Indonesia:

At the BRI units, most loan rejections are based on character, not the business assessment. Rejection occurs if the credit officer learns that the applicant is not respected in the community or has misrepresented himself in the application. Almost without exception, the unit staff interviewed for this research identi-fied the neighbor's assessment of the applicant's character as the most impor-tant means of predicting a new applicant's future repayment behavior—more important than the business assessment.

At ADEMI in the Dominican Republic, credit officers also check the sta-bility of home life, based on their finding that "troubled homes often become troubled borrowers" (Churchill 1999, 56). At Financiera Cálpia in El Salvador, agricultural extension workers are important inform-ants about some borrowers' character, and accordingly credit officers build ongoing relationships with extension workers.

Thus, even where group lending is not used, novel mechanisms are in place to generate information. Credit officers get out of their branch offices and get to know the neighborhoods in which they work. Microlenders find that the views of shopkeepers, bartenders, schoolteachers, and other central figures in communities can be as helpful in assessing borrower's creditworthiness as a stack of business plans.

Cross-Reporting

Gathering information from neighbors can be helpful at many stages in the loan process, not just at the application stage. One problem faced by microlenders using the threat not to refinance defaulters is that it's a strong penalty. It's particularly strong when coupled with group lending, since, in principle at least, the entire group should be cut off when any member fails to repay. Rai and Sjöström (2004) argue that these punishments are inefficiently tough, and that "cross-reporting" can improve performance.

Cross-reporting refers to statements made by one borrower about another. If Mrs. Haq is willfully refusing to repay (despite having the necessary resources), the bank can take appropriate action if Mrs. Rahman speaks up about it. If Mrs. Haq's troubles are not self-imposed, Mrs. Rahman can provide helpful input then too (preventing the bank from coming down too hard on Mrs. Haq). Rai and Sjöström describe how cross-reporting can be reliable and improve efficiency. While their focus is on improving group lending schemes, cross-reporting can have wider applications.

In order to work, the bank must credibly commit itself to a system of reward for truthful reports, and the bank must itself check on its borrowers' monitoring activities. One fear is that formalizing such a system may create tensions among individual borrowers or a strong incentive for them to collude. Still, cross-reporting seems promising in a variety of settings, and, as Rai and Sjöström argue, it is already an informal feature of banking relationships, especially coupled with group lending.

SUMMARY AND CONCLUSIONS

Group lending with joint responsibility is far from the only innovation in microfinance. Successfully creating dynamic incentives and creating products that are built around households' cash flows have been as important. Good dynamic incentives are created through attractive long-term relationships. When forward-looking customers know that default means risking losing the relationship, incentives to work hard are strengthened.

Helping customers to manage cash flows is also critical, since it helps banks to give banks access to customer resources before they are spent or otherwise dissipated. Weekly or monthly repayment schedules, although a sharp break from traditional banking practices, have been particularly critical in allowing customers to repay loans in manageable bits. Strategic microlenders often attempt to break repayment installments into pieces that are small enough that cus-tomers can, if needed, repay loans from household funds other than profits from the given investment project. The bank's risks are consid-erably reduced as a result.

In order to work effectively in sparsely populated rural areas, in highly transient urban areas, and with more mature clients, it has been necessary to develop additional mechanisms. Even where group lending has been central (e.g., in the densely populated villages of Bangladesh), the additional mechanisms have been put to good use.

These additional mechanisms include flexible approaches to collateral (where what matters most is the value that the customer attaches to losing the item, rather than the value that the lender expects to recover from selling the item) and having public repayments, even when joint responsibility is not a part of credit contracts. It is not clear in the end how important group lending is to the continued success of microfinance. We expect that the future will see much more innovation, and the beginning point should be better understandings of existing mechanisms.

But, to date, the innovations described here have been studied far less than group lending, and we know of few systematic attempts to sort out which mechanisms have most power in practice, or how the mechanisms operate together. Progress could be made by experiment-ing with different mechanisms in a way that would allow researchers to properly infer causality—say, by using different methodologies in different, randomly chosen branches. Microlenders will understand-ably be reluctant to give over their decision making to a random number generator, but building some elements of randomization into research and development can allow more systematic product testing and piloting—and cleaner answers on what really drives microfinance performance.

6

Savings and Insurance

INTRODUCTION

In the beginning, microfinance was called *microcredit*, and lending was the focus. The previous two chapters of this book reflect that empha-sis. The change reflects more than mere terminology: The transition from *microcredit* to *microfinance* has brought a change of outlook, a growing realization that low-income households can profit through access to a broader set of financial services than just credit. Practitioners are taking the lead in the transition, stepping out ahead of mainstream economic research. Notably, new initiatives are under way to create deposit accounts with terms and features that appeal to low-income customers. *Safe*Save, a cooperative working in the slums of Dhaka, for example, sends its sixty staff members out on daily rounds, during which customers are visited in their homes or busi-nesses. Each day, customers can choose to make deposits, pay down loans, or to make no transactions all. There are no limits to how big or small the daily transactions must be.

The bank in this case comes to the customers, placing convenience and flexibility for customers above convenience for the staff, and after six years *Safe*Save has established a client base of about 7,000 people who live and work in Dhaka's poorest neighborhoods. On a far larger scale, Bank Rakyat Indonesia (BRI) has built a customer base of over 25 million depositors by reducing minimum opening amounts and required balances, and by creating a network of over 3,900 small suboffices. Most Indonesians can now find a BRI location in the nearest town center. Thailand's large state-owned Bank of Agriculture and

Agricultural Cooperatives (BAAC) is follow-ing BRI's lead, and the model is being discussed as a prospect for bank reforms in India and China. In other countries, postal savings services are allowing customers to easily make deposits at their local post office.

The amounts accumulated are not large in absolute terms, but they can make a relative difference in the lives of customers. By the middle of 2003, the average savings balance at *Safe*Save was $22. The average savings balance at BRI at the end of 2002 was about $75. Neither $22 nor $75 is much from the vantage of a more affluent country. But $22 is substantial in a country like Bangladesh where the per capita gross domestic product is about $400, and the annual income in its slums is even lower. Moreover, even if the average household does not accu-mulate vast sums from year to year, saving can still be an important way to manage resources within a year and across seasons. Evidence on BURO Tangail, a microfinance institution in Bangladesh, for example, shows that even when average balances do not grow much, an open-access savings account may be very popular and very inten-sively used. At the end of 2000, BURO held just under 27 million taka in general savings, a figure that had grown by less than 2 million over the year. But the owners of these accounts hadn't been idle—they had deposited more than 62 million and withdrawn more than 60 million during the year. Similarly, simulations of consumption-smoothing behavior (reducing year-to-year consumption swings by saving and dissaving), described by Deaton (1992), show that effective and active consumption-smoothing may be achieved even with low levels of average assets.

Implicit in the push to create better ways to save is the assumption that households at present have limited and imperfect ways to do so. If the assumption is right, it can help explain some puzzles. One is why rotating savings and credit associations are so popular as informal financial mechanisms, and more-over, why ROSCAs do not fall apart—a tale to be unraveled further below. Another puzzle that can be explained is why we see credit con-straints in the first place. Economic theory dictates that forward-looking households ought to be able to save their way out of credit constraints if given enough time. Does the existence of credit rationing thus stem from a more fundamental constraint in the ability to save? Are poor households too impatient to save? Do they require a differ-ent "savings technology"? To the extent that this is the case, it is not clear that providing microcredit need be the main answer to credit market problems. Promoting microsaving is another—albeit slower— route to the same end, and thus it is presented as another tool in the antipoverty arsenal.

This line of thinking is a major departure for the microfinance world. It also challenges assumptions routinely made in academic devel-opment economics. Microfinance grew from innovations on how to provide affordable, reliable credit without collateral. From the start, microlenders like the Grameen Bank created savings accounts for all clients, but the accounts came with so many strings attached that they hardly looked like savings accounts. Most important, a fixed fraction of loans disbursed had to be deposited into the accounts, and funds in those accounts could only be withdrawn upon leaving the program. For example, in the Shakti Foundation for Women—a replicator of the Grameen model in the slums of Dhaka and Chittagong, Bangladesh—compulsory savings in 2000 included a group tax of 5 percent of the loan principal and weekly compulsory savings of 10 taka (about 20 cents), half of which went into the Centre Fund and half of which went into a personal account. The latter account could be accessed at any time, but the other accounts could only be touched when the client left the program—and only if the client had been in for five years or more. A survey of over nine hundred women showed that only 13 percent of its current clients were dissatisfied with this arrangement, but 40 percent were unhappy among those who dropped out.

In principle, the compulsory saving program is meant to help clients build up assets over time and develop the discipline of saving. But to many, these involuntary savings accounts look instead like a way for the bank to acquire relatively cheap capital and to secure a form of col-lateral from borrowers (since the microlender can seize accumulated savings if the borrower tries to quit the program while in default). It seems like a smart strategy for the microbank, but it is several steps removed from providing the kind of fully vol-untary savings possibilities that more affluent customers of traditional commercial banks take for granted (and that are featured, for example, by Bank Rakyat Indonesia). These compulsory savings programs are also several steps away from the kinds of commitment savings devices that customers may voluntarily opt into and that typically last for no more than a year before all savings can be withdrawn. With little available in the way of client-driven savings products, it is under-standable that most people in the field spoke of microcredit rather than microfinance.

Today, though, the term *microfinance* is used far more frequently (even in the title of this book), and most practitioners accept that low-income households deserve better (i.e., more flexible and conven-ient) ways to save and insure on top of better ways to borrow. The Grameen Bank itself has radically reversed course, for example, and introduced "Grameen Bank II" in 2001. In addition to new, flexible loan products, "Grameen Bank II" introduces new, flexible savings products (and a popular way to save over the long-term, the Grameen Pension Scheme). The savings products are marketed to a broader community than just current borrowers, and by July 2003 Grameen was holding deposits equal to three-quarters of its loan portfolio, allowing it to sub-stantially reduce reliance on external financing.

The potential benefits of these steps are large. Indeed, some, such as Robinson (2001, 21), argue that deposit services are more valuable than credit for poorer households. With savings, not only can house-holds build up assets to use as collateral, but they can also better smooth seasonal consumption needs, finance major expenditures such as school fees, self-insure against major shocks, and self-finance investments.

The first part of this chapter examines savings in greater detail, and, in the process, illuminates tensions in modern views of household economies in impoverished regions. The final part of the chapter turns briefly to microinsurance, a concern that has only gathered steam in the past five years. There is great potential here to address market failure, and progress has been made with sorting out institutional forms.

Why Save?

Households save for many reasons. Table 6.1 reports on a survey of households in Indonesia, for example, that shows that low-income households planned to use their savings for business uses, building up assets, and for future consumption.

Nearly as many were saving for working capital (13 percent) as were saving to pay school fees (14 percent) and for general household con-sumption (13 percent). Savings are mainly used to facilitate large, lumpy expenditures occurring in the short or medium term, but they are also used for long-term needs. Most academic work on the eco-nomics of saving begins with these latter needs, building analysis around the "life-cycle" model which describes "low-frequency" saving behavior over the very long term.

Table 6.1: Reported uses for savings

	Percentage reporting as primary use
Business uses	*16*
Working capital	13
Finance new business	0
Buy building, equipment	2
Buy vehicle	1
Nonbusiness consumption	*35*
School fees	14
Medical expenses	3
Household consumption	13
Purchase jewelry	0
Wedding/funeral/etc.	2
Religious holiday	3
Finance and assets	*6*
Purchase land	1
Purchase housing	5
Pay loan	0
Other use or not applicable	39

Source: 2000 survey of 201 BRI clients. Calculations by the authors. The sample was drawn from representative regions; results are not weighted to reflect different popula-tion levels across sampling units.

"Low-Frequency" Saving

Most households in high-income countries proceed in similar ways: get educated (perhaps borrowing in order to pay for it), get a first job, start saving for later in life, start a family, move up the ladder at work (or move on to other jobs), raise the family, continue saving, retire, then draw down savings, and possibly, leave a bequest. The model in its starkest form implies that households should borrow when very young, save aggressively when in middle age, and dissave when older. Optimal behavior should yield fairly flat consumption over time, rather than ups and downs associated with the ups and downs of income and retirement.

The model does a reasonable job in explaining savings behavior in middle-income and higher-income countries. It's not perfect. For example, just when the model predicts households should save most for retirement (in the peak-earning years of middle age), households tend to be hit with large demands like college tuitions for their children, the costs of weddings, and so forth. And since much saving takes the form of investing in one's own house, only tracking financial assets will miss much of the story. Also, when young, risk-averse households are typically reluctant to live much beyond their means, even if they might reasonably predict that their incomes will be much higher in the future. Still, all in all, the model provides a reasonable benchmark.

The model's predictive success is much worse in lower-income coun-tries. One of the often-cited reasons is that the model is designed to describe the behavior of nuclear families, not the complex, multi-generational households that often live and eat together in more tradi-tional economies. Instead of a standard household with two parents and children, we are as likely to see households that combine grand-parents, parents, and grandchildren all living under the same roof or in the same compound. So in multigenerational households, as family members age, as some are born and others die, the average age of the household may hold fairly steady over time. Thus the ups and downs of income (followed by retirement) experienced by a typical household head poorly represents the income flowing into the household as a whole. Another reason that the life-cycle model has less bite in impov-erished regions is that retirement periods tend to be shorter than in more affluent countries, with older family members often working close to the end of their lives.

Kochar (1996) takes a close look at cross-sectional data on 4,734 households in Pakistan, in a survey collected as part of the World Bank

Living Standards Measurement Survey (LSMS) project. She finds that if you plot the incomes of intergenerational households over time (i.e., as the household head gets older), you don't find the pattern of increas-ing and then decreasing income that emerges when doing the same plot for nuclear households. In fact, the plot for intergenerational house-holds looks as if there was a single, infinitely lived household with steady income over time. That is, it looks as if households continually rebundle themselves as they add and lose members, doing so in a way that minimizes variation in the household's average age and demo-graphic structure. It seems that rather than smoothing consumption by borrowing and saving, the household smoothes its income by rebundling; in this case, if the household simply consumed all of its income in each period, consumption patterns would also be similarly smooth. And if a household can smooth its income, it has little motivation to save for life-cycle purposes; that is, it has little need to borrow and save to make consumption smoother. Simple within-household transfers (e.g., from adult child to his coresident elderly parents) should instead be the best means to achieve optimal con-sumption patterns. If this is the case, life-cycle saving motives are weak in this population.

Remember, though, that the evidence comes from a cross-section of households. The plot has household income on the vertical axis and the household head's age on the horizontal axis; the plot does not actually map changes over time for the same households—since, unfortunately, we lack such data. Instead, the plot shows patterns of different house-holds at a single point in time. The question is whether the cross-sectional plot closely approximates what happens over time to a single family. Kochar (1996) argues that it does not, and this is because, as described previously, relatively few people spend all of their lives in intergenerational households. Kochar finds that household heads under forty-five are in fact most likely to reside with their nuclear fam-ilies. This is so for about 80 percent of household heads in their thir-ties. But after the age of forty-five, the picture shifts sharply so that about 80 percent of household heads who are in their fifties and sixties live instead in intergenerational households (defined as having at least one father coresiding with an adult son or son-in-law). Nuclear house-holds average six members while intergenerational households average nine (three of which are, on average, adult males). In a typical pattern, newly married men live with their parents (and maybe wife and children), but by about age thirty, the young family splits off to form their own nuclear household. Later, as the sons of the nuclear family grow older and marry, an intergenerational household is formed again. The result is that at various points in the life cycle (particularly in one's thirties and forties) there may remain a keen desire to save up over the long term—even in a place like Pakistan where intergenera-tional households are so common.

The observation helps to explain the popularity of the Grameen Pension Scheme in Bangladesh, where intergenerational households are also prevalent. The GPS was introduced in 2001, and although it is called a "pension," the GPS can be used by people of any age. In the GPS, every Grameen borrower with a loan larger than 8,000 taka (about $138) must contribute at least 50 taka (86 cents) per month. Ten years later, the borrower will receive nearly twice the amount (Yunus 2002), earning 12 percent per year in compound interest and ultimately getting back 187 percent of their deposits at the end of the decade (Grameen Bank 2002, note 13.02). Given a low rate of inflation, the return is generous and clients will be able to build up tidy sums through the power of compound interest.

As points of comparison, Grameen's Fixed Deposit savings scheme, for example, which was started in May 2000, pays 8.75 percent to 9.5 percent in annual interest for deposits of one- to three-year durations (Grameen Bank 2002, note 13.01). ASA's deposit rate is 6 percent (Ahmmed 2002, 91), and turning to external sources of funds for com-parison, the *Palli Karma Sahayak* Foundation (PKSF) a Bangladesh apex organization, provides microcredit institutions with funding at 7 percent per year. The commercial loan rate is roughly 10–11 percent at minimum (and some businesses pay about 14–15 percent)—and that does not entail the cost of collecting and administering millions of small deposits. The GPS is thus relatively generous, but the high return must be balanced against the restrictions on withdrawals.

While the GPS is compulsory, it also turns out to be popular with customers in its own right. Attractive features are a low minimum monthly installment and a mechanism built around a fixed, structured commitment to saving. In this, the GPS shares features of the ROSCAs described in chapter 3. Unlike the ROSCAs, though, the commitment to the GPS is not short-lived. Ten years is a long time, and the GPS has not yet been operating long enough to know how households will manage to meet their obligations in stressful times. From a financial perspective, the scheme provides a steady inflow of cash for the bank, with reports that it is bringing in over 100 million taka (U.S. $1.75 million) each month (Yunus 2002, 14). If Grameen can keep costs down, its clients will benefit considerably from the ability to stow away the money—and Grameen will gain access to a new trove of funds with a bill not due for years.

"High-Frequency" Saving

Low-frequency saving (steady, long-term accumulation) is only part of the savings picture. Another important part is "high-frequency" saving to fund short-term investments and to smooth consumption from month to month or from season to season. High-frequency saving has generated the most interest by academics investigating saving in lower-income economies, following the lead of Deaton (1992). By and large, they have found that households are both eager to save in the face of recurrent shocks but also that households have problems doing so.

Evidence comes mainly from tests of the permanent-income hypoth-esis using household survey data. The permanent-income hypothesis was developed by Milton Friedman in the 1950s as a simple charac-terization of how a rational, forward-looking household would choose to borrow and save in the face of uncertain future income. Friedman observed that incomes go up and down over time, but some of the changes are permanent (e.g., you get a promotion at work based on your newly acquired skills) while some are transitory (e.g., sales were unusually good this year and your firm gives everyone an especially plump end-of-year bonus). Friedman argues that you should enjoy the permanent changes (assuming they are positive) and increase your expenditures accordingly. But a prudent household should save the transitory increases, expecting downturns later. And when transitory downturns happen, rational households will draw upon savings or borrow in order to maintain fairly steady consumption levels over time. Households facing a lot of income variability—for example, farmers in the semi-arid tropics that stretch across Africa and South Asia— will thus find themselves spending a lot of time trying to smooth consumption.

How well do they do? Before getting to the evidence, we describe the simple idea at the heart of empirical approaches, and then apply it to reality. The basic idea is that if you know that in one year you will earn $4,000 and in the next you will earn $6,000—and if your consumption needs are identical in both years—you would do better to borrow $1,000 and to consume $5,000 each year. The insight in economic terms is that you want to "equalize the marginal utility of consumption in each period." Rather than starting with the idea that you necessarily want to equalize consumption, start with the idea that if spending a dollar now will give you more benefit than holding on to that dollar until later, you should spend it today. And you should keep on spending today until you get to the point when you are just indifferent between spending the extra dollar now or saving it for later. In our simple example, this is the point at which you consume $5,000 in both years. However, in more complicated models that take changing needs into account, consump-tion levels need not be equalized—but the "marginal utility" of con-sumption in all periods should be. Conversely, you should save today if you will benefit more from spending the dollars later—again, up to the point when marginal utility is equal in all periods.

Your choices, of course, must not lead you to exceed your total life time resources, which include your current income as well as your assets and any future income that you are able to borrow against. Making the example more realistic involves bringing in (a) the interest rate for borrowing and saving; (b) a discount rate wherin future con-sumption may be judged to be intrinsically less valuable than con-suming right now; and (c) the fact that when you make choices today you don't know how tomorrow will turn out—you only have your best guess.

Putting this together yields a formal representation of the solution to how much to borrow and how much to save. If you could perfectly smooth consumption, you would want to set the marginal utility of consumption in period *t* equal to the *expected* marginal value of con-sumption in a later period £ + 1 (where the expectation is formed in period):

$$MUj = (1+r)/(1+<5)E_{(}[MUt_{+}1], \qquad (6.1)$$

Where MU_f is the marginal utility of consumption in period f; *r* is the net interest rate on loans or deposits (assumed to be identical) between the two periods; *8*is the discount rate; and $E_{(}[]$ indicates that we are interested in the expected value of the item within brackets.

The equation yields a striking conclusion: If you could make choices without constraint (i.e., if you can borrow and save without restriction as long as you don't end up consuming more than you earn or inherit over your lifetime), your consumption choices should be fully inde-pendent of when your income arrives. If this year is an unusally bad year, you should borrow—or draw down your savings—to maintain desired consumption levels. And, similarly, you should save when income is unusually good. Equation (6.1) should hold perfectly if markets work perfectly. But imagine that you had difficulty borrowing and saving (for all of the reasons discussed in this book). Then,

$$MUj = (1+r)/(1+<5)E([MUt+1] + At+1, \qquad (6.2)$$

where *t+1* ^ 0 reflects the extent of difficulties. When you have diffi-culty borrowing and saving, your consumption patterns over time will mirror your income patterns more closely than you would like. When that is so, Aj+1, the measure of how much your consumption choices depart from the optimum degree of smoothness, should be correlated with your transitory income. After making assumptions about the shape of utility functions, it is possible to learn about *Xt+1* in practice.

The trouble is that we do not actually observe *t+1,* thus we have to make inferences indirectly. There are two relevant cases. In the first, you face a constraint on the amount that you wish to borrow. Going back to the example we started with, say that this year your income is $4,000, and next year it is $6,000—and again ignore interest rates, dis-count rates, and expectations error. You would like to borrow $1,000, but are unable to find a willing lender. So, in the extreme case of absolutely no borrowing possibilities at all, you end up consuming \$4,000 this year and \$6,000 the next. In terms of marginal utility, the marginal utility of consuming an extra dollar today exceeds that of consuming that same dollar next year. You would like to set $MU_t = E_t[MU_{t+1}]$, but instead $MU_t > E_t[MU_{t+1}]$. So it must be, by equation (6.2), that $l_{t+1} < 0$. Conversely, if you face difficulty saving and this year's income is \$6,000 and next year's is \$4,000, $MU_t < E_t[MU_{t+1}]$ and by equa-tion (6.2), it must be that $l_{t+1} > 0$.

With these pieces in place, we can see that when you face a borrow-ing constraint—that is, in the first example here—the lower your initial income, the faster consumption levels will grow between periods. Here, the \$4,000 first-year income meant a \$2,000 jump between periods from \$4,000 to \$6,000. If, instead, income had been distributed \$3,000 in year one and \$7,000 in year two, there would have been a \$4,000 expected jump. Thus, lower initial income is associated with a larger jump in consumption. To bring matters back to the measure of borrowing constraints, the more negative the correlation is between initial income and consumption growth, the greater the likelihood is that $l_{t+1} < 0$. If there is no correlation between initial income and consumption growth, it is fair to assume that $l_{t+1} = 0$, and there are no systematic borrowing constraints. An important hypothesis is that where borrowing constraints are likely to bind most tightly—for the most impoverished citizens with least collateral—the negative correlation between initial income and consumption growth should be greatest. For higher-income households, the correlation should be noticeably smaller.

This is indeed the pattern typically seen. It turns out that for higher-income households, even in lower-income areas like the rain-fed villages of South India, constraints turn out to be small. But for poorer households, the constraints can bind tightly as demonstrated by a large, negative coefficient on the initial income variable in a regression that captures the spirit of the previous discussion. Morduch (1994), for example, reports that landless and near-landless households in rural South India are able to smooth away just a small part of transitory income shocks. This pushes the households to try smoothing income by making more conservative agricultural choices, pushing them to more likely adopt traditional cropping choices, for example, rather than riskier but more profitable high-yielding varieties. Similarly, in rural China, Jalan and Ravallion (1999) find that the bottom 10 percent of households can protect themselves from only 60 percent of adverse income shocks, while the top 10 percent cope well with all but 10 percent. Accumulating evidence from other parts of the world is telling similar stories: The poorest households seek means to address high-frequency fluctuations, but the means are far from perfect.

Before we leave this discussion, we return to the issue of savings con-straints. While most researchers in the consumption-smoothing litera-ture interpret the negative coefficients on initial income as evidence of borrowing constraints, the evidence can also be explained by the pres-ence of savings constraints. In the case of savings constraints, $l_{t+1} > 0$, and households with transitorily high incomes are forced to consume more today than they would like. Consumption growth between today and later periods is thus negative, so again, a negative correlation is generated between income today and subsequent consumption growth. This negative correlation is generally interpreted as a sign that there are borrowing constraints ($l_{t+1} < 0$), but the evidence is consistent with $l_{t+1} > 0$ as well. It remains for future work to better distinguish between the cases.

TAKING SAVING CONSTRAINTS SERIOUSLY

The preceding discussion points to the existence of both saving and borrowing constraints. Our discussion of informal rotating savings and credit associations in chapter 3 pointed to the use of ROSCAs as methods of saving rather than primarily as means to borrow, an obser-vation given support by a survey of ROSCA participants in Bangladesh (Rutherford 1997). One can go further, though, and argue that the very existence of ROSCAs—why they do not fall apart—must rest in their value as vehicles for saving (at least for the kinds of ROSCAs that we see most commonly).

In the ROSCAs described in chapter 3, a group of neighbors join together to raise funds, with each person contributing a fixed amount to a pool of money collected weekly or monthly. Each member of the group gets one turn to receive the entire pool until everyone in the group has had an opportunity. One problem with this scheme is that the very last recipient of the pot would appear to have no incentive to participate—because she could instead simply save the money on her own, week after week, and in the end be just as well off as she would have been if she had participated in the ROSCA. The last recipient may even be better off on her own, since she would be free from the rigid structure and schedule of the ROSCA rules. Hence, there is no clear economic gain from ROSCA participation for the last recipient.

The problem is that someone has to be last. And if no one is willing to be last, there can be no ROSCA. The thing falls apart. But ROSCAs are common around the globe, serving as a mainstay of informal economies. Why? One explanation is that the last recipient may not in fact be able to "simply save the money on their own" as previously assumed. As Anderson and Baland (2002) suggest (based on a survey in Nairobi), married female ROSCA members would otherwise have difficulty protecting savings from their husbands' grabbing hands. Or, as Gugerty (2003) argues (also based on data from Kenya), the disci-pline of the ROSCA helps participants accumulate savings in a regular, structured way. In short, ROSCAs may well owe their existence to poor households' desires to save—and their very imperfect alternative options. ROSCAs may thus be a response to the failure of the "market for savings" as much as they are a response to credit market failure.

Such savings constraints do not have a prominent place in academic explanations of why poor people stay poor, and responsibility rests with two somewhat conflicting attitudes, both of which are due a reassessment. First is the assumption that there is little desire by lower-income households to save: namely, that very poor households are simply too impoverished to save (e.g., Bhaduri 1973). At one level, the logic seems tight: Immediate consumption needs must take priority for households at the brink of subsistence, leaving little (or no) surplus to save for tomorrow. According to this logic, the need to save is far less important than the desire to borrow.

The second assumption, in contrast, is that there are plenty of infor-mal ways to save for those who want to; so, once again, the lack of a formal savings bank is not an immediate cause for concern. House-holds do indeed use a wide array of informal mechanisms for accu-mulation, including using money guards (typically a reliable neighbor who holds on to extra cash, and importantly, gets it out of one's house and away from temptations); rotating savings and credit associations described here and in chapter 3; purchasing jewelry and other fairly liquid assets; and, simplest of all, hiding places to stash money at home.

More important may be the less visible ways of saving, such as self-financing a business and purchasing equipment and livestock that—similar to jewelry—can be sold in times of need. In principle, if lower-income households are constrained in their abilities to borrow, they should simply put extra cash directly into their own businesses, typically earning far higher returns than that on money put in the bank. For these reasons—and for the fact that borrowing can yield faster access to a bigger lump of money than waiting to accumulate it by oneself—it was perceived that improving the ability to borrow should take precedence over improving the ability to save.

So, why are these positions now up for grabs? First, even very poor households seem eager to save. Basu (1997) points to a logical flaw in Bhaduri's (1973) argument: If they are forward-looking, even the poorest households should see the virtue of saving (even if it is just a bit at a time) so that over the long term they can escape from the con-straints imposed by being so close to subsistence. Probably more important in practice is the fact that most households below the poverty line are in truth fairly far from the brink of subsistence. They would have little scope for saving if measures of poverty could be taken literally (where the poverty line is rooted strictly in a notion of minimal needs for subsistence), but poverty measures are only approx-imate tools. Evidence is mounting that many households well below the poverty line are indeed interested in saving. The slum dwellers of Dhaka who day-by-day contribute their pennies to *Safe*Save accounts testify to the demand once a well-designed program is in place.

The second statement, that households have sufficient informal means to save, has also been taken apart. Many households are reluc-tant to tie up all their money in their own risky businesses. Those busi-nesses may not function all year, and investments may be difficult to withdraw in times of need. Other informal means to save may also be risky or may be otherwise burdensome. When a locality as a whole is hit with a crisis, for example, the local market can get flooded with jewelry and assets as households desperately try to generate income. As Dercon (1999) finds in data from Africa, the returns to the assets used by households for "saving" are often positively correlated with incomes. So, when incomes fall, the value of assets fall in turn, and the savings strategy ends up being of only limited help. Saving cash under the mattress or in a secret hiding place would be a better strategy when many in a region are affected by shocks at the same time, but cash is vulnerable to erosion through inflation, and, often more important, through theft or the simple inability to keep temptation at bay. One study (Wright and Mutesasira 2000) in Uganda showed that for 99 percent of households the average loss in savings *per year* was 22 percent.

The figure from Uganda helps to put into perspective the implicit interest rates charged by deposit collectors. Consider the case of Jyothi, a deposit collector in the southeastern Indian town of Vijayawada described by Rutherford (2000). Jyothi works in the slums, and mainly with women. Her job is to take clients' surplus funds, hold them securely, and return the funds (less a fee) at the end of an agreed-upon period. In a typical pattern, Jyothi's clients agree to save a little bit each day for 220 days. The daily amount is fixed, and at the end of the 220 days Jyothi gives her clients the money that they have accumulated—less the fee, which in this case is 9 percent of the total. So if, as in Ruther-ford's example, a client agreed to save five rupees each day for 220 days, she would end the period with 1,100 rupees. Jyothi then keeps 100 rupees as a fee and hands over the remaining 1,000 rupees to the client. In the meantime, Jyothi holds the savings. The effective cost of her services (taking into account the timing of transactions and putting figures into annualized terms) is equivalent to an annual interest rate on deposits of roughly negative 30 percent per year. The poor women in the slums of Vijayawada are clearly willing to pay well in order to secure safe, convenient savings services.

Are Credit Constraints Ultimately Saving Constraints?

Microcredit proponents insist that credit constraints pose fundamental problems for poor households. So why don't households just save their way out of credit constraints? Economic theory argues that households should, for the same reason that Basu (1997) argues that households should save their way out of subsistence constraints. Theoretical work by Bewley (1976) shows that a credit-constrained household that acts with foresight will always slowly and steadily accumulate until credit constraints are overcome. A similar argument is made by de Meza and Webb (2001) in the context of adverse selection in credit markets. De Meza and Webb argue that when households face credit constraints due to adverse selection, the house-hold always does better if it can wait a bit before investing. Waiting allows the household to accumulate more wealth; and thus to invest more and generate higher income. De Meza and Webb show that it is prudent to prolong waiting until credit constraints disappear alto-gether. In practice, then, if households can save, we should never see binding credit constraints in equilibrium. These results come from theoretical models and rely on abstractions from reality, but they pose an important challenge: Why does reality seem to look so different? Why are credit constraints so commonly cited in practice?

One immediate response, again from a theoretical perspective, is that households may simply be too impatient to save enough. As Deaton (1992) demonstrates, as long as households are suitably keen to consume today rather than waiting until tomorrow, credit con-straints can persist. Specifically, Deaton's notion of impatience flows from the assumption that the rate at which a household discounts future consumption is greater than the interest rate on deposits. In the context of equations (6.1) and (6.2), this means that d > r.

In this case, households will prefer to consume the marginal dollar rather than save it for later. But why assume that households are so impatient? The assumption stretches plausibility if it is true that house-holds "save" largely by self-financing investments that have large mar-ginal returns to capital (an assumption that is consistent with the typical interest rates on loans charged by microlenders; *Safe*Save, for example, charges 36–48 percent per year). On the other hand, if we take seriously the idea that households have difficulty finding convenient, reliable means to save, and, as in the case of Jyothi the deposit collec-tor, are even prepared to receive *negative* interest on deposits, Deaton's framework becomes perfectly plausible. Discount rates exceed interest rates on deposits because effective interest rates are so low, not because discount rates are necessarily so high. A different explanation for the inability to save one's way out of credit constraints involves risk. Persistent negative shocks can keep wiping out assets and make accumulation all but impossible. In theory, households should still be able to adequately accumulate in the very long term, but in a risky environment this could require an implausibly long horizon.

A final explanation is put forward by Platteau (2000) based on obser-vations of village institutions in Africa. Platteau argues that difficulties in saving may have origins in social arrangements. Consider, for example, informal risk-sharing arrangements based on reciprocal claims such that you agree to help your neighbors and family when they need assistance, and they agree to help you in return. A problem arises, though, when your neighbors and family assert that they are in need and put claims on your surpluses, preventing you from saving for your own personal gain. Their incentives may in fact be to keep you from accumulating since, once you get wealthy enough, your own incentive could be to bow out of the mutual insurance arrangement and to self-insure. In order to keep the arrangement together, your surpluses thus get "taxed" by the community, making it difficult to save over the long term.

BUILDING BETTER SAVINGS BANKS

The earlier arguments explain why households may have difficulty accumulating for personal or social reasons. Part of the problem may also be that households lack safe, secure, convenient institutions in which to save. Putting the two issues together takes us to product design. Given the many purposes that individuals save for, and given the varying constraints and objectives they face, one product design is surely not best for all. Some individuals will do best with a savings account that maximizes flexibility. Others will do better with an account that is more rigid. Insights from behavioral economics suggest that others may do better with both.

Ashraf, Karlan, and Yin (2004) provide an interesting study of the way that rigidity can help some customers build their savings. Working together with the Green Bank of Caraga, a small rural bank in Mindanao in the Philippines, they conducted a field experiment to test the efficacy of a commitment savings product. The researchers began by administering a comprehensive household survey of the 1,767 clients of the bank. Then, half of the clients were randomly selected to be offered a new type of account, called a SEED account. The account restricted access to deposits according to the customer's instructions at the time that the account was opened. No other extra benefits or costs were imposed.

For the other half of the bank's customers, they were either put into a control group and received no contact at all about savings products, or they were put into a group that received promo-tions about the bank's existing savings products—but received no offer of the SEED account. Of the 710 individuals offered a SEED account, 202 (28 percent) opened one. After six months, average bank account savings increased by 86 percent for those who opened the account, a figure substantially higher than seen in either of the control groups over the same period. For those who felt they most needed a com-mitment product, access to it had an economically and statistically significant impact on financial savings. The findings are particularly interesting in light of Gugerty's (2003) interpretation of the value of rigidity in the design of ROSCAs in western Kenya.

Independent of the nature of the savings product, successful banks that provide savings will face institutional design issues as well. From an institutional perspective, collecting deposits appears to be easier than making loans. Most important, the risk lies entirely with the depositor, and the informational asymmetries that undermine bankers when making loans are absent here. Here, the table is turned: Now it is the banker who may be subject to moral hazard, and it is the customers who are unsure whether they can trust the financiers. Will the banks adequately safeguard deposits? Will the bank allow withdrawals when needed? Will the bank still exist in a decade? Five years? It has been left to regulators to assuage those concerns and banks must then deal with paperwork, reserve requirements, and other products of regulation. So, one explanation for the lack of deposit services is that regulation makes it too costly to profitably serve small-scale depositors.

Another constraint is that—putting aside regulatory costs—collect-ing small deposits generates higher transaction costs per dollar trans-acted than collecting large deposits. As a result, banks often exclude poorer depositors through the use of high minimum balance require-ments. Richardson (2003), of the World Council of Credit Unions, cites evidence that many banks claim that it is impossible to profit on deposit accounts smaller than $500, leaving many small savers to rely on informal mechanisms.

The track record of credit unions shows that the $500 limit is exces-sive, though (Richardson 2003). Indonesia's BRI provides one coun-terexample: The bank successfully (and profitably) collects deposits while insisting that opening balances be only 10,000 rupiah (just over one dollar), with minimum balances equivalent to 57 cents. Most accounts are far larger—although still well below $500. As noted earlier, the average balance at the end of 2002 was $75. By simplifying its mechanisms, BRI is able to serve over 1,200 customers per staff member on average (Hirschland 2003, Figure 1) and keep operating costs below 3 percent.

Another challenge is to find adequately high returns for the funds that are deposited. Taking deposits—especially when they are frequent and small—is only profitable if investments are available that offer sufficiently high returns. Finding such returns, while at the same time keeping funds sufficiently liquid, is difficult. The most obvious way to use deposits is to add to the microlender's capital pool for lending to other customers, but this is little help for programs that are running large deficits on the lending side. Improving financial performance in lending may thus be a key to success in taking deposits.

Cost control is an ongoing struggle, and it is made more complicated by the premium that low-income depositors place on convenience and liquidity. One of the lessons from Jyothi, the deposit collector pre-viously described, and from BRI, is that convenience matters. Convenience matters because clients are often trying to convert bits and pieces of income that flow into the household into a useful, large sum to be spent on a major purchase or investment (an observation that Stuart Rutherford built into the design of *Safe*Save). If a bank is not convenient, it is less likely that the little bits of daily savings will make their way into a deposit account. Thus, serving low-income households means finding ways to reduce travel time and hassles for both customers and staff members. In the case of *Safe*Save, for example, staff members are recruited from the slums where they work so that salary costs are relatively low and travel costs are nonexistent.

Another source of costs is the demand for liquidity. Consider the case of BRI. Its important innovation occurred in 1986 after a year of field-work, when BRI introduced its "village savings" product, *Simpanan Pedasaan* (SIMPEDES). It quickly became popular, even though BRI paid no interest at all on small deposits. While the largest deposits were paid an interest rate of 12 percent per year, this rate was smaller than the top rate offered on BRI's competing savings product, TABANAS. But TABANAS had the disadvantage of restricting withdrawals to two times per month, while SIMPEDES offered unlimited withdrawals. Patten and Rosengard (1991, 72) argue: "Although very few TABANAS savers actually withdraw funds twice a month, this limitation is an important psychological barrier to the people in rural areas, who seem to fear that they will not have access to their TABANAS savings when they need them." Managing liquidity remains a major concern, but the problem appears to be easily kept within bounds.

As more programs turn toward microsaving, a greater range of lessons and models will be produced, and those will surely spawn new innovations in short order. There is still much that is poorly understood about the saving behavior of low-income households. But the impor-tant step of the past decade has been to recognize that the demand for saving services exists, even among the most impoverished households. Providing convenience and flexibility appears critical to creating a solu-tion that works for customers; the interest rate on deposits, it turns out, is most often a secondary concern.

Microinsurance

The push to provide microcredit started because too many low-income households could not get access to loans on "fair" terms. Government banks provided some credit to low-income households (but inefficiently and at major losses), while credit from informal-sector money-lenders was in short supply and costly. This reasonably characterizes the insurance sector too: not much access by poor households, inefficient government providers running large losses, and informal mechanisms that are often very costly. And the problems are similar as well: Providing insurance has all of the incentive problems associ-ated with providing credit—and worse Most notable, moral hazard and adverse selection are ongoing problems (in ways that parallel our discussion in chapter 2); transactions costs are high; and contract enforcement is difficult. Consider the data on state-supported crop insurance programs collected by Hazell (1992); he finds that for these government programs, costs exceeded revenues by 4.6 times in both Brazil and Japan, by 3.7 times in Mexico, and by 2.4 times in the United States.

Can we do better? So far there has yet to be a breakthrough innova-tion (of a kind that parallels the innovations described in chapters 4 and 5) that could propel a "microinsurance" movement to become a global phenomenon. Still, a growing movement within microfinance is pushing to provide insurance on top of loans and deposit services. Life insurance has been most successful to date, but health insurance plans are being tried, as well as property and crop insurance.

Life insurance is typically offered as part of a microcredit package. So-called credit-life contracts pay off any outstanding loans and provide the family with a fixed payout in the event of death. The program run by FINCA Uganda, for example, provides about $700 to the dependents of the client should the client die an accidental death; their outstanding loan balance is also repaid (Cohen and Sebstad 2003, Table 5). If the death is not accidental (e.g., from illness), dependents get only $175 and again the loan is paid off. Should the client's spouse die by accident, the client receives $350. And should any of the client's children die by accident, the payout is $175 per child (up to 4 children). In return for the coverage, clients pay an extra 1 percent on top of inter-est for each loan that is disbursed. So far, clients have been pleased with the arrangement, particularly as it ensures that their own death does not impose an undue burden on their families. But it is not particularly cheap and the coverage is restricted—for example, there are no payouts if a spouse or child dies of illness.

For FINCA Uganda the benefits are dual. First, the product gener-ates profit. The actual coverage is provided by the American Insurance Group (AIG), one of the world's largest insurers, and AIG gets 45 percent of the premia collected. FINCA keeps the rest to defray the administrative burden and to supplement general revenues. The other benefit for FINCA Uganda is that loans are paid off when clients die, sparing the difficulty of having to chase down relatives during a time of mourning. Cohen and Sebstad (2003) found that insur-ance premiums (for similar coverage) are even higher at other pro-grams. In Tanzania and Kenya, for example, microlenders charged 2.25 percent and 2 percent of loans disbursed, respectively, for credit-life insurance.

The idea of life insurance is greatly welcomed by clients, supplant-ing private efforts to insure against loss through joining informal burial societies that pool resources and pay out to participants in the event of a loss. But Cohen and Sebstad (2003) argue that the way these programs are implemented has led to ambivalence about their value.

One tension is that as loan sizes increase, so do premia. But benefits increase less than in proportion, since a large part of the benefit includes fixed-size payouts in the event of death (the value of the other part, repayment of outstanding balances, grows in proportion to loan size). Small-scale borrowers thus get a better deal than large-scale bor-rowers, and the large-scale borrowers perceive the inequity. Another tension is that coverage only lasts during the duration of a loan; so if you take a break between loans, your coverage lapses. A third tension is that insurance purchases at FINCA Uganda are mandatory. This is a wise response to adverse selection—since the program avoids facing a self-selected pool that is riskier than average—but it means that clients who perceive themselves as being fairly safe (e.g., young, healthy bor-rowers) end up cross-subsidizing their riskier neighbors. None of these problems are insurmountable, however. At the cost of adding slightly to administrative burdens, premia could be adjusted for age; coverage between loans could be instituted straightforwardly; and cost schedules could be adjusted so that large-scale borrowers get a better deal. Even in its present form, though, credit-life insurance is generally workable (and very often profitable).

A major part of the success for FINCA Uganda stems from the part-nership with AIG. The partnership spares FINCA staff from having to deal with the technical side of insurance provision (calculating actuar-ial tables, calculating appropriate reserves), avoids extra regulation, and ensures that risks are diversified. As a large insurer, AIG has the means to spread risks across its many policies and can reinsure with ease (reinsuring occurs when an insurer sells a fraction of its policies to another insurer in order to reduce exposure). Were FINCA to go it alone, it would not only be exposed to major administrative burdens, it would also have to find a way to protect itself in the event of larger-than-expected obligations.

Health insurance programs have been less successful. Part of the problem is that adverse selection is rampant in voluntary programs, a long-known problem. (See the classic articles by Arrow [1963] and Pauly [1968].) When programs are voluntary, less healthy households tend to be overrepresented among those seeking insurance; and insur-ers, bogged down by imperfect information, are unable to set prices appropriately for different clients. Jowett 2002, for example, shows that in a voluntary health insurance program in Vietnam, individuals self-reporting as being healthy are 41–55 percent less likely to purchase insurance (Jowett 2002, 225), saddling insurers with a client base that is less healthy than the population average.

Moral hazard can also be a problem, and it tends to take two main forms. First, once insured you may be less likely to take due precau-tions. Second, you may overuse facilities, seeking medical attention for ailments that are minor and can be treated (if treatment is necessary at all) without a doctor's intervention. In theory, the way to alleviate the problems is to impose a deductible (so that the patient is only reim-bursed for expenses over a given minimum) and a co-payment (so that the patient also pays some fraction of the overall bill). Somewhat sur-prisingly, though, insurers have been reluctant to lean heavily on these mechanisms. Part of the reason is that clients insist on seeing quick returns for their premia, and high deductibles discourage clients that are just purchasing formal insurance for the first time. There is also a fear that high deductibles and co-payments may discourage clients from seeking necessary preventive care—and could end up being costly to the insurer in the long run.

In order to control costs, insurers have thus imposed restrictions on the diseases that they are willing to cover. While, for example, the MicroCare Health Plan of Uganda covers a range of outpatient and inpatient services—including surgery, X-rays, laboratory analysis, and prescription drugs—there is no coverage for common (and growing) problems like high blood pressure, diabetes, and ulcers, nor for alco-holism or long-term care associated with chronic illness (Cohen and Sebstad 2003, Table 7 and footnote 18). Other programs, like the health insurance program of the Self-Employed Women's Association (SEWA) of Ahmedabad, India, have controlled costs by limiting coverage and relying on public hospital care.

Without a new innovation that can cut costs, insurers find themselves with few other options for the time being. Similarly, customers complain that insurance only helps them pay for medical care that, for now, is often of low quality (Cohen and Sebstad 2003). This has deterred some households from signing up for insurance programs.

Paradoxically, though, as more people buy health insurance, the demand for higher-quality medical care—combined with the new ability to pay for it—may be great enough to push providers to make quality improvements such as more widely avail-able medicines, better-trained doctors and nurses, and easier access to facilities. But getting to scale will first involve greater participation despite the existing low-quality services, creating a coordination failure that might be unremediable without appropriate interventions by donors or governments.

In addition to health and life insurance, there have been some attempts to provide other forms of insurance, like property insurance. At SEWA, for example, clients pay an annual premium of $1.50 for cov-erage against loss of property due to catastrophic circumstances. Soon after SEWA initiated the plan, it found itself paying out 630 claims against loss due to flash flooding (totaling $5,000), followed the next year by 2,000 claims in the wake of the massive earthquake in Gujarat in January 2001 (totaling $48,000). The insurance delivered $10 to members for each wall that collapsed in their house, and $60 in the event that a member's house was beyond repair. The experiences show that property insurance can work, but they also highlight the impor-tance of having adequate reserves and reinsurance policies in place before big catastrophes hit.

One of the most promising new insurance lines in recent years is rainfall insurance, and pilot programs are underway in Morocco and

India (implemented by the microlender BASIX). The idea of rainfall insurance is to avoid the moral hazard and adverse selection problems associated with crop insurance (not to mention the high transactions costs). The strategy is to abandon trying to insure against bad crop yields and instead to insure against bad weather directly. In a typical plan, tamperproof rain gauges are installed in a region; contracts are then written that guarantee payouts in the event of specific events of bad weather (e.g., lack of rainfall by a certain date or, in other cases, too much rainfall).

The contract works well as long as bad crop yields are closely cor-related with bad weather. The correlations, though, are not as high as some would imagine. For example, the research underlying the Morocco pilot focused on cereals—the basis of Moroccan agriculture. The correlation between cereal revenue and rainfall was found to be 60–80 percent. At the low end of that range, a great many farmers could suffer losses without getting payouts—or, by the same token, may have a good year but still get a payout. The extent of such "basis risk" will be the main limit to how widely rainfall insurance can substitute for traditional forms of insurance. Given failure after failure of crop insurance, though, experts are guardedly optimistic about the new approach, and in 2002 the World Bank's International Financial Corporation invested $80 million to establish a Global Weather Risk Facility in partnership with Aquila, Inc., a Kansas City–based trader in weather-based derivatives (World Bank 2002).

If successfully implemented, rainfall insurance will yield another advantage: You don't have to be a farmer in order to buy it. Thus, shop-keepers, craftsmen, traders, and others whose livelihoods are condi-tioned by the weather will have a chance to gain added protection, even if they do not themselves work the fields.

MICROLOANS AND RISK

The turn to microsaving and microinsurance springs from the recog-nition that vulnerability goes hand in hand with having low incomes. As with microcredit, the fundamental problem is lack of access to the kinds of financial services that most of us take for granted. The idea of broadening the scope of interventions has had immediate appeal and sets challenges for both practitioners and academics.

Some observers, though, have worried that microloans themselves may actually be sources of risk—so the proposed solution to one problem (low earning power) worsens the other (vulnerability). To sharpen the point, Dale Adams, a longtime critic of subsidizing micro-credit, routinely uses the term *microdebt* instead of microcredit. His point is that lenders provide loans, not gifts, and this creates obliga-tions. When misfortunes strike, those obligations cannot always be met, putting the borrower into even greater jeopardy.

From this vantage, the professionalism that microlenders have worked hard to achieve—which translates into uniform treatment of clients and persistent efforts to make sure that borrowers repay their loans—can, in some cases, mean being tough on clients in times of need. Before Grameen Bank instituted its new reform (Grameen Bank II), there were many cases in which clients ran into difficulty repaying, and loan officers were often strict with clients—thus generating ill will and often pushing the clients to seek help from others, including the local moneylender. At its worst, debt spirals of the sort described by Matin (1997) can occur, in which Grameen customers turned to moneylenders for help, borrowed more from Grameen to pay the moneylenders, and so forth until the the mountain of unrepaid debt became too unmanageable. Grameen II was created in part to help customers—and the bank—pick up the pieces and reestablish work-able relationships.

The bottom line is that while microfinance providers tend to stick by hard and fast rules in order to reduce costs and enhance transparency, costs can be imposed on clients. In contrast, moneylenders are much more flexible, and borrowers may opt to pay more to a moneylender in exchange for knowing that if difficulties make it hard to repay on time, the moneylender will typically extend the loan duration, often without extra interest charges. In Irfan Aleem's (1990, Table 7.3) sample from Pakistan, for example, loans were routinely extended by half a year when needed. Grameen Bank II, with a new "easy" loan product that allows rescheduling with ease, builds this idea into microcredit contracts. It is designed instead to create "tension free" microlending by giving staff ways to accommodate clients in temporary crises. (Another help, of course, is the development of microinsurance that can alleviate stresses directly.) As long as rescheduling is used as a last resort, borrower discipline faces little threat of weakening.

On a more positive note, traditional group lending contracts may foster mutual insurance relationships so that before the loan officer is forced to intervene, problems are addressed by neighbors bound together in a group contract. Drawing on contract theory, Sadoulet (2003) argues that group lending can foster mechanisms in which borrowers down on their luck can get help from fellow group members—in return for helping others later. If this is so, borrowers do better when groups are more diversified; and Sadoulet and Carpenter (2001) show that in a sample from Guatemala, borrowers do sort themselves into fairly diverse groups (although it cannot be nailed down whether the sorting stems from insurance motives or from other reasons).

A different way that microloans may help to reduce risk is by allow-ing customers as individuals to reduce exposure to income fluctuations by diversifying income streams and facilitating borrowing for con-sumption purposes. Microlending can thus aid consumption smoothing in part by facilitating income smoothing. Empirical evidence from Bangladesh is consistent with that observation, showing that across seasons households with access to microloans have smoother income streams (and thus smoother consumption patterns) relative to control groups (Morduch 1998).

SUMMARY AND CONCLUSIONS

Microfinance practitioners and policymakers are coming around to the view that facilitating savings may often be more important than finding better ways to lend to low-income customers, especially for the most impoverished households. This is a welcome shift in that many poor households have strong desires to save and often find ingenious ways to do so, but, in general, they lack convenient and secure deposit facilities.

Meanwhile, we see no evidence to support the general premise that having better ways to save is *more* critical than having better ways to borrow. The two are complementary, and in section 6.6 we added into the mix the value of reasonable possibilities to purchase insurance. Being able to save and borrow is, in itself, an important way to self-insure against uninsurable events.

Much can be learned from the experience with microcredit as we turn to microsavings and microinsurance. In particular, the microcredit experience shows the advantage to allowing households to make fre-quent, small-sized transactions, rather than repaying loans (or deposit-ing funds, withdrawing savings, and paying insurance premia) in large lump sums. The microcredit experience also shows the importance of building strong institutions. Here, the problem is harder as customers' savings must be protected and insurers must be able to deliver pay-ments reliably and quickly when troubles emerge. Regulation and diversification are thus far more imperative when it comes to savings and insurance.

In discussing microsavings, we have turned to the broader literature on saving in low-income communities. In that literature, it is often argued that because households are often formed as intergenerational units, the demand for low-frequency saving is small. Important low-frequency events include predictable changes that occur through the life-cycle—such as starting a family, raising children, and retiring. It is argued that for intergenerational households, within-household trans-fers can do the job that saving has to do in a nuclear household. This is true to some degree, but we need to be careful. Even in places like rural Pakistan where intergenerational households are the norm, indi-viduals still spend substantial parts of their lives in nuclear households. They form into intergenerational households only at later stages. Thus, the demand for low-frequency saving can remain important—and this should inform the design of new savings products. The Grameen Bank's new pension products, which have been very popular in the first few years since their introduction in 2000, are a case in point.

High-frequency saving refers to saving and borrowing with the purpose of obtaining insulation from the vagaries of income. When income is highly variable, foresighted households can build up and draw down assets to stabilize consumption levels. Access to con-sumption loans—rather than loans strongly tied to microenterprise investment—is an important complement to flexible opportunities to save. *Safe*Save, for example, a cooperative working in the slums of Dhaka, has made the combination of savings opportunities and con-sumption/investment loans the center of its operation, with the aim of helping households to better manage their finances—and not neces-sarily to build particular businesses.

These microsaving initiatives lead us to question assumptions com-monly made by economists, even if implicitly—most important, that borrowing constraints are far more serious than savings constraints. As a theoretical matter, the persistence of bor-rowing constraints is difficult to explain without invoking the possi-bility of savings constraints as well. In turning to empirical tests for borrowing constraints, we argue that evidence that is taken to be a sign of borrowing constraints can also be explained by the presence of savings constraints. We set out these arguments as a prod to academics, who have yet to see what practitioners are observ-ing in the field: namely, that many low-income households have genuine difficulties saving and, for lack of effective institutions, are forced to take costly measures to build up assets.

As with microcredit, informa-tion problems create inefficiencies due to adverse selection and moral hazard, and transaction costs are high. The area has also been plagued by ill-advised and expen-sive government interventions directed at giving farmers relief from crop failure. New initiatives include providing life insurance tied to loans, health insurance, and insurance against bad weather rather than bad crop outcomes.

Returning to microcredit, describes ways that the design of loan contracts affects customers' exposure to risk. Group lending, for example, can in principle be a way to cement informal, reciprocal self-help agreements among neighbors. But the rigidity of contracts can also penalize customers just at the moment when they are most in need of flexibility. Taken together, the topics in this chapter suggest the value of focusing on a broad set of financial services, rather than focusing on narrowly defined microenterprise finance.

7

Gender

INTRODUCTION

To many, microfinance is all about banking for women. Pioneers such as BancoSol and the Grameen Bank were built around serving women, and microfinance networks such as Women's World Banking and NGOs such as Pro Mujer cement the association. Not all microfinance institutions focus specifically on women, but a recent study found that women make up 80 percent of the clients of the thirty-four largest microlenders (Mody 2000). The Microcredit Summit Campaign Report for the year 2000, "Empowering Women with Microcredit," reports on a 1999 tally of over 1,000 programs in which 75 percent of clients were women (Microcredit Summit Campaign 2000).

So far we have only touched briefly on gender in microfinance, but in this chapter we address issues directly. We begin by asking why most microfinance borrowers are women, especially the most impoverished. We then ask whether targeting women is efficient in the strict eco-nomic sense. Does it help microfinance enterprises to attain their self-sustainability goals? Does it favor more equality within the household? How might microfinance help to promote social capital and women's empowerment?

The Grameen Bank's history is instructive. From the start, Muham-mad Yunus recognized the importance of women when confronting poverty. But cultural norms, especially the Muslim practice of *purdah* (which guards a woman's modesty and limits her mobility and social interactions), made it difficult to approach potential female clients. At first, Yunus struggled to serve at least 50 percent women; but now, with barriers fallen, 95 percent of Grameen's clients are women (Yunus 2001). When the bank started, most borrowers were men; just 44 percent of clients were women in October 1983 (Yunus 1983, 11). The bias in favor of women was reinforced by experience showing that, relative to male borrowers, women had better repayment records. But the com-parative advantage of women as microfinance customers did not stop there; it extended to other dimensions of performance as well. For example, Khandker (2003) finds that a 100 percent increase in the volume of borrowing by a woman would lead to a 5 percent increase in per capita household nonfood expenditure and a 1 percent increase in per capita household food expenditure, while a 100 percent increase in borrowing by men would lead to just a 2 percent increase in nonfood expenditure and a negligible change in food expenditure. Thus, evidence shows that serving women turns out to have stronger impacts on households. Serving women thus seems to accord well with the dual objectives of maintaining high repayment rates and meeting social goals as proxied by the higher household expenditures.

The importance of women in microfinance in places such as Bolivia and Bangladesh has been helped by other social transformations that started far earlier. Data on fertility rates and illiteracy show how dra-matic those changes have been. Table 7.1 shows that fertility rates have fallen steadily in both countries—as they have in Indonesia, another country thick with microfinance, and for low-income countries overall. In 1970, women in Bangladesh had seven children on average, leaving limited time for extra work. By 2000, fertility in Bangladesh had fallen to nearly three children per woman, a dramatic decline with clear eco-nomic and social implications. The change means that women have more time and resources for self-employment, and it shows that impor-tant transformations were already under way within households well before microfinance burst onto the scene. Another important change has been falling illiteracy rates for adult women, from 54 percent to 21 percent in Bolivia between 1970 and 2000, and from 88 percent to 70 percent in Bangladesh. The role of microfinance has been to extend and develop the ongoing transformations, more than to initiate them.

Table 7.1: Falling fertility and female illiteracy rates, selected countries 1970–2000

	Bolivia	Bangladesh	Indonesia	All low-income
Fertility rate				
1970	6.5	7.0	5.5	5.9
1980	5.5	6.1	4.3	5.3
1990	4.8	4.1	3.0	4.4
2000	3.9	3.1	2.5	3.6
Female adult illiteracy rate				
1970	54	88	56	73
1980	42	83	41	65
1990	30	77	27	56
2000	21	70	18	47

Source: World Bank World Indicators 2002, CD-ROM. Fertility rate is average number of births per woman. Illiteracy is the percentage of women fifteen years and older who cannot read or write.

Why Women?

Formal-sector commercial banks tend to favor men, mainly because men run the larger businesses that commercial banks favor, and men tend to control the assets that banks seek as collateral. Microfinance is a totally different business, though. It is about small businesses which most often involve self-employment in the informal sector, and women make up a large and growing segment of informal-sector businesses.

On the demand side, women tend to be more credit-constrained than men and, therefore, more likely to select themselves into microcredit contracts with all kinds of strings attached—namely, small loans, training sessions, weekly meetings, and joint responsibility. From the microlender's viewpoint, serving women has at least three potential advantages.

The first advantage is purely financial: Women are often more con-servative in their investment strategies, and are often more easily swayed by peer pressure and the interventions of loan officers—making women more reliable bets for banks worried about repayment. As we described in chapter 5, evidence from Grameen Bank—and replications elsewhere in Asia—shows that women are better about repaying loans. For example, Khandker, Khalily, and Khan (1995) find that 15.3 percent of male borrowers were struggling in 1991 (i.e., missing some payments before the final due date), while only 1.3 percent of women were having difficulties. That finding is echoed in studies elsewhere in Asia. The field experience of Grameen replications in southern Mexico indicates a similar pattern, and evidence from credit scoring regressions using data from Latin American microlenders confirms this tendency too. (These are studies of repayment rates, in which gender is an explanatory vari-able.) While the advantage of women in the credit scoring studies falls after considering factors such as age, income, region, and other covari-ates, it is the simple correlation that is most important in determining the attractiveness of women as customers. In this line, Kevane and Wydick (2001), for example, find that at a group lending institution in Guatemala, female borrowing groups misused funds least often, and, as a result, outperformed male borrowing groups.

The next two advantages pertain to institutions pursuing social objectives—namely, aiming resources to women may deliver stronger development impacts. One reason is that women tend to be more concerned about children's health and education than men (e.g., Blumberg 1989). The second reason is that women are overrepresented among the poorest of the poor, and are too often oppressed by their husbands and by prevailing social norms. In its 1990 *World Development Report*, the World Bank reports that women are lagging behind in many key indicators of economic development. Literacy rates, for example, were found to be 61 percent of that of men in Africa, 52 percent in South Asia, 57 percent in the Middle East, 82 percent in South East Asia, and 94 percent in Latin America. Moreover, the report finds that, relative to men, women in low-income countries face far greater social, legal, and economic obstacles. In addition to everything else, microfinance is thus seen as a road to "gender empowerment."

Region-specific studies on gender bias abound. One stark example is provided by population sex ratios that are so skewed that Sen (1992) has written of a crisis of "missing women." While in developed coun-tries there are approximately 105 females for every 100 males, the ratios are lower in South Asia, the Middle East, and North Africa, due to exceedingly high female mortality rates. The very large female-to-male death ratio in these regions is attributed to parents' neglect for their female infants and, in some cases, to selective abortion of female fetuses. Sen (1992) estimates that the number of missing women (those who died prematurely or who were selectively aborted) in the early 1990s was over 100 million people.

Among the reasons that young girls are discriminated against is that they are not viewed as an important source of income and, in some instances, are seen as a burden due to dowry obligations. Less extreme forms of discrimination are mani-fested in day-to-day living. Poor women, for example, tend to work longer hours for less pay. The World Bank (1990) reports: "Women typ-ically work for longer hours, and when they are paid at all, will be so at lower wages." Studies in numerous developing countries emphazise that when unpaid home-production activities are included, women seem to work even longer hours than men.

Ethical considerations aside, the gender bias has clear implications for policy. Unequal access to health, nutrition, and educational status of women in low-income households has been linked to high fertility rates, low labor force participation, low hygiene standards, and the increased incidence of infectious diseases. And all these variables are clearly related to productivity and household income.

Against this are arguments that male entrepreneurs may more aggressively expand enterprises when given access to credit. There may thus be a trade-off between lending to women in the name of poverty reduction and lending to men in the name of economic growth. Kevane and Wydick (2001), though, find that gender differences in eco-nomic responses to credit access are small in the Guatemalan group lending program they investigate.

While they find that young male entrepreneurs tend to be more aggressive in generating employment than older male entrepreneurs, older women tend to be more aggres-sive in generating employment than younger women or older men. Holding all else constant, Kevane and Wydick thus find no statistically significant overall difference in the way that credit affects the ability of female and male entrepreneurs to generate increases in gross sales within an enterprise.

NEOCLASSICAL APPROACHES TO HOUSEHOLD DECISION MAKING

The traditional neoclassical economic approach to household decision making leaves no room for analyzing conflict between men and women. Households are seen as acting as a single unit, making choices as if household members were in full consensus. Even here, though, a case for targeting on the basis of gender can be made.

The so-called unitary approach goes back to seminal work started by Gary Becker in the 1960s. In particular, in his *Treatise on the Family*, Becker (1981) assumes that male and female preferences can be aggre-gated into a common household objective function to analyze decisions about expenditures and "noneconomic" investments such as the number, education, and health of children. Households maximize their joint objective utility function subject to constraints on time use, tech-nology, and joint resources. While the time allocation of each house-hold member between the production of market and household output matters (since it may affect total household output), the distribution of income among family members is totally irrelevant. A dollar is a dollar, no matter who in the family earns it. The approach, so focused as it is on efficiency, is sometimes called the "pure investment" model; and it leaves no scope for intrahousehold conflict.

One of Becker's objectives was to understand how households allo-cate individuals to activities, with household members seeking to gain from their comparative advantages. According to this approach, if the wage in the market sector is higher for males than for females, it would be efficient for men to work more in the market sector and for women to stay in the household (or to work in the informal sector). Becker argues that this is the best way to increase the household's total output, and he claims that this is a good representation of patterns seen in the United States in the 1960s.

In principle, Becker's predictions also apply to developing countries. In most agricultural economies, there are a number of high-wage activ-ities that require certain skills, such as physical strength, for which gender matters. Becker's framework in this case suggests that it is optimal for men to benefit from their comparative advantage by spe-cializing in strength-intensive marketable agricultural activities outside the house. Women, on the other hand, should devote more time to unpaid household work and those marketable activities that require considerably less physical strength, even if the monetary rewards are often low due to market discrimination. It remains unclear whether such unequal specialization within the household truly reflects women's preferences.

Rosenzweig and Schultz (1982) provide early evidence on the pure investment model, finding that survival probabilities for female infants in rural India are higher in areas where opportunities for female employment are greater. Their argument is that asymmetric mortality patterns result because parents are forced to invest in children with the greatest earning potential. It is argued that such strategic decision-making results from the need to sometimes make tragic, brutal choices in the struggle for basic survival.

But microfinance advocates repudiate the helplessness that is implied. First, by helping to raise incomes, advocates argue that micro-finance can lift the constraints that force households to make such life-and-death choices. As important, advocates argue that microfinance can also change the nature of basic trade-offs. Rather than taking the structure of wages and employment as given, microfinance advocates aim to improve opportunities and the economic returns to women's work, and thus to change the economic value of females within the home. Raising those returns can, in principle, reduce discrimination of the sort documented by Rosenzweig and Schultz (1982).

The pure investment model is a useful starting point, but microfinance advocates go further. They argue that by raising women's status within families, the nature of decision making can change too. Rather than assuming that households work by consensus, as argued by Becker, economists have recently started deconstructing household choices, finding them to be driven often by inequalities, bargaining, and conflict. Browning and Chiappori (1998), for example, derive implications of a model in which bargaining power is driven by the ability of women to credibly threaten to leave the household. The cred-ibility of those threats will depend on factors like earning power and other factors that affect women's relative power within the household, such as divorce or employment legislation. Access to microfinance can potentially be part of this equation.

To venture further, we first need to turn to a framework in which parents care intrinsically about the education and health of their chil-dren (rather than as in the pure investment model, where concern is purely instrumental, restricted to how improving health and education raises earning power). A simple approach is given by Behrman, Pollak, and Taubman (1982), and we follow Strauss's and Beegle's (1996) expo-sition. We assume that there are two children in a household, a girl and a boy. If the mother is exceedingly averse to inequality in the well-being of her children, she will care most about the child that is worst off. Diagramatically, at the extreme her preferences are L-shaped, or, in the public finance jargon, the mother's preferences are "Rawlsian." This is shown as an "L-shaped indifference curve", where the mother has preferences over the health of her son and daughter.

In the case depicted, if the daughter's health improves, we will see a hori-zontal move from *A* to *B* in the diagram. This change will not improve the mother's condition, though, because she dislikes inequality. In con-trast, take the opposite extreme in which the mother does not care about inequalities between the two children. In this case, the indiffer-ence curve will be completely linear, as shown in the downward-sloping line *I–I*. Here, the mother will invest more in household members whose returns are the greatest (which is the case emphasized by Becker). Preferences between these two extremes are captured by the more plausible indifference curve *C*, where preferences for equal-ity are traded off against the need to ensure earning capacity.

Such trade-offs shift with income. In particular, at very low income levels, the household may favor males for survival reasons, and mothers may support that decision. Take the example of food, which is often controlled by women. At very low incomes, women's prefer-ences may be biased against females because survival is all that matters, and sons may represent higher earning opportunities for the household. Women may therefore allocate more food to males who can potentially bring a higher level of income to the household. Distribu-tions become more equal, though, as the general level of income increases.

Berhman (1988), for example, shows that household nutrient intakes and health outcomes in his sample from India are positively correlated with earning profiles. He also shows that the pro-male bias is more severe during the "lean" seasons, when resources are tight. In particu-lar, households tend to allocate food to members who receive the great-est returns in the labor market, resulting in greater intrahousehold inequality in the lean seasons, but they are more egalitarian in surplus seasons.

Another layer of complexity is added by allowing that men and women may have different preferences, and that conflicts are resolved through negotiation. The more power a woman has in the household, the more the household's decisions reflect her preferences. Increasing income can thus lead to households changing the pattern of allocations for reasons that get mediated through the bargaining process. Browning and Chiappori (1998), for example, show that in bargaining contexts, preferences tend to shift with income. Microfinance may thus affect household choices through a variety of channels: by changing bargaining power, by raising overall resources, by affecting the returns to investments in human capital, and by influencing attitudes and norms.

Are Women Better Customers?

There are at least three reasons that lending to women may have advan-tages for the bank—and may enhance efficiency in a broader economic sense. The first has to do with poverty, the second with labor mobility, and the third with risk. We address the poverty-related argument first. Women are poorer than men. According to the UNDP *Human Develop-ment Report* (1996), 70 percent of the world's poor, about 900 million people, were women. Under the standard neoclassical assumptions about the production function, if women have less access to capital than men, returns to capital for women should therefore be higher than for men. Endowing women with more capital can thus be growth-enhancing in principle.

This assumes, though, that capital is not completely fungible within households—that is, the money of all members is not fully pooled and treated as a common resource. Given that the once common assump-tion of full within-household resource pooling has come under steady attack, the case for a gender focus in microfinance is strengthened. While there is concern that credit directed to women might end up being re-directed to male household heads (who are the ones that actu-ally carrying out investment projects of their own, with the resources borrowed by women), evidence from Bangladesh delivers a reassuring response. Goetz and Sen Gupta (1996), for example, report that 40 percent of women in their survey have little or no control over their own investment activities, but optimistic observers respond that this means that 60 percent have full or partial control. Thus, investments do seem to be undertaken by women, despite norms that place restric-tions on women. To the extent that—as reported by Goetz and Sen Gupta—women already enjoy a comparative advantage in small-scale microenterprise activities, the efficiency-augmenting argument by neo-classical theorists is further enhanced.

The second argument hinges on labor mobility. Women tend to be less mobile than men and are more likely to work in or near the home. Bank managers can therefore monitor women at a lower cost. Moreover, less mobility facilitates delegated monitoring under group lending methodologies. Typically, peer borrowers who under-take investment activities at home—and stay at home most of the time—can more easily monitor each other. Similarly, lower mobil-ity reduces the incidence of strategic default under the fear of social sanctions.

This brings us to the third argument in favor of a pro-female bias. Because women are less mobile and more fearful about social sanctions, they tend to be more risk-averse than men and more conservative in their choice of investment projects. This makes it easier to secure debt repayments and create a reputation for reliability.

Why May Impacts Be Greater When Lending to Women?

Khandker's (2003) evidence suggests that lending to women yields greater social and economic impacts than lending to men. Policymakers have long been aware of the potential impact of delivering aid for disadvantaged households to women. Food stamps in the United Kingdom and Sri Lanka, for example, and staple food and cash deliv-eries under the PROGRESA (now called Oportunidades) program in Mexico were directed to women rather than their husbands. The fear is that if such aid was given to men, they might sell the food stamps and misspend the resources—possibly wasting money on gambling, tobacco, and alcohol. Skoufias (2001) reports that Oportunidades in rural Mexico indeed led to sharp social improvements: Poverty decreased by ten percent, school enrollment increased by four percent, food expenditures increased by eleven percent, and adults' health (as measured by the number of unproductive days due to illness) improved considerably as well.

Similarly, Thomas (1990) reports that child health in Brazil (as meas-ured by survival probabilities, height-for-age, and weight-for-height) along with household nutrient intakes, tend to rise more if additional nonlabor income is in the hands of women rather than men.

With respect to survival probabilities, income in the hands of a mother has, on average, twenty times the impact of the same income in the hands of a father. In a subsequent study, also on Brazil, Thomas (1994) reports that increasing the bargaining power of women is associated with increases in the share of the household budget spent on health, educa-tion and housing as well as improvements in child health.

Engle (1993) similarly studies the relationship between a mother's and father's income on child nutritional status (height-for-age, weight-for-age and weight-for-height) for hundreds of households in Guatemala, and reports that children's welfare improves as women's earning power increases relative to their husbands'.

Schultz (1990) finds that in Thai-land nonlabor income in the hands of women tends to reduce fertility more than nonlabor income possessed by men. He also finds that the impact of nonlabor income has different effects on labor supply, depending on which household member actually controls that income.

An overwhelming majority of the women responded that the principal objective for joining a ROSCA was to save, and nearly all of the respon-dents were married. Anderson and Baland conclude that an important motive for women joining ROSCAs is to keep money away from their husbands. Other studies, not necessarily confined to ROSCAs, suggest that savings considerations (and protection of assets) apply as well to women's involvement in microfinance institutions.

Udry (1996) provides related evidence. Using panel data from Burkina Faso, he finds that, controlling for soil quality and other vari-ables, agricultural productivity is higher in plots that are cultivated by men. He also finds that relative to plots cultivated by women, the higher yields of male-cultivated plots are due to a greater intensity of productive inputs (including fertilizer and child labor).

He thus con-cludes that productivity differentials are attributed to the intensity of production between plots cultivated by men and women, and not to inherent skill differentials. This outcome is not efficient since there are sharply diminishing returns for fertilizer.

Not only are resources not fully shared, they are allocated in ways that diminish total household income. Udry suggests that input reallocation toward plots cultivated by women can thus enhance efficiency. Another solution (i.e., the microfinance solution) is to provide women with credit sufficient to purchase additional inputs. A second way that microfinance can poten-tially address problems like this is by tackling the social norms that prevent women from having adequate access to inputs and marketing facilities in the first place. This could be done through demonstration effects or from pressure created by the microlender to ensure high returns to borrowers' investments.

GENDER EMPOWERMENT

Advocates argue that microfinance can increase women's bargaining power within the household. Women will become "empowered" and enjoy greater control over household decisions and resources. To the extent that group lending in microfinance entails peer monitoring by other borrowers in the same group, microfinance is likely to provide protection to women within their households.

In particular, violent acts and abuses by men against women can now be subject to third party scrutiny as peer borrowers will want to find out why a woman in their group has stopped attending repayment meetings. This, in turn, should act as a deterrent against domestic violence, and, more generally, as an instrument for women to promote their rights and improve their bargaining power vis-à-vis their husbands or other male family mem-bers. Rising household incomes in general can also diminish conflicts between husbands and wives by loosening constraints. Evidence on the effect of microfinance on women's rights delivers an unclear picture, however.

Hashemi, Schuler, and Riley (1996) and Kabeer (2001), on the one hand, report that microfinance in Bangladesh has indeed reduced violence against women. Kabeer argues that the rationales for targeting women, over and above the desire to empower, include the observations that (1) men are less likely to share their loans with women than women are likely to share loans with men; (2) loans to women are more likely to benefit the whole family than loans to men; and (3) loans to men have little impact on intrahousehold gender inequalities—in fact, they can reinforce them by providing men with a base to prevent wives from engaging in income-generating self-employment.

But the opposite conclusion is reached by Rahman (1999), albeit with evidence from just one village. As many as 70 percent of Grameen borrowers in his survey declared that violence in the house-hold had increased as a result of their involvement with microfinance. Rahman's explanation for the upsurge in violence is that microfinance exacerbates tensions because men feel increasingly threatened in their role as primary income earners in traditional societies.

Another way in which microfinance can affect women's empower-ment is with regard to the use of contraceptives. Especially in Bangladesh, microfinance has been promoted as a way to limit the number of children, and positive impacts have been found on contra-ceptive use (e.g., Rahman and Da Vanzo 1998; Schuler, Hashemi, and Riley 1997).

This can be explained by the fact that microfinance increases the opportunity cost of women's time. This effect may be rein-forced by peer pressure as women are urged to reduce family size in order to increase education and health expenditure, and to better manage the ability to repay.

On the other hand, Pitt et al. (1999) argue that microfinance could be positively associated with *higher* fertility as access to microfinance raises income (holding all else constant this should increase the demand for children), but may only raise oppor-tunity costs slightly (since, unlike factory work, women can engage in self-employment activities from home while simultaneously caring for children). They show confirming evidence from a cross-sectional survey in Bangladesh.

While microfinance can potentially empower women within the household, there is less evidence that it has been effective in transforming social norms and traditions. Mayoux (1999), for example, reports on a survey of fifteen different programs in Africa, finding that the degree of women's empowerment is household- and region-specific, and thus, she argues, depends on inflexible social norms and traditions. The findings have to be weighed against the fact that impacts on empowerment will, of course, also depend on how well the particular programs were designed.

Criticisms

We have argued earlier that microloans have played an important role in the promotion of self-employment in traditional activities where, relative to men, women already enjoy a comparative advantage. By enhancing women's specialization in those activities, microfinance may thus improve efficiency.

The focus on gender empowerment as a broader goal has come under fire from a variety of angles. The ever-provocative Adams (Adams and Mayoux 2001, 4), coming from the right, argues that the widespread use of the term "empowerment" by the microcredit crowd makes me uneasy. To the unwashed it conveys the impression that smearing a dab of additional debt on a poor woman will transform her into Super Woman.

Those who insist on using this bloated term grossly overstate the contribution that indebting crusades play in easing poverty. More debt does not cure malaria or HIV/AIDS. It does not provide clean drinking water or prevent flooding. It does not improve law-and-order or eliminate weeds in a borrower's crops. It does not make crops grow in barren soil or provide secure title to land that squatters occupy. It does not provide schools or teachers for the poor...

A loan provided by the microdebt industry, for say $100, is no more an empowerment tool than is a similar loan from an evil moneylender or a rela-tive, unless the intent of the lender somehow transforms the usefulness of the money borrowed—which it doesn't. The critique mirrors Adams's broader critique of microfinance as a poverty alleviation tool, discussed earlier in chapter 2.

The argument hinges on the (much-disputed) assertion that poor women have ade-quate access to credit through informal means, so that microfinance might change the terms on which credit is obtained, but it does not open access. The argument also dismisses the role of training or social capital that may be generated through participation in microfinance programs. Mayoux takes Adams to task, but agrees that credit alone is not enough to bring meaningful change to women; empowerment "also depends on how far [programs] are able to build on group organ-ization to enable people to organize on other issues" (Adams and Mayoux 2001, 5).

Mayoux's critique of minimalist, banking-only approaches is taken further by observers from the left. Rankin (2002), for example, argues that microfinance may entrench—rather than challenge—traditional gender roles.

First, she cites the Goetz and Sen Gupta (1996) evidence that it is often men, not the women borrowers, who actually control the microenterprise investments and income. Second, even when women maintain control, Rankin argues that "they are often encouraged to take up enterprises such as sweater knitting that do not disrupt practices of isolation and seclusion within their households (Rankin 2002, 17)."

This raises a more complicated question: Is increased specialization within the household a good thing from an equity standpoint? Many critics, notably, Gibbons (1995), Goetz and Sen Gupta (1996), and Dawkins-Scully (1997), forcefully argued that it isn't. Within-household special-ization, the argument goes, reinforces women's reliance on male family members due to women's limited access to inputs, supplies, and mar-keting facilities.

One answer to these criticisms is that unskilled women have very few working opportunities outside the household (in the formal sector, at least). So microfinance helps women to make the most out of the traditional activities that they are restricted from in the short run. Meanwhile, the hope is that they acquire new skills and accumulate resources that improve their family's living conditions. Thus, microfinance advocates who stress gender empowerment tend to look to programs that add training and consciousness-raising—such as the training program organized by BRAC, the largest microlender in Bangladesh, or the credit with education strategy of Pro Mujer in Latin America. BRAC not only provides lessons on new productive activi-ties, but they also hold sessions on legal and social rights and basic health practices. Such training is costly, though, and BRAC defrays expenses through funds from the government and international donors.

SUMMARY AND CONCLUSIONS

In this chapter we first argued that enhancing opportunities for women can be good for both efficiency and intrahousehold equity. Advocates argue that microfinance can also improve long-term development, as women are the main brokers of children's health and education. In particular, we highlighted the potential for microfinance to play a role in increasing the scale and scope of self-employment opportunities and skill acquisition, protecting women's rights through monitoring by third parties, for facilitating savings, and for enhancing social capital. These are not achievements that will necessarily arrive as a matter of course. Rather, to be achieved, programs need to be designed with these outcomes in mind. When and whether the goals can be met without sacrificing other goals—such as financial performance— remains an open question. Microfinance practitioners who are most interested in building strong financial systems have viewed discussions of gender empowerment with a wary eye—quite understandably, given the lack of systematic data—but we find a great deal of evidence from other quarters to support the potential of microfinance to make a difference here.

In many ways, the discussion in this chapter just scratches the surface, and more research is needed on at least three important dimen-sions. First, the empirical evidence is scattered and incomplete. In par-ticular we would like to learn more about the relationship of gender and social capital in microfinance; about the impact of microfinance on skill acquisition, education, and women's access to the formal sector; and about the effect of microfinance on intrahousehold income distri-bution. The broader interrelationship of gender and class also deserves consideration within the microfinance context.

Second, how does the emphasis on gender affect the design of microfinance institutions? Should financial services be bundled with the provision of complementary inputs and training by NGOs, governments, and/or donor agencies? How should the lending con-tract or savings devices be modified to increase women's opportuni-ties within the household and the broader community? A third question involves the extent to which microfinance can contribute to changes in social norms, rather than being a vehicle for reinforcing existing norms. These are all "frontier" issues, and will no doubt be revisited regularly.

8

Measuring Impacts

INTRODUCTION

Anecdotes on the benefits of microfinance abound and inspiring stories from around the globe have helped to turn microfinance from a few scattered programs into a global movement. Consider the story of Mrs. Braulia Parra, who lives with a family of seven in a poor neigh-borhood in Monterrey, Mexico, in a home with cardboard walls and dirt floors. Illiterate and inexperienced in the workplace, Mrs. Parra took her first $150 loan from ADMIC, a local microlender. The loan allowed her to buy yarn and other sewing supplies to make handsewn decorations. Each week she sells about one hundred handmade baskets, dolls and mirrors, going door-to-door in her neighborhood. After ten loans, Mrs. Parra had earned enough to install a toilet in her modest home, as well as an outdoor shower. Building a second floor was next in her sights.

Anecdotes like this are not a substitute, however, for careful statisti-cal evidence on impacts from large samples. For every Braulia Parra, was there another customer who fared poorly? The number of careful impact studies is small but growing, and their conclusions, so far, are much more measured than the anecdotes would suggest. Microfinance is touted as a way to raise incomes for the very poor, but studies of SEWA Bank in India, Zambuko Trust in Zimbabwe, and Mibanco in Peru sponsored by the United States Agency for International Devel-opment (USAID), for example, found that on average borrowers had net income gains only in India and Peru. In Zimbabwe, there were no measurable increases in average incomes relative to those in control groups (Snodgrass and Sebstad 2002). This should not be surprising: The anecdotes are culled to show the potential of microfinance, while the statistical analyses are designed to show typical impacts across the board. Inevitably, some customers will thrive, others will be unchanged, and some may slip backwards. One study of Bolivia's BancoSol, for example, reports that staff estimated that in any given cohort roughly 25 percent showed spectacular gains to borrowing, 60–65 percent stayed about the same, and 10–15 percent went bankrupt (Mosley 1996b).

Increasing income is, of course, not the only metric by which to judge microfinance. Microfinance participation can affect households in many ways. Researchers have analyzed a range of social and economic outcomes beyond household income and consumption—including business profits, nutrition, schooling, fertility, contraception, risk, asset holdings—and a range of measures of empowerment and changes in social consciousness. In the USAID study of Zimabwe, for example, clients were shown to diversify their income sources more than others, a potentially important means of risk diversification.

No matter what the outcomes of interest are, the most difficult part of evaluating impacts is to separate out the causal role of microfinance (which requires stripping out the various "selection" and "reverse causation" biases common to nearly all statistical evaluations). Even if earnings from microfinance participation are funding new houses, further education for children, new savings accounts, and new busi-nesses, we have to ask whether these changes are more remarkable than what would have happened without microfinance.

If we see that richer households have larger loans, we have to ask whether the loans made the households richer—or do richer households simply have easier access to credit (or both) without actually being made much more productive by the loans. Ultimately, the question that every careful evaluation seeks to answer is how would borrowers have done without the programs.

In practice, it's a surprisingly difficult question to answer cleanly. One major problem is that many microfinance clients already have initial advantages over their neighbors. In examining village bank pro-grams in Northeast Thailand, for example, Coleman (2002) finds that households that will later become microfinance borrowers tend to already be significantly wealthier than their nonparticiping neighbors before the village bank starts its operations. Moreover, the wealthiest villagers are nearly twice as likely to become borrowers than their poorer neighbors; the wealthiest are also more likely to use their power to obtain much larger loans than others. Alexander (2001) similarly finds that microfinance borrowers in Peru start off considerably wealth-ier than their nonparticipating neighbors.

In a small sample from Bangladesh, Hashemi (1997) also finds impor-tant underlying differences between borrowers and nonborrowers in villages served by Grameen Bank and BRAC.

Over half of those who chose not to participate did so because they felt that they could not gen-erate adequate profits to reliably repay loans. Another quarter opted out due to religious and social sanctions that restricted the ability to participate in meetings outside of the home with nonfamily males. If sufficient care is not taken to control for such self-selection into micro-finance programs, estimated "impacts" on income and "empower-ment" will be misleading. The microfinance interventions will seem more positive than is indeed the case.

Unfortunately, this is not an esoteric concern that practitioners and policymakers can safely ignore. It is not just a difference between obtaining "very good" estimates of impacts versus "perfect" esti-mates—the biases can be large. In evaluating the Grameen Bank, for example, McKernan (2002) finds that not controlling for selection bias can lead to overestimation of the effect of participation on profits by as much as 100 percent. In other cases discussed later, controlling for these biases reverses conclusions about impacts entirely.

In many ways, the problems and solutions are no different from eval-uations of health and education interventions, say, so microfinance researchers can learn much from the broader literature on evaluation. But, by the same token, the best empirical work on microfinance holds lessons for researchers with interests beyond the financial sector. In this chapter, we take up important issues around evaluation methods, chal-lenges, and solutions.

HOW MICROFINANCE AFFECTS HOUSEHOLDS

First, researchers have to ask: What are we trying to measure? Microfi-nance may affect household outcomes through a variety of channels. Most immediately, microfinance may make households wealthier, yield-ing an "income effect" that should push up total consumption levels and, holding all else the same, increase the demand for children, health, children's education, and leisure. But running microenterprises may also take time (and make that time relatively more valuable than other activities), yielding "substitution effects" that may counterbalance the effects of increased income.

With increased female employment, for example, time spent raising children can become costlier in terms of fore-gone income, pushing fertility rates downward. The need to have chil-dren help at home (to compensate for extra work taken on by parents) could decrease schooling levels; and leisure, in this case, may fall if the return to working rises sufficiently. Only evaluating impacts on business profits, for example, may thus miss out on other important changes within the household.

The fact that it is often women that are earning the income is not inci-dental. As described in chapter 7 on gender and microfinance, another way that microfinance can affect household outcomes is by tipping the balance of decision making. With added income, women may gain clout within the household, using it to push for greater spending in areas of particular concern to women.

Microlenders may also make direct, nonfinancial interventions that affect client outcomes. Some programs use meetings with clients to advise on family planning, and to stress the importance of schooling and good health practices, taking advantage of group meetings to hold communal discussions and training sessions. Village banks that are run on the "credit with education" model developed by the NGO Freedom From Hunger have made this a mainstay of their approach, for example, and other microlenders like Latin America's Pro Mujer have added training and education components in various ways (Dunford 2001). Taking these kinds of extra benefits into account, McKernan (2002) finds that being a member of the Grameen Bank is associated with a 126 percent increase in self-employment profits *after* accounting for the direct benefit of access to capital. The increase, she presumes, is due to increased social and human capital derived from group meetings.

The multiplicity of channels means that it is typically impossible to assign a given measured impact to the strictly financial elements in microfinance; although there have been attempts to analyze programs that are essentially similar but which differ in specific, limited ways. In order to separate out the role of education programs, for example, ideally one would want to run programs without the "credit with edu-cation" training sessions and compare them to similar programs that use the integrated approach. Smith (2002) does this with data on Project HOPE's "health banks" in rural Ecuador and urban Honduras. He finds that the health interventions did indeed improve health care for the participants relative to the health care received by those in credit-only programs, and the health interventions did not diminish the the banks' financial performance. There is also hope that health interven-tions like this might have impacts on household income and spending by reducing the incidence of illness and raising productivity, but results on that score are mixed in Smith's sample. Much could be learned by following Smith's example to gauge the impacts of business training, marketing, "consciousness-raising," and other interventions that are sometimes delivered alongside financial services.

Evaluation Basics

To be concrete, we focus on attempts to measure the causal impact of microfinance on borrower income. Income can be attributed to many sources. Most immediate, those sources are your job, your business, your pension, and so forth. But here we take one step backward in order to focus on more basic sources such as your age, education, and experience. These attributes are generally measurable. Another cate-gory of attributes is far harder to measure, such as your entrepreneur-ial skills, your persistence in seeking goals, your organizational ability, and your access to valuable social networks. In this latter category, we also include "shocks" such as whether you had a bad flu last winter or a falling out with your boss. Another set of attributes has to do with where you live—for example, in a city or village (measurable) or in a place with a thriving local market (measurable, but typically not actu-ally recorded in surveys). A final broad category includes income deter-minants that tend to be broadly felt, like political upheavals, rampant inflation, or economic booms.

Calculating the impacts of microfinance requires disentangling its role from the simultaneous roles of all of these attributes. The challenge is made harder by the fact that the decision to participate in a microfinance program—and at what intensity—will likely depend on many of those same attributes. Thus, there is likely to be a high correlation between microfinance participation and, say, your age and entrepre-neurial ability. Since researchers can record your age, there are simple ways of controlling for age-related issues. But since entrepreneurial ability is typically unmeasured, researchers need to be careful in making comparisons or else the impact of being a better entrepreneur could misleadingly be interpreted as an impact of microfinance access.

ADDRESSING THE SELECTION PROBLEM IN PRACTICE

In the following sections, we consider a series of related approaches to impact evaluation. The overview is not exhaustive and we do not aim to provide a full survey of impact surveys to date. Rather, we aim to point to key methodological issues and to gather several important results. The results to date are decidedly mixed, with some evidence of modest positive impacts of microfinance on income, expenditure, and related variables, while other studies find that positive impacts disap-pear once selection biases are addressed. There have been few serious impact evaluations of microfinance so far, though, so a collection of definitive results is still awaited. All the same, the existing studies provide useful insights and directions for future research.

Using Data on Prospective Clients in Northeast Thailand

A number of recent studies use novel research designs to address selec-tion biases. One approach is to use information on borrowers before the microfinance program enters. Coleman (1999) and (2002) takes advantage of a particular way a microfinance program was imple-mented in Northeast Thailand, providing a unique way to address selection bias. He gathered data on 445 households in fourteen villages. Of these, eight had village banks operating at the start of 1995. The remaining six did not, but village banks would be set up one year later. Interestingly (and critically for the evaluation), at the beginning of 1995, field staff from the village bank programs organized households in these six villages into banks, allowing the households to self-select according to the village bank's standard procedures. But then the households were forced to wait one year before getting their first loans. The unusual procedure on the part of the programs allows Coleman to analyze who joins and who does not *before* the village banks start running. Moreover, it allows him to estimate the following regression equation:

$$Y_{ij} = X_{ij}a + V_j b + M_{ij}g + T_{ij}d + h_{ij}, \qquad (8.1)$$

where the variable to be explained Y_{ij} is a household-level outcome—income or profit—for household *i* in village *j*. The regression approach allows a refinement of the difference-in-difference approach. Here, "dummy-variables" (i.e., variables that only take the values of zero or one) are used to control for location and partici-pation status. Other variables control for factors like age and educa-tion. The variables X_{ij} capture household characteristics (and a constant term); and V_j is a vector of village dummy variables that control for all fixed characteristics of the village. The two variables of most interest are M_{ij} and T_{ij}. The first is a "membership dummy vari-able" that equals one for both actual members of the village banks and those villagers who have opted into the programs (in the control vil-lages) but who have not yet received loans. Coleman argues that M_{ij} controls for selection bias so that d, the coefficient on T_{ij}, is a consistent estimate of the causal treatment effect. In his application, the variable T_{ij} is the number of months that village bank credit was available to (actual) members, which is exogenous to the household.

Controlling for selection makes an important difference. Coleman (1999) finds that average program impact was not significantly differ-ent from zero after controlling for endogenous member selection and program placement. When he extends the estimating framework to dif-ferentiate between impacts on "rank-and-file members" and members of the village bank committee (who tend to be wealthier and more pow-erful), he finds again that most impacts were not statistically signifi-cant for rank-and-file members, but there were some noted impacts for committee members, particularly on wealth accumulation. Coleman cautions, though, that the results need to be put into the context of the larger financial landscape. Thailand is relatively wealthy (at least compared to Bangladesh), and villagers have access to credit from a range of sources—some at low interest rates from government-backed sources. Strikingly, survey households held over 500,000 baht in wealth on average and had over 30,000 baht of "low-interest" debt (excluding village bank debt). Thus, the village banks' loans of 1,500 to 7,500 baht may be too small to make a notable average difference in the welfare of households; in fact, complaints about small loan sizes prompted some women to leave the banks. Coleman argues that one reason that wealthier borrowers may have experienced larger impacts was because they could commandeer larger loans.

Attrition Bias: Problems When Using "New Borrowers" as a Control Group in Peru

A problem in trying to replicate Coleman's approach is that it's not often that a researcher comes upon programs that go through the trouble of organizing villagers but then delay credit disbursement for a period. So instead, researchers have tried to capture the flavor of the approach by comparing "old borrowers" to "new borrowers" within the same area. Typically this is done with cross-sectional data, yielding an approach that is simple and relatively inexpensive (and which does not require surveying nonborrowers). This procedure has been pro-moted by USAID through its AIMS project (more on this to come) and by other microfinance organizations (Karlan 2001).

Assuming that the characteristics of people who enter into programs are unchanging over time, the method should account for the fact that borrowers are not a random group of people. But assuming that the relevant characteristics are similar over time requires a leap of faith. Why didn't the new borrowers sign up earlier? Why were the older borrowers first in line? If their timing of entry was due to unobserv-able attributes such as ability, motivation, and entrepreneurship, the comparisons may do little to address selection biases—and could, in fact, exacerbate bias.

Karlan outlines two additional problems based on his experience evaluating village banks organized by FINCA Peru. Assume that the conditions of selection *are* constant over time so that the same kinds of people become clients today as who became clients five years ago. All seems well, but there are still two potential biases, both of which are most pronounced when assessing impacts using cross-sectional data. Both are also due to dropouts.

Dropouts are an ongoing microfinance reality. Sometimes borrowers leave because they are doing so well that they no longer need microfinance; but, more often, it is the borrowers in trouble who leave. Wright (2001) gives evidence that dropout rates are 25–60 percent per year in East Africa. In Bangladesh, Khandker (2003) estimates rates for three leading lenders of 3.5 percent per year between 1991 and 1992 and 1998 and 1999 (which is much smaller than the numbers cited by Wright, nonetheless, they can add up over time). Gonzalez-Vega et al. (1997, 34–35) provide parallel data for Bolivia. They investigate the fraction of people who ever borrowed from a given microlender that are still active borrowers at the time of their suvey (the end of 1995). The result-ing proxy for retention rates shows that just half of BancoSol clients were still active. In rural areas, two-thirds of borrowers from PRODEM were still active, possibly reflecting the fact that there are fewer alter-native lending sources in the countryside.

It is likely that these "older borrowers" (i.e., those who remain active) have the positive qualities of survivors, while "new borrowers" have yet to be tested. If the failures are more likely to drop out, comparing old to new borrowers will overestimate impacts. We suspect that this patten is most often the case, but, as suggested earlier, the prediction is not clear-cut. If it is mainly the successes that move on (leaving weaker clients in the pool), the sign of bias will be reversed, under-estimating causal impacts. The second problem is due to nonrandom attrition independent of actual impacts. If richer households are more likely to leave, the pool of borrowers' becomes poorer on average. Then it could look like microfinance borrowing depletes one's income, when in fact it may have no impact at all. Conversely, when lower-income households leave in greater numbers, impacts will be overstated.

Karlan argues for hunting down the dropouts and including them in the analysis along with the other older borrowers, though it may be costly. A cheaper improvement would be to (1) estimate predictors of dropout based on observable information on older borrowers; then (2) form a prediction of who among the new borrowers is likely to (later on) drop out; and (3) use the prediction to weigh the new borrower control group. The method is not perfect, though: In particular, dropouts who made their decision based in part on the size of impact are not addressed by the reweighing scheme.

Longitudinal Data: USAID AIMS Studies in India, Peru, and Zimbabwe

Some biases can be mitigated by using data collected at several points in time, allowing "before versus after" comparisons. Under certain conditions, the approach controls for both nonrandom participation and nonrandom program placement. But when those conditions are not met, the approach is subject to biases due to unobservable variables that change over time—hard-to-observe characteristics such as entrepreneurial spirit and access to markets that are likely to be correlated with borrowing status.

The most ambitious longitudinal studies to date are those sponsored by USAID in the late 1990s, with the hope to demonstrate methods and generate benchmarks. Teams analyzed impacts on members of SEWA (a labor organization and microlender serving women in the informal sector in Ahmedabad, India), Mibanco (an ACCION International affiliate in Peru), and the Zambuko Trust in Zimbabwe. Baseline data was collected and then the same households were resurveyed two years later. Case studies were also conducted alongside the statistical analyses.

The teams selected clients randomly from lists provided by the programs. The trick was then to identify control groups. In India and Peru, the control group was a random sample drawn from nonparticipants in the same regions who met program eligibility criteria. In Zimbabwe, enumerators instead used a "random walk procedure" in which they set off in a given direction to find nonclient households for the control group. As Barnes, Keogh, and Nemarundwe (2001, 19) explain, "For example, when the client's business was in a residential area, from the front of the house the interviewer turned right, went to the first road intersection, turned right and walked to the third intersection and then turned left; from there the interviewer asked a series of questions to identify who met the criteria for inclusion in the study." The criteria used to match treatments and controls were gender, enterprise sector and geographic location, as well as additional criteria added by Zambuko Trust: "a) never received credit from a formal organization for their enterprise, b) be the sole or joint owner of an enterprise at least six months old, and c) not be employed elsewhere on a full-time basis" (Barnes, Keogh, and Nemarundwe 2001, 19).

The data have potential, and the researchers followed dropouts as best they could to avoid the attrition biases described earlier. With two years of data, the researchers could have analyzed impacts by investi-gating how changes in microfinance participation affect changes in out-comes.

But, surprisingly, the AIMS researchers chose *not* to analyze variables converted to changes over time, which would have elimi-nated all biases due to omitted variables that do not change over time (i.e., to analyze differences-in-differences as described in section 8.3). The stated rationale is that the "differencing" procedure also eliminates the chance to analyze the roles of variables such as gender and enter-prise sector that are also fixed through time, and so alternative methods (analysis of covariance) were used (Dunn 2002). In our view, the costs of that choice far outweigh the benefits.

To see the differencing method (i.e., the method not used), we can modify equation (8.1) to specify that the variables are measured in a given time period *t*:

$$Y_{ijt} = X_{ijt}a + V_j b + M_{ij}g + T_{ijt}d + h_{ijt}. \qquad (8.2)$$

As before, we are interested in estimating the value of d, but here it is the coefficient on the value of loans received. (The two variables, value of loans and length of membership, are typically very similar since loan sizes and length of time borrowing often move closely together.) The dependent variable, Y_{ijt}, is a household-level outcome (income or profit) for household *i* in village *j* at time *t*. The variables X_{ijt} capture household characteristics at *t* (and a constant term), and V_j is a vector of village dummy variables *that are assumed to be unchanging over time.* The dummies will capture village-level features like distance to the closest major city, proximity to major transportation and markets, and the quality of local leadership.

Similarly, we assume that the individual-specific variable M_{ij}, the variable that captures nonrandom individual selection into the program, is also unchanging over time. It may reflect, for example, an individual's energy level, management ability, and business savvy. In this case, though, we do not assume that it is observable. Thus, there is a potential bias stemming from its omis-sion when equation (8.2) is estimated.

The problem can be addressed by estimating in differences. Assume that we have the same variables collected in period $t + 1$:

$$Yijt+1 = Xijt+1a + Vjb + Mijg + Tijt+1d + hijt+1. \quad (8.3)$$

Then, we can subtract equation (8.2) from (8.3) to obtain

$$DY_{ij} = DX_{ij}a + DC_{ij}d + Dh_{ij}, \quad (8.4)$$

where D indicates the difference in the variables between periods t and $t + 1$. Here, the village dummies drop out, as do the fixed (and unob-servable) individual-specific characteristics (which was the concern that prompted the AIMS researchers not to follow this method). The benefit, though, is considerable: A consistent estimate of the impact d can be obtained (which is the most important aim).

It turns out that the omitted unobservables in equations like (8.2) do make a large difference, and not addressing them undermines the cred-ibility of the AIMS impact studies. When Alexander (2001) returns to the AIMS Peru data and estimates the equations in differences (akin to equation 8.4), she finds that estimated impacts on enterprise profits fall.

In fact when she controls for reverse causality by using an instrumen-tal variables approach (more on this to follow), the estimated impacts shrink and are no longer statistically significant. Selection bias is clearly a major problem, but results might be different if the two surveys had been collected more than two years apart or if other instrument vari-ables had been used. Below we address why finding instrumental vari-ables continues to be a challenge.

Using a Quasi-Experiment to Construct Instrumental Variables: Bangladesh Studies

A different way of approaching the problems above would have been to search for an instrumental variable for microfinance participation. The instrumental variables method allows researchers to address prob-lems posed by measurement error, reverse causality, and some omitted variable biases. The instrumental variables strategy involves finding an additional variable (or set of variables) that explains levels of credit received, but that has no direct relationships with the outcomes of interest (like profit or income). Then a proxy variable can be formed based on the instrumental variable, and it can be used to tease out the causal impact of credit access.

The interest rate is a potential instrumental variable—or simply "instrument"—since it can explain how much credit a borrower desires while not being a direct determinant of income in itself (that's testable, at least). The trouble is that interest rates seldom vary within a given program, and the statistical techniques are impossible without some variation. And, while it is true that interest rates vary when compar-ing clients of different institutions—both formal and informal—it is likely that the variation partly reflects unobserved attributes of the bor-rowers, undermining the use of interest rates as instruments. Lender characteristics are also candidates for instrumental variables. Similar to all other community-level variables, though, they will be wiped out when including village dummy variables in specifications when there is no variation in program access within a village. In short, the instru-mental variables approach can be powerful, but finding convincing instrumental variables for credit has been frustrating.

But when there is within-village variation in program access, rules determining eligibility can be the basis of an evaluation strategy, an approach employed in a series of studies of microfinance in Bangladesh. Over the years 1991 and 1992, the World Bank–Bangladesh Institute of Development Studies surveyed nearly 1,800 households in eighty-seven villages in Bangladesh; most villages were served by microlenders but fifteen were not. In 1998 and 1999, teams were sent back to find the same households, but by then all of the villages were served by microlenders. After losing some households through attri-tion, 1,638 households were left that were interviewed in both rounds. In a sign of the rapid spread of microfinance in Bangladesh, about one quarter of the sample included a microfinance customer within the household in 1991–1992, but by 1998–1999 the figure had jumped to about half. The jump makes program evaluation more difficult, but not impossible. To complicate matters, about 11 percent of customers were members of more than one microfinance institution in 1998–1999.

Estimates from the 1991–1992 Cross Section

The first round of data has, on its own, generated a series of papers; the most impor-tant results have been compiled in Khandker's (1998) *Fighting Poverty with Microcredit.* Completing impact studies with just a single cross-section requires ingenuity and some important assumptions, and the task was made more challenging by the desire to estimate impacts of borrowing by men and by women separately. The studies are sophis-ticated in their use of statistical methods to compensate for the funda-mental limitations of the data set. One large limitation arises because the researchers were eager to generate results with the first wave of the data rather than waiting for the second. That the studies use heavier statistical artillery than other microfinance studies does not necessar-ily mean that they deliver results that are more reliable or rigorous than other studies. In fact, as we describe later, the studies are open to ques-tions about the validity of the underlying assumptions that prop up the statistical framework.

On the face of it, it would seem impossible to get far with just a single cross-sectional data set and without a special setup like that of Coleman (1999). But the way that microlenders in Bangladesh implement their programs opens a door for researchers. To capture the basic insight, figure 8.3 shows two hypothetical villages, one with a program (the treatment village) and one without (the control village). The villages are separated into distinct groups based on their eligibility and par-ticipation status; we discuss how eligibility is determined shortly. The groups within the thick black lines are eligible to borrow (or, in the case of the control village, *would be* eligible). As a first step, researchers could compare the incomes and other outcomes of microfinance participants to nonparticipants just using data from the treatment village, but it is impossible to rule out selection biases of the sort described in section 8.3. It is also possible to use the control villages to compare participants from the treatment villages served by microfinance to the eligible households from the control villages, but even here there are potential selection biases since the participants are still a select group.

A more satisfactory approach is to compare eligible households (all households within the thick black lines) between the two villages. Here, the goal is to estimate the impact of microfinance access rather than actual participation. The benefit is that a clean estimate of the average impact of access may be more useful than a biased estimate of the impact of participation. Moreover, if there are no spillovers from participants to nonparticipants, it is possible to recover a clean estimate of the impact of participation from the estimate of access (by simply dividing the latter by the fraction of households in the village that par-ticipate). The assumption that there are no spillovers is strong, though, and Khandker (2003) finds evidence against it.

The fault with the latter approach is that while selection biases at the household-level are addressed, it does not address biases stemming from nonrandom program placement. As mentioned earlier, villagers served by microlenders may seem to do poorly relative to control groups just because the microlender chooses to work in isolated, dis-advantaged villages. In other cases, villages may be doing better than average even without the microlender, so the bias would go in the other direction; estimated impacts would be too high.

A potential solution is at hand, though, provided by the particular way that the selected microlenders determine eligibility for program access. Pitt and Khandker (1998) develop a framework for estimating impacts using the 1991-1992 cross-section. The starting point is the observation that the three programs being studied—Grameen Bank, BRAC, and the state-run RD-12—all share the same eligibility rule. In order to keep focused on the poorest, the programs restrict their serv-ices to the "functionally landless"; this is implemented through a rule declaring that households owning over half an acre of land are not allowed to borrow. The individual programs place some additional restrictions, but the half-acre rule is the common criterion. So, in terms of figure 8.3, the functionally landless are encompassed by the thick black lines, and the noneligible lie outside. The fact that there are ineligible households within villages with programs means that there is another control group that can help alleviate concerns that the microlenders choose villages that are special in one way or another.

An improved estimation strategy—but *not* the one adopted by Pitt and Khandker—is to compare differences-in-differences as described in section 8.3. It involves comparing the outcomes of households with microfinance access to the outcomes of households that are ineligible, but living in treatment villages. The strategy then turns to the control villages where the ineligible are compared to those who "would be" eligible. Finally, those two comparisons are pitted against each other. The result tells us if households with access to microfinance are doing better than their ineligible neighbors, relative to the difference in out-comes between functionally landless households in control villages versus *their* ineligible neighbors.

One can do even better by implementing this strategy in a regression framework that also accounts for a broad range of household charac-teristics. In the regression framework, the difference-in-difference strat-egy would be implemented as

$$Yij = Xij(\propto + Vj/3 + Eijj + (Tij \ \% \ E_y)<5' + r/y, \qquad (8.5)$$

The idea is very similar to that of equation (8.1), but two important changes are made. First, E_y is a dummy variable that reflects whether or not a household is functionally landless and thus eligible to borrow from a microlender (whether or not there is in fact a microlender present in the village).

The variable equals one if a household is within the thick black lines in either village in figure 8.1. The other important change is the variable $(T_{r_i} \cdot E_y)$, which is the product of E,y and a dummy variable that indicates whether or not the household is in a treatment village; it equals one only if the household is within the thick black lines in the village with a microlender. The coefficient on the dummy variable gives the average impact of credit access—after controlling for being functionally landless, living in a particular village, and having specific household characteristics.

Morduch (1998) takes the approach in equation (8.5) and finds no sharp evidence for strong impacts of microfinance on household con-sumption, but he finds some evidence that microfinance helps house-holds diversify income streams so that consumption is less variable across seasons. The estimates, though, rely on the assumption that the village dummy variables perfectly capture all relevant aspects about the villages that would influence microlenders' location decisions. In this setting, though, the village-level dummies only control for unob-servables that affect all households in a village identically (and lin-early). Nonrandom program placement thus remains an issue if, as is plausible, the functionally landless are noticeably different from their wealthier neighbors (noticeable to bank staff but not the econo-metrician), and if the programs take this into account when deciding where to locate. In that case, the dummy variable $(T_{ij} \cdot E_{ij})$ could pick up the effects of those inherent differences, thus biasing estimated impacts.

Morduch (1998) also takes a closer look at the eligibility rule on which the strategy rests. As Pitt and Khandker (1998) point out, it is important that landholdings are exogenous to the household—that is, households are not, for example, selling land in order to become eligi-ble to borrow. If that was the case, selection biases would creep back in—even when estimating using equation (8.5)—since unobservably promising borrowers would be taking special steps to switch their eligibility status. Pitt and Khandker cite the fact that in southern India in the 1980s, village land markets tended to be thin, and most land was acquired through inheritance. In that case, landholdings were exoge-nous to the household and unlikely (or at least much less likely) to be correlated with unobserved potential.

But Bangladesh in the 1990s is not southern India in the 1980s, and land markets in the study area turn out to be fairly active—and this is evident upon closer inspection of the landholding module of the data set. On the other hand, Morduch (1998) finds no evidence that households are selling land in order to meet microfinance eligibility criteria. If anything, successful borrowers are buying land, and one explanation for Morduch's inability to find sig-nificant impacts on household consumption could be that funds were instead going to land (and other asset) purchases.

The reason that households are not selling land to gain access to microfinance raises another tricky issue. It turns out that the microlenders were not following the eligibility criteria strictly; so many house-holds owning over a half an acre were nonetheless borrowing in 1991-1992. As a result, there was no reason to sell land to become eli-gible. Khandker (2003) acknowledges the problem and finds that 25 percent of borrowers were over the half-acre line in 1991-1992 and 31 percent were over in 1998-1999. Pitt (1999) follows up on the issue and suggests that households with more land have lower quality land, so they still may be impoverished, even if they are not (strictly speak-ing) functionally landless. But a problem remains: the eligible house-holds in the control villages were surveyed on the basis of a strict interpretation of the half-acre rule, while the eligible households in the treatment villages include the mistargeted households. Morduch (1998) adjusts the samples in order to maintain comparability, and Pitt (1999) does robustness checks to show that the Pitt and Khandker (1998) results change little when mistargeting is taken into account.

These issues should be borne in mind when turning to the Pitt and Khandker (1998) framework. We start by noting that equation (8.5) (which can be run using ordinary least squares) is closely related to the following instrumental variables approach estimate instead:

$$Yij = Xij(\propto + Vj/3 + Eijj + QjS'' + r/y, \qquad (8.6)$$

where C_y is the amount of credit received and $T_{i;} \cdot E_{i;}$ is employed as an instrumental variable. Estimating equation (8.6) using ordinary least squares would bring trouble since households who have received more and larger loans can be expected to be different in unobservable ways from those who have received fewer loans (leading to a variant of selec-tion bias associated with loan size). The instrumental variables method addresses the problem and leads to a clean estimate of *8''*, the average impact of credit access (subject to the same caveats as village dummy variables noted earlier).

Before moving on to the method used by Pitt and Khandker (1998), note that the instrument *Ty·Ey* is a dummy variable that only reflects credit access. The estimate of *8''* thus does not draw on variation in *how much* credit is received, it only depends on whether credit is received.

The step taken by Pitt and Khandker is to expand to a larger set of instruments, in effect, by using $X_{i} \cdot T_{i} \cdot E_{i}$ as instruments. The step yields as many instruments as there are X's. (The X's include education and various aspects of household demographics.) The move means that the estimate of d d'' takes advantage of variation in how much credit house-holds receive.

An important identifying assumption is that the specification in equation (8.6) is correct so that education and demographics affect household outcomes in exactly the same way for the whole sample; otherwise, biases enter back in. In other words, it is assumed that there are no important nonlinear relationships in the ways that age, educa-tion, and the other variables influence outcomes of interest.

Another critical identifying assumption stems from their use of a Tobit equation to explain credit demand in a first stage in which they are effectively creating the instrumental variables used in the final regressions.

The Tobit provides a way to efficiently handle variables with many zero values (like credit); but it requires that, in the second stage estimation, all microfinance impacts are assumed to be identical across borrowers, an assumption that is often made out of necessity but that stretches plausbility here. It also implies (implausibly) that marginal and average impacts of credit are equal. Estimating using a simpler two-stage least squares method would lead to consistent estimates without requiring these assumptions, but the method is less efficient (i.e., coefficients would tend to have larger standard errors). By using the Tobit, the efficiency of the estimators is improved.

Pitt and Khandker take one more step to investigate credit received by men separately from credit received by women. Tc do this, they take advantage of the fact that microlending groups are not mixed by gender in Bangladesh. In the eighty-seven villages surveyed in 1991–1992, ten had no female groups and twenty-two had no male groups (and forty had both, leaving fifteen villages with no groups). Identification in this case comes from comparing how the roles of age, education, and so forth for men with access to male groups compare to the roles for men without access. Similarly, for the characteristics of women with and without access. Pitt and Khandker's most cited result from the 1991–1992 cross-section is that household consumption increases by eighteen taka for every one hundred taka lent to a woman. For lending to men, the increase is just eleven taka for every one hundred taka lent. Men, according to the estimates, take more leisure when given the chance, explaining in part why household consumption rises less when they borrow. Nonland assets increase substantially when borrowing is by women, but not by men. Schooling of boys increases in general with borrowing, but schooling of girls only increases when women borrow from Grameen—but not when women borrow from the other pro-grams. It cannot be ascertained from the estimates why loans to women have higher marginal impacts than loans to men. Pitt and Khandker interpret is as an indication of a lack of fungibility of capital and income within the household (which is plausible assuming that their basic result is correct). A very different interpretation is supported by the fact that loans to males tend to be larger so that the smaller relative impacts may be explained, at least in part, by the standard theory of declining marginal returns to capital. However, marginal returns would have to be very sharply diminishing, since loan sizes are in the same general ballpark.

The 1991–1992 cross section has also been used to analyze noncredit program impacts, fertility and contraception choices, and impacts on seasonality and nutrition (for an overview, see Morduch 1999b). Khandker (1998) has used the basic impact numbers described earlier (imperfect as they be) to estimate broad impacts on poverty and to com-plete cost-benefit analyses. The work is ambitious; but, as the previous discussion suggests, the underlying setup is far from perfect. The basic imperfections are not the fault of the researchers, but they do necessitate more structure, greater econometric sophistication, and a heavier load of assumptions than would otherwise be necessary. The second round of data collected in 1998–1999 provides hope that simpler methods may be able to deliver more robust, transparent results, but initial results are just being circulated as we write this book.

Estimates from the Full Panel, 1991–1992 and 1998–1999

With the two rounds of data, Khandker (2003) estimates an equation along the lines of equation. As with the work on the cross section, he modifies the equation slightly, to allow for separate impacts when women borrow versus when men borrow. And in other specifications, he explores spillovers to nonborrowers who live in the same villages as borrowers.

Table 8.1: Falling poverty in Bangladesh: Program participants versus nonparticipants

	Headcount for moderate poverty			Headcount for extreme poverty		
	1991–1992	1998–1999	Difference	1991–1992	1998–1999	Difference
Program area						
All program participants	90.3	70.1	20.2	52.5	32.7	19.8
Target nonparticipants	91.1	72.0	19.1	58.9	44.0	14.9
Nontarget nonparticipants	69.8	50.8	19	23.6	19.3	4.3
Total	83.7	65.5	18.2	45.0	31.4	14.6
No program in 1991–1992						
All program participants	90.8	71.6	19.2	56.6	43.8	13.2
Target nonparticipants	87.4	82.9	4.5	57.0	51.2	6.8
Nontarget nonparticipants	72.7	53.2	19.5	35.5	26.0	9.5
Total	80.3	67.7	12.6	46.6	38.3	8.3

Source: Khandker 2003, Table 14, and calculations by the authors.

Note: Program and nonprogram area is based on 1991–1992 program placement. All villages had programs by 1998–1999.

As noted earlier, the control villages from 1991 to 1992 all have programs by 1998–1999, so simple before and after compar-isons in treatment versus control villages are not possible. In addition, the extent of mistargeting became more severe by the end of the 1990s. The panel data allow us to see trends that help put the microfinance revolution in Bangladesh into perspective. Table 8.1 compiles data from Bangladesh in Khandker (2003). If we just look at the top panel of the table, we see that in program villages, microfinance participants saw important declines in poverty rates (as measured by moderate poverty), from a rate of about 90 percent in 1991–1992 to about 70 percent in 1998–1999, roughly a 20 percentage point decline. But eligi-ble nonparticipants saw a similar decline (roughly 19 percentage points), as did noneligible nonparticipants (roughly 20 percentage points). Pessimists may thus argue that the poverty declines for micro-finance participants would have happened even without microfinance. Optimists, on the other hand, will argue that the impacts of microfi-nance have been far-reaching, spilling over to nonparticipants as well. This, they will argue, explains the broad and similar progress in villages with programs.

If the results for program villages are compared to results for those without programs in 1991–1992, we see similar patterns: Poverty rates all fell by around 19 to 20 percentage points; except in this case, eligible nonparticipants only saw a poverty decline of about 5 percent-age points. Khandker's conclusions, based on his new set of economet-ric estimates, balances the optimistic and pessimistic vision: He argues that microfinance contributed to roughly one third to one half of these poverty declines. Overall, Khandker finds that (at most) lending 100 taka to a woman leads to an increase in household consumption by as much as eight taka annually. This is considerably less than the 18-taka increase that he found in the earlier cross-section. But it is still mean-ingful. Khandker's (1998) much-cited finding that microfinance might cause as much as a 5 percent per year drop in poverty thus appears to be far too optimistic, and we have already discussed caveats about the cross-sectional estimation on which that calculation was based.

The World Bank and Bangladesh Institute for Development Studies surveys have yielded a broad range of interesting data, and they will surely generate a series of interesting studies and much discussion. Of important note, the emerging results from the full panel are much more muted than the initial results based only on the cross-section. Those initial results have also raised methodological issues. And, given the complicated scene on the ground in Bangladesh (where microlending has spread far and wide, leaving little scope for identifying control groups), we suspect that the ultimate resolution of how large an impact microfinance can have will be settled by data from elsewhere.

SUMMARY AND CONCLUSIONS

The microfinance movement was born of the ideal to create new banks with social and economic missions. Completing impact evaluations is an important way to determine if those missions are being achieved. As we have described, there is no study yet that has achieved wide consensus as to its reliability; and this reflects the inherent difficulty in evaluating programs in which participation is voluntary and different customers use the services with varying degrees of intensity.

Still, a set of solid impact evaluations are within reach. Incorporat-ing experimental designs into the program implementation will be one way to achieve more reliable estimates, and useful lessons can be drawn from the experimental design of Mexico's PROGRESA educa-tion and health program. The discussion in this chapter shows that it matters to get details right, and that, for analytical purposes, having one very reliable evaluation is more valuable than having one hundred flawed evaluations.

The challenges in evaluation arise because no microfinance program lends to random citizens. Instead, lenders carefully select areas in which to work and clients to whom to lend. When the characteristics that make borrowers different from nonborrowers are observable, the relevant conditioning variables (age, education, social status, and so forth) can be accounted for in impact evaluations. Often, though, what makes clients different is not measured—borrowers may, for example, have a more entrepreneurial spirit, enjoy better business connections, or be more focused than nonparticipants. Because these kinds of unobservable attributes are correlated with having credit, what seems like an impact of getting access to credit may in fact largely reflect these unobservable attributes. Estimated impacts of microfinance will be biased if nothing is done about the problem. And the biases can be large.

An important source of selection bias stems from where institutions and their branches are located. Are they set up specifically to serve the underserved in atypically isolated areas? This may lead to apparent negative impacts if control areas are not similarly isolated. Alterna-tively, the programs may set up where there is good complementary infrastructure (highways, markets, large towns), biasing estimates upward. When evaluating large programs, programs may be placed in different areas for different reasons, so comparisons with control areas need to be made carefully. Some approaches, such as those based on comparisons of outcomes at more than one point in time, can address those characteristics of program location that do not change over time. But they have limitations too—and often unobservable characteristics do change over time.

Still, while some observers have despaired at the impossibility of generating reliable evaluations, their despair is misplaced and too pes-simistic. It is true that rigorous statistical evaluations are seldom easy. But an often heard early concern—that since money is fungible within the household, it is impossible to trace the impact of a particular loan to a particular change in enterprise profits—turns out to be a minor limitation; this has been called the "attribution dilemma" by Ledgerwood (2001). Even if a given loan cannot be attached to a given change in profit, it is still possible to evaluate how profits change with capital (i.e., to measure the marginal return to capital) and how borrowing affects household-level variables such as income, con-sumption, health, and schooling. In many ways, these are more inter-esting policy questions anyway, relative to narrow issues around sources of microenterprise profit.

Useful evaluations need not be enormous in scale, involving surveys of thousands of households. All else the same, the larger the sample, the better. But some of the smaller studies discussed here turn out to yield more reliable evidence than larger studies that are imperfect in one dimension or another.

There is currently a movement afoot to design evaluations that are rough but that let practitioners quickly gauge their broad impacts by tracking indicators of outcomes for borrowers only. This approach, led by the Imp-Act project based at the Institute of Development Studies at Sussex, will surely provide users with a great deal of helpful data that will lead to program refinements; but they should be distinguished from impact assessments (of the kind described in this chapter) which also track control groups. The latter studies attempt to answer the question: What would have happened to the participants had the program not existed?

Our argument is not that practitioner-friendly steps should be aban-doned. Far from it: The Imp-Act tools are helping organizations to better understand their clients, to improve targeting, and to develop appropriate products and marketing. Rather, our argument is that the approach is not a sufficient way to learn from microfinance. Obtain-ing more careful, credible impact studies that can garner universal acceptance is also vital to push conversations forward. Reliable studies need not be complicated, they only need to be well-designed, as, for example, Coleman's interesting study in Thailand suggests.

The road does not end with impact evaluations, however. Even with a spotless, perfect impact evaluation, interpreting the results is another matter, and one that has received even less attention. Consideration of the worth of programs typically stops too soon. A clear showing of a positive net impact does not necessarily mean that a program is a good candidate for support. Cost-effectiveness matters too. As described in chapter 9, the microfinance programs that are being evaluated should be judged against the costs and benefits of alternative approaches, including other ways of doing microfinance.

9

Subsidy and Sustainability

INTRODUCTION

The August 20, 2003, *Wall Street Journal* carried a short article on micro-finance in Latin America (Kaplan 2003). The article starts with the story of Mrs. Esther Simone Garcia, a shopkeeper in rural Mexico. Mrs. Garcia's $130 loan from Pro Mujer, a leading microlender founded in Bolivia, was enough to improve the range of offerings in Mrs. Garcia's small grocery store. With the debt repaid and business expanding, the *Wall Street Journal* reports that Garcia has started raising her ambitions, and even thinks of sending her daughter to college.

"Now, one of the highly praised tools in the global fight against poverty is also proving it can be a viable business," the article con-tinues, "increasingly drawing investors who seek profits along with the loftier goal of social development." BancoSol's 1996 $5 million bond issue in Bolivia and Compartamos's 2002 $10 million bond issue in Mexico are cited by the *Wall Street Journal* writer to support the case, along with the news of Bank Rakyat Indonesia's plan to sell 30 percent of its equity through an initial public offering in late 2003. These banks are proving part of the promise of microfinance—that microlending can be profitable.

The other part of the promise of microfinance is that it can deliver critical benefits to underserved borrowers such as Esther Garcia in Mexico. Some programs have achieved both promises (sustainability *and* deep outreach to the underserved), but most have not—even though many microlenders are now well-established and run impres-sively efficient (if not actually profitable) operations. On the other hand, BancoSol, Compartamos, and Bank Rakyat Indonesia (BRI) all serve underserved low-income populations, but their outreach to the most impoverished falls short of the leading programs in Bangladesh and India.

The South Asian programs, on the other hand, have not been as commercially successful as BRI or the top Latin American programs. The challenge remains to find ways to deliver small loans and collect small deposits while not sending fees and interest rates through the roof. And if that objective cannot be met, the challenge is then to develop a framework for thinking about microfinance as a social tool that may need to rely, to some degree and in some places, on continu-ing subsidies.

The reality is that much of the microfinance movement continues to take advantage of subsidies—some from donors, some from governments, and some from charities and concerned individuals. The *Microbanking Bulletin* (Microbanking Bulletin 2003), for example, shows that sixty-six out of 124 microlenders surveyed were financially sus-tainable, a rate just over 50 percent. For microlenders focusing on the "low-end," just eighteen of forty-nine were financially sustainable as of the July 2003 accounting, a 37 percent rate. On one hand, the data show that even programs reaching poorer clients can do so while cov-ering the full costs of transactions. But, on the other hand, the norm remains subsidization.

Not only that, but bear in mind that these 124 microlenders in the *Microbanking Bulletin* data are a relatively impressive bunch, sustainability-wise. They only include programs that have indicated particularly strong commitments to achieving financial sustainability, and have allowed their financial accounts to be reworked by *Bulletin* staff to improve numbers' conformity with international accounting principles. Bangladesh's Grameen Bank, for example, is not included. In terms of financial management, the programs are thus skimmed from the cream of the global crop. We lack comparable data on the 2,572 programs counted by the Microcredit Summit at the end of 2002, but the bulk presumably show weaker financial performances than the select 124 in the *Microbanking Bulletin.*

Given the role of subsidies in microfinance, one might expect to find a mini-industry of consultants with expertise in cost-benefit analysis, plying their trade on data from program after program, quantifying whether the subsidies are used well or not. In a perfect world, microfinance cost-benefit analyses would be routinely pitted against cost-benefit studies from other poverty reduction efforts, following well-established modes in the study of public finance—such as Rosen (2002). These studies could usefully frame policy debates. In chapter 1, for example, we reported the finding of Binswanger and Khandker (1995) that during the 1970s the state banking system in India appeared to have caused increases in nonfarm growth, employment and rural wages. But those programs were inefficient and badly targeted, and there were just modest benefits on agricultural output and none on agricultural employment. Binswanger and Khandker conclude that the costs of the government programs were so high that they nearly swamped the economic benefits.

Microfinance promises to improve on state banks by reducing costs, improving targeting, and maintaining (or expanding) benefits. Even to get a snapshot of microfinance performance, measuring benefits alone is clearly inadequate. To test the full promise, cost-benefit studies pit independent assessments of subsidized program costs against meas-ured benefits. Cost-benefit studies can show that even if a microfinance program delivers less impact than alternative uses of funds (e.g., for schools or health clinics), supporting the microlender could still end up being a more effective use of funds if the microlender delivers more impact for a given budget.

But in fact, we know of just two serious cost-benefit analyses of microfinance programs—and those were completed by researchers rather than by donors. Microfinance is not an outlier with regard to the lack of rigorous evaluations. As Lant Pritchett argues in his paper "It Pays to Be Ignorant," rigorous impact studies of health and education interventions are few as well. Pritchett argues that the general lack of rigorous impact analyses is no accident: Most programs have little incentive to be seriously evaluated. After all, why risk a negative assessment? So programs fail to collect the kinds of data required, espe-cially data on appropriate control groups. Collecting data also takes resources away from programs' core missions: *doing* microfinance. In the end, for most programs the costs outweigh the benefits of under-taking cost-benefit studies.

Donors, on the other hand, should be keen on cost-benefit analyses since the studies promise to show donors how to get the most bang for their buck. But donors to date have also shown only limited interest in cost-benefit analyses. One explanation flows from the logic of the promise of financially sustainable microfinance. According to this view, cost-benefit studies pushed in the public finance approach are of limited value since subsidies are only a short-term aid to get microfinance programs up and running. It is of little interest to know the current benefits that subsidies deliver, the argument goes, since subsidies should in the end have no place in microfinance. The *Microbanking Bulletin* data show that indeed older lenders do look better on average (in terms of financial sustainability) when compared to newer programs—although most older programs remain subsidized.

There are two main reasons that this argument is inadequate. First, it is still useful to assess the costs and benefits of the start-up subsidies relative to alternative uses that they could be put to—building health clinics, buying school textbooks, paving roads, and so forth—even for the programs that eventually achieve financial sustainability. And second, since reality shows that subsidies remain an ongoing part of doing microfinance for nearly all programs, cost-benefit analyses should nevertheless be a routine part of the evaluation tool kit. An additional concern is that older programs perform worse in terms of depth of outreach, as measured by average loan size in the *Microbank-ing Bulletin*. The trend may simply reflect that maturing clients seek larger loans over time or it could reflect "mission drift"; the full story is not clear without more careful studies.

That said, it is far from clear that cost-benefit studies by themselves will resolve key debates. First, doing clean cost-benefit studies can be difficult and costly, and it is often impossible without collecting new data. Inevitably, assumptions must be made in counting costs and ben-efits, and results will always be open to criticism. Second, even if it can be shown that a dollar used to subsidize an existing microfinance program helps poor households more than the same dollar does in other uses, it might also be that the microfinance program would ulti-mately help more poor people if it was not subsidized (or if it was sub-sidized at a much lower level). Thus, demonstrations that benefits of subsidies outweigh costs may not be enough to satisfy critics of subsidies.

More and different kinds of data are required to make a clear policy analysis, and completing a comprehensive quantitative assessment may be daunting. The essential problem is that evaluating microfinance is not like evaluating whether a new bridge should be built or whether a school should expand. In those cases, there are typically clear, fixed projects that are under consideration (or sometimes a limited number of alternative models). Each can be evaluated on its own terms and then be accepted or rejected.

But microfinance programs are not like bridges or schools. They are still evolving, and how they use subsidies affects the nature of prod-ucts and services that can be offered. Interest rates are in part rationing mechanisms (determining who chooses to borrow and who does not), and microlenders' interest rate policies may also affect competitors working in the same markets. Since getting more subsidy generally means that microlenders can keep interest rates lower than otherwise, removing subsidy will, by the same token, put upward pressure on fees charged to clients. Not only that, but the degree of subsidy has implications for how staff are hired and treated, how quickly programs can expand, how large loans can grow, and so forth. (We describe the relationships further in section 9.4.) Thus traditional approaches to evaluation based on the notion of a given, unchanging project (with given, unchanging subsidy levels) fall short.

So, even when faced with a well-done analysis showing that bene-fits exceed the costs of subsidies, critics will argue that the case for subsidization is still not nailed down. The fundamental problem is that a single cost-benefit study from a given program at a given moment cannot address the value of the existing program versus the continuum of alternative models that would emerge if subsidies were reduced.

In this chapter we lay out a research agenda for getting to the root of arguments, and we describe how far-existing work can help us sort out questions.

COUNTING SUBSIDIES: EVIDENCE FROM THE GRAMEEN BANK

A logical starting point for conversations about subsidies is to figure out how large the subsidies are. This turns out to be harder than it seems. Microlenders take in subsidies in many ways—even those who claim to earn profits. The Grameen Bank, for example, advertises in its annual reports that it has earned profits almost every year since it was started. The sum reported between 1985 and 1996, for example, was $1.5 million (converted into 1996 dollars). These are modest profits, and are in line with Grameen's focus on poverty reduction.

But during this period Grameen also took advantage of subsidies from a variety of sources. Sometimes subsidies are direct—for example, grants to help pay for staff training. Other subsidies are indirect, and teasing them out often requires reading the bank's income statements with a calculator at hand. (The amounts cited here are the best approx-imations feasible given the available published data, but they are nevertheless approximations.)

Grameen's annual reports, for example, indicate that between 1985 and 1996 their direct subsidies totaled $16.4 million. Since these grants are included as income in the bank's income statement, it's clear that when Grameen management writes that they make profits each year, they simply mean that the bank took in more revenue than it spent. By subtracting the $16.4 million in grants from the $1.5 million in reported profits, we can see that in this period Grameen clearly did not earn profits as traditionally calculated. To get a richer picture, we need to look at other sources of subsidy too. Other forms of subsidy come via "soft loans" from donors. A donor might prefer to support a microlen-der by making a loan to be repaid in twenty years at an interest rate of 1 percent per year. The subsidy comes in when the interest or loans obtained through the market would be much higher. In Gramee case, between 1985 and 1996 the bank paid an average nominal inte rate of about 3.8 percent per year on the money it borrowed inflation adjustments are made, the average real rate was -1.8 per year. Commercial businesses in Bangladesh that have funds at a rate close to the interbank interest rate, on the would have paid nominal interest rates greater than 10 pe

The implied subsidy in this case is the net gain to the microlen-der due to their access to cheap capital from the donor. The implicit subsidy amounts to roughly $80.5 million for Grameen between 1985 and 1996. At other times, the subsidy may take the form of tax holi-days, loan guarantees, "soft equity," or the assumption of exchange rate risk. The soft equity portion of Grameen's balance sheet, for example, adds another $47.3 million to the bank's effective subsidy in 1985–1996. The total of these direct and implicit subsidies was about $144 million for the period 1985–1996, on average amounting to about 11 cents for every dollar in Grameen's average loan portfolio. We do not take the position that these subsidies are necessarily good or bad—we would need reliable data on social and economic benefits to make that judge-ment. But we recognize that, in principle, well-targeted subsidies can generate much benefit, and Grameen has had an influence that has spilled far beyond Bangladesh's borders.

The subsidy dependence index, created by Jacob Yaron, a finance specialist at the World Bank, is one attempt to systematically account for all of these kinds of subsidies in a clear, concise, policy-relevant way. The measures of "financial self-sufficiency" described by Ledgerwood (2001) have a similar goal—and are subject to similar caveats. The subsidy dependence index attempts to answer the question: How much higher would the interest rates charged to borrowers need to be in order for the bank to operate without subsidies?

To see how it works, start with a break-even (net) interest rate r^* that solves the equation

$$L(1+ r^*)1 - d)+I = L + C + S, \qquad (9.1)$$

where L is the volume of loans outstanding before adjustments are made for problem loans, $(1 - d)$ is the fraction of the portfolio that is expected to be repaid, I is total income from other investments, C cap-tures total costs (including the cost of capital), and S is the total value of implicit subsidies. The left side gives expected income and the right side gives costs (in the absence of soft loans). To break even the two sides must be (at least) equated. Rearranging yields that the break-even interest rate is thus

$$r^* = [C + S - I + dL]/[L(1 - d)], \qquad (9.2)$$

and the percentage increase in the current interest rate required for the bank to break even is

$$(r^*-r)/r = [C+S-I+dL-r(1-d)L]/[rL(1-d)] = (S+K-P)/[rL(1-d)] \quad (9.3)$$

where P is reported net profits and K is direct grants and the value of dis-counts on expenses (see section 4 of Morduch 1999c). Reported profits are gross revenues from lending, grants, and investments (less repay-ment of principal and all associated costs). This final formula is identical to Yaron's subsidy dependence index (SDI), given that appropriate adjustments are made to reported profits and to the volume of loans out-standing. (In Yaron's formula, the default rate d is assumed to be folded into L through appropriate provisioning and it is also assumed implicitly that nonpayment rates of interest are identical to nonpayment rates of principal; see Yaron 1992; Schreiner and Yaron 2001).

Morduch's (1999c) SDI calculations suggest that Grameen Bank would have needed to increase their lending rates by about 75 percent in order to break even without subsidies between 1985 and 1996—holding all else the same. The calculation is roughly in line with SDIs calculated by others for the same period. More recently, Grameen has been able to take advantage of returns to scale and has turned increas-ingly to members' savings as a source of capital, so we expect that the SDI in 2005 should be substantially lower than the SDI a decade beforehand.

The SDI is a useful tool, but there are important caveats about the approach described here. The SDI has the merit of systematically answering a narrowly defined question. That question is: Holding all else the same, how much would a lender have to increase its revenue by in order to cover costs if the lender had no access to subsidized resources? The calculation thus sheds light on how institutions such as Grameen would fare if they were truly commercial lenders. But the "holding all else the same" condition is a strong one—and it applies also to other widely used measures of financial self-sufficiency. A tension arises because if Grameen had not had access to such plentiful and cheap capital, it surely would have organized its business differ-ently. In this sense, the SDI gives an upper bound on how much revenue would have to rise. Once faced with commercial conditions, lenders such as Grameen would surely find ways to adapt as best they could in order to minimize costs.

Second, it is important to note that lenders such as Grameen are driven by their social missions as much as by their economic missions. When subsidized resources are made available to them, it would seem foolish (some might even say unethical) to turn down the resources and not try to pass along the gains to customers. But doing so lowers the SDI. It would be wrong then to infer from their current lack of prof-itability that lenders such as Grameen would collapse if the subsidized resources dried up. Instead, Grameen could survive in principle, but the nature of services received by clients might have to change in the process. The SDI thus only partially answers the question about how institutions such as Grameen would fare as commercial lenders. By holding constant the lender's current business structure, the answer is unrealistically static. It's more important to know whether the institu-tion has a realistic long-term strategy to remain viable—Grameen's has involved the steady shift from donor finance to obtaining capital from savings deposited by customers within Bangladesh. But gauging the viability of strategies is far harder than measuring whether the short-term financial snapshot involves subsidy or not. As the previous numbers demonstrate, the SDI approach is at the least an important check on accounts presented by lenders who calculate profits in "non-standard" ways.

Costs and Benefits of Subsidies

So how do subsidies compare to benefits? We only know of two serious attempts to calculate the costs and benefits of microfinance. Those two studies, reviewed later, show that support for microfinance has indeed been a good social investment in Thailand and Bangladesh. As noted earlier, though, this does not nail down the case for continued subsi-dization. In section 9.5 we discuss additional data we would want in order to make broader policy judgments.

Costs and Benefits in Thailand

The BAAC is a state-run bank that is Thailand's largest microlender, serving about 3.5 million borrowers. Townsend and Yaron (2001) start by accounting for BAAC's subsidies, which means careful analysis of the bank's revenues. In 1995, the bank collected fees and interest from its clients, amounting to 11 percent of the outstanding loan portfolio; this is the "portfolio yield," a rough proxy for the average effective interest rate. Using the SDI method devised by Yaron (e.g., Yaron 1992; Schreiner and Yaron 2001), Townsend and Yaron argue that BAAC would have had to raise its portfolio yield by 35.4 percent in 1995 in order to be able to survive without subsidies—assuming that all else was unchanged. This means that the resulting financially sustainable portfolio yield would have to be raised from 11 percent to 14.9 percent, still a moderate average interest rate.

Given that the total yield on the 1995 portfolio was 18.5 billion baht, Townsend and Yaron calculate the total subsidy received in 1995 as approximately 4.6 billion baht per year. Much of this subsidy is received directly from the government, but other parts come from the implicit subsidies on soft loans and equity. (The Japanese government was a major source of soft loans in the 1990s.)

The next question is whether or not these subsidies yielded com-mensurate benefits. Townsend and Yaron do not try to complete a full assessment of BAAC's impacts. Instead, they draw on work by Townsend and Ueda (2001) that considers the benefits that BAAC's 4.5 million customers derive from risk reduction only. (Considering the impacts on average incomes and broader measures of economic and social change would presumably lead to an even larger benefit figure than that reported in this section.)

Townsend and Ueda begin their estimation with a theoretical model that focuses on ways that access to banking helps customers cope with risks such as illness, local weather problems, and other idiosyncratic shocks. The mathematical model is based around a fully dynamic general equilibrium characterization of a hypothetical economy that shares characteristics of rural Thailand, and Townsend and Ueda are interested in its real-world plausibility. Accordingly, they form predictions from the hypothetical world and compare them to the per-formance of the actual Thai economy between 1976 and 1996. The results are mixed, and in general, households do better in theory than they do in practice. Townsend and Ueda speculate that the problem is barriers of access to banking, and they calculate that the associated loss in welfare is about 7 percent of average household wealth (about 10 percent for middle-income households). Since wealth averaged 876,000 baht in the sample, the 7 percent loss is equal to 61,000 baht. Taking that 61,000 baht loss (which implies a 61,000 baht improvement over the status quo once households get access to BAAC), converting it into annualized terms, and multiplying it times the 4.5 million BAAC bor-rowers yields a final figure for benefits that BAAC delivers in terms of risk reduction: 13.86 billion baht. Townsend and Yaron conclude that "clearly some nonzero subsidy could be justified."

Assumptions have to be made along the way to deriving the cost (4.6 billion baht) and benefit (13.86 billion baht) figures, and subsequent studies may move the numbers up or down. Monthly data on finances (rather than annual data) might refine the subsidy side, and the benefit figures may look different if estimated directly rather than making inferences from the application of a stylized theoretical model. When Townsend (2000) looks directly at how BAAC access affects risk reduc-tion (during the Thai financial crisis of 1997–1998), he does indeed find evidence that BAAC helps customers cope better, but it is not possible to link that finding to the 13.86 billion baht estimate. Still, the Townsend and Yaron (2001) study puts together the available evidence in an inter-esting and considered way, and provides evidence that subsidies have been meaningful.

COSTS AND BENEFITS IN BANGLADESH

The Grameen Bank has been in the vanguard of the microfinance movement, reporting repayment rates of 98 percent and modest profits while serving over two million functionally landless borrowers. As noted these self-reported figures exaggerate Grameen's financial successes, however. Closer examination of the data shows that while the bank reports profits that sum to $1.5 million between 1985 and 1996, the profits rest on $175 million in subsidies, both direct and implicit. These include $16 million of direct grants, $81 million of implicit subsidies via soft loans, $47 million of implicit subsidies through equity holdings, and at least $27 million in delayed loan loss provisions. The real (i.e., inflation-adjusted) costs of borrowed capital paid by Grameen averaged

-1.8 percent during 1985–1996, a time when Grameen would have had to pay real interest rates of 5–10 percent to get access to capital had soft loans been unavailable. In 1996, Grameen received a major concessional loan from the Japanese government, but Grameen has received no important external funds since then, and their goal is to shift to self-financing through deposit mobilization within Bangladesh.

Taken together, Grameen's subsidies are relatively modest relative to its scale of operation. The average amount of subsidy as a fraction of the loan portfolio fell from over 20 percent in the mid-1980s to 9 percent by 1996. What have these subsidies allowed Grameen to do? Like most of the microlenders in Bangladesh, Grameen is committed to serving the poorest households, and their first concern is with fostering eco-nomic and social transformation. Studies have linked Grameen's oper-ations to improvements in income, stability, child schooling, and family planning practices.

Khandker (1998) combines estimates of Grameen's subsidies with estimates of impacts to yield a cost-benefit ratio of 0.91. Benefits are measured by the extent of increased household consumption when women borrow from the bank, and Khandker's calculation (which is based on a 1991–1992 survey) implies that it cost society 91 cents for every dollar of benefit received by clients. If instead the resources were directed toward male borrowers, the cost-benefit ratio would be 1.48. The ratio is higher since lending to men appears to have a smaller impact on household consumption (based on estimates by Pitt and Khandker [1998]) showing an 18-cent average increase in total con-sumption when lending a dollar to women, but just an 11-cent average increase when lending a dollar to men). Even the ratio for male bor-rowers, though, compares favorably to cost-benefit ratios from alter-native poverty alleviation programs in Bangladesh. For example, the World Food Programme's Food-for-Work scheme had a cost-benefit ratio of 1.71, and CARE's food-for-work program had a cost-benefit ratio of 2.62.

The microfinance programs of BRAC compare less favorably in Khandker's analysis. Khandker reports cost-benefit ratios of 3.53 when lending to BRAC's female customers and 2.59 when lending to BRAC's male customers. But BRAC staff respond that the costs used here are unduly inflated by including expenses not related to microfinance when accounting for BRAC's subsidies. When accounting is done according to their allocating protocols, BRAC's subsidies shrink—and in the late 1990s BRAC's microfinance operations claimed to be fully financially sustainable. But Khandker may well be right: If the nonmi-crofinance activities (like training programs and providing productive inputs to clients) raise BRAC's estimated impacts, then there is a good argument to include the attached subsidies when calculating cost-benefit ratios too.

Khandker (2003) produces new estimates of Grameen's effectiveness. In his new research (which combines the earlier data with data from 1997–1998) he reports that the impact of lending to a woman is found to be an increase in household consumption by 10.5 cents for each dollar lent to a woman (and results for men are small and mixed in sig-nificance). This 42 percent decline has striking implications for cost-benefit ratios. If subsidies are unchanged, it is no longer true that it costs society 91 cents for every dollar of benefit to clients. Instead, 91 cents only buys 58 cents of benefit. Still, a cost-benefit ratio of 1.57 (ninety-one divided by fifty-eight) continues to look favorable relative to alternative uses. Moreover, since 2000 Grameen has changed its funding strategies in order to reduce subsidy dependence. New data that account for changing subsidy levels may well show that although the estimated impact is lower, so too are subsidies. Updated data will indicate if shifts in cost-benefit ratios have been advantageous.

Discussion

Townsend and Yaron (2001) and Khandker (2003) provide first cuts at taking costs and benefits seriously. The two studies suggest that invest-ing in microfinance can yield social benefits that beat the costs—although Khandker's estimates are equivocal. Like all simple calculations, though, the studies rest on a series of simplifications. Most immediate, only measurable benefits can be considered: The impact on gender empowerment discussed in chapter 7, for example, is difficult to put into monetary terms, and thus hard to feed into a cost-benefit ratio. Other limits hinge on how the measurable impacts are quanti-fied. For example, Khandker's 0.91 ratio for lending to women by Grameen draws on an estimated 18 cent increase in household con-sumption for every additional dollar borrowed by women from Grameen (Pitt and Khandker 1998). The estimate is a marginal impact of an additional dollar lent; but the average impact is more appropri-ate here since the entire program is being evaluated, not just the expan-sion of scale.

Simple cost-benefit ratios also fail to capture dynamics. Imagine that borrowing allows a client to purchase a sewing machine. Owning the machine (and being able to set up a small-scale tailoring business) creates benefits into the future, and using impacts on current house-hold consumption fails to capture the full value of borrowing since in this case cost is best thought of a stock variable, while benefit is a flow. In principle, costs should be compared to the present value of the flow of future impacts, not the current impact, and doing so will lower cost-benefit ratios, thereby improving the program's appeal.

Perhaps the most difficult problem—and the one most relevant from the vantage of the current debate into microfinance—is that simple cost-benefit calculations fail to provide insight about all of the relevant counterfactual scenarios. As argued below, cost-benefit ratios will be changed by reducing subsidies slightly, and the simple cost-benefit ratios provide no sense of the optimality of such a move.

Moving Debates Forward

What kinds of information are needed to move forward on debates about susbsidy? First, a clear sense of objectives and social weights. Are impacts on poorer households, for example, weighed in the social calculus more than the same impacts on richer households? The answer must combine both subjective social weights and judgments about the way that marginal increases in income and consumption translate into well-being for different groups.

Second is the impact of subsidy on credit demand and supply. There are two competing effects. One is that demand for loans by current bor-rowers may fall as interest rates rise, which is the standard result from demand theory. The competing effect emerges in contexts with credit rationing: As programs untether themselves from subsidies, they can increase the supply of loans to the underserved, delivering the oppo-site result.

The third major impact is on average returns to borrowers. Again there are two competing possibilities. One is that raising interest rates will screen out poor projects and raise average returns, while the com-peting possibility is that raising rates will exacerbate moral hazard and adverse selection, and instead worsen net returns.

The fourth major concern is the impact on other (nonsubsidized) lenders, as manifested by changes in their interest rates. One view is that subsidized lenders squeeze out other lenders, so that removing subsidies should both expand overall credit supply and allow those lenders to raise their rates. A contrasting view is that subsidized lenders helpfully segment the credit market; and when subsidies fall, other lenders may be forced to lower their rates given a more diverse pool of potential clients.

The ultimate impact of reducing subsidies is thus the sum of a range of possible mechanisms. There are bits and pieces of data on each, but there is little consensus on the size or sign of the general relationships, and there is clear need for better empirical understandings.

Despite the lack of evidence (or perhaps because of it), experienced practitioners on both sides of the debate strongly hold their views. Dis-cussion about the role of microfinance in development thus remains stalemated early in the game, with assertions checked by coun-terassertions and no immediate route to resolution. Those who oppose subsidization tend to assume a relatively flat distribution of social weights, low sensitivity of credit demand to interest rates, positive impacts of interest rates on returns, very low returns to investments by poorer households, and negative externalities of subsidized credit pro-grams on other lenders. Those who are open to strategic subsidization, on the other hand, tend to put greater social weight on consumption by the poor, assume highly sensitive credit demand to interest rates, low impacts (or perhaps negative impacts) of interest rates on returns, moderately high (but not extremely high) returns to investments by poor households, and small or beneficial spillovers onto other lenders.

Fortunately, apart from the social judgments, these are all issues that can be resolved by fairly straightforward empirical studies, and chapter 8 has outlined guidelines and concerns for the research. The question is whether donors, who have been eager to spend on new programs and who have had ample funds available for subsidization, are willing to divert funds to assess the value of their interventions.

Smart Subsidies

Despite the optimistic cost-benefit studies previously discussed, the cheap credit policies of failed state banks have tarred the idea of using subsidies in microfinance (Adams, Graham, and von Pischke 1984). Cheap credit has long been a problem. Lenders charging interest rates that are far below rates available elsewhere in the market are associated with inefficiency, mistargeting, and low repayment rates. The problems stem in part from the low interest rates themselves; and they are reinforced by other aspects of poor program design and management.

When subsidized credit is much cheaper than loans available else-where in the market, getting hold of those loans is a great boon. Loans meant just for the poor are thus frequently diverted to better-off, more powerful households. Even when the loans go to the poor, the fact that highly subsidized loans have typically come from state-owned banks (and the fact that the loans are so cheap) make them seem more like grants than loans, and repayment rates fall sharply as a consequence. And because state-owned lending institutions are seldom expected to earn profits, there are few incentives for bank workers and their man-agers to seek efficiency gains. Political pressures in fact often work against cost-cutting and vigilant loan collection. Poor households may still benefit from loans (especially if there is little pressure to repay loans), but in the long-term the institutions waste precious resources and eventually fall into crises.

That said, the jump from criticizing this kind of cheap credit to crit-icizing other kinds of subsidies is made far too quickly by leading microfinance advocates (e.g., Adams and von Pischke 1992). These advocates emphasize the need to strengthen financial systems over more immediate efforts to reduce poverty. (The so-called financial systems approach has been associated with the Rural Finance Program at Ohio State University). While there is wide acceptance of subsidies to help institutions get through initial start-up periods wherein costs are high before scale economies can be reaped, there is much less acceptance of the idea of using subsidies in an ongoing way to aid clients. From a theoretical vantage, the argument for using ongoing subsidies is solid, and, in practice, well-designed subsidies may be easy to implement and effective for borrowers. Even skeptics of subsidies recognize that institutions currently use subsidies as integral parts of their programs. With that in mind, we turn to a discussion of "smart subsidies": carefully designed interventions that seek to minimize distortions, mistargeting, and inefficiencies while maximizing social benefits.

"Subsidize the Institution, Not the Customer"

We start with short-term subsidies. Some donors argue for a strategy wherein the aim is to "subsidize the institution, not the borrower." If taken literally, the statement is nonsensical: A program without subsi-dies must pass along all costs to customers one way or another. Thus, any subsidy to the institution means that fewer costs have to be passed on to customers; directly or indirectly customers gain through lower prices.

But, if not taken literally the strategy has some appeal: It simply translates as "subsidize start-up costs, not ongoing operations". In terms of customers, consider a long-term situation in which the insti-tution can be financially self-sufficient when charging an interest rate of, say, 30 percent per year to customers. But, in the first eight years of business, 30 percent would not cover all costs; instead the lender would have to charge, say, 45 percent. Then, the strategy here would be to charge the customers 30 percent from the very first day of operation (and for all time thereafter) and to take a subsidy of fifteen cents per dollar lent for the first eight years.

Figure below depicts the strategy in a setting where average costs fall over time. The figure shows initial costs start at r_0 but fall steadily until time *£**, at which time costs have reached the long-term level r^*. *A* subsidy that covers all costs greater than r^* that are incurred before t^* allows the program to charge borrowers interest rates of r^* from the very start of operations. After time t^*, the program can continue to charge customers r^* and exactly cover the ongoing costs of lending without subsidy. The initial subsidies mean that the customers do not have to help shoulder start-up costs. As mentioned in chapter 1, the argument echoes the "infant indus-try" arguments for tariff protection familiar from the theory of inter-national trade.

The case is sound in principle, but lessons from trade in practice are less favorable: It has proved hard to wean industries off protection once it starts, and some protected industries are far from their infancy. To be effective, donors need a credible exit strategy based on clear benchmarks (based, for example, on achieving efficiency gains by set dates) that push microlenders to achieve cost reductions in time for the withdrawal of subsidies.

Another form of subsidization that is less controversial than others is to subsidize public goods that the institution might otherwise not provide (notably, data collection and impact evaluations from which others in the field might also benefit). Subsidizing technical assistance (e.g., for setting up a new management information system or design-ing incentive schemes) also carries little of the negative weight of long-term subsidies since, by its nature, it is short-term and fosters institution-building.

STRATEGIC SHORT-TERM SUBSIDIZATION OF VERY POOR CLIENTS

A more interventionist approach would recognize that clients may also benefit from subsidies in a broader way. One approach, which is again limited, is to subsidize those clients that are not yet ready to borrow from microlenders at "market" interest rates. They may, for example, need training first, or they may need time to build businesses that reach a minimum scale.

An example is given by the Income Generation for Vulnerable Group Development (IGVGD) program of BRAC in Bangladesh. BRAC builds their program around a food aid program sponsored by the World Food Programme. The resources of the food aid program are integrated into a program that provides both eighteen months of food subsidies and half a year of skills training, with the aim of developing new liveli-hoods for the chronically poor. Participants are also expected to start saving regularly in order to build discipline and an initial capital base. When the training program is completed, households are expected to be able to graduate into BRAC's regular programs.

The program focuses on households headed by women or "aban-doned" women that own less than a half acre of land and that earn less than 300 taka ($6) per month. The training includes skills like livestock raising, vegetable cultivation, and fishery management.

After an 80 percent success rate in a pilot program with 750 house-holds, BRAC rolled out the program throughout Bangladesh, and IGVGD had served 1.2 million households by 2000. A follow-up study by Matin and Hulme (2003) showed that the program was associated with dramatic increases in income for households just after complet-ing the program. But within another three years, average income had fallen by nearly 60 percent from its peak. Part of the cause was that when the food subsidy was removed, households sold business assets and used BRAC loans to purchase food rather than invest in businesses, leaving households not much better off than they had been in the beginning. Matin and Hulme thus argue for additional measures to help households from slipping back and to account for the different speeds at which households progress. Hashemi (2001), though, stresses that we should not lose sight of the fact that two-thirds of IGVGD par-ticipants graduate successfully to regular microfinance programs, although it is not clear how to best support the remaining third (Not to mention the 10 percent of applicants rejected for being old, disabled, or otherwise unpromising in microbusiness.)

The IGVGD strategy is akin to the infant industry strategy described earlier—only here the point is to subsidize the *client's* start-up costs, and, as long as there are vulnerable and very poor clients that meet the program criteria, subsidies to the institution could continue for a long time.

The subsidies at BRAC are not large in the scheme of things. Taken together, Hashemi (2001) estimates that IGVGD subsidies per person amount to about 6,725 taka (about $135 in 2001). The largest compo-nent is 6,000 taka for the food subsidy (provided by the World Food Programme), and the remainder is about 500 taka for training costs and 225 taka to support making small initial loans to participants (the first loans are typically about $50). For $135 per participant, BRAC aims to forever remove the need for participants to require future handouts. To achieve that aim, efforts to ensure sustainable impacts must be imple-mented and success rates improved, but, even as it stands, the IGVGD is an important model for other programs. BRAC itself has launched a new initiative, Targeting the Ultrapoor, that builds on the IGVGD and also combines training and subsidy for the very poor.

Strategic Subsidization over the Long-Term

Programs like the IGVGD take us closer to considering strategic sub-sidization over the long-term. Part of BRAC's costs stem from the fact that initial loans are so small (just Taka 2,500) that BRAC loses money servicing them at the given interest rate (15 percent charged on a flat basis, roughly equivalent to a 30 percent per year effective interest rate). At loan sizes of 4,000 taka and more, BRAC can recover costs with inter-est earnings, but small loans are too costly per taka lent. The subsidy of 225 taka on a 2,500 taka loan suggests that BRAC would need to raise effective interest rates by about 9 percentage points for small loans; but BRAC fears that effective interest rates of 40 percent would be unaf-fordable for the poorest borrowers and could undermine social goals. Figure 9.2 illustrates the general situation. In the figure, servicing small loans costs the microbank more per dollar lent than servicing larger loans, and some of the costs are passed on to customers. But part of the added costs are paid for with subsidy in order to keep interest rates from going too high. Costs start at r_0 but fall until loan size L^*, at which time interest rates have reached the long-term level r^*. At loan size L^*, the program can charge customers r^* and cover all their ongoing costs. In the figure, borrowers seeking small loans pay more than those seeking large loans, but, as with BRAC, it could be that all borrowers are charged the same rate. Or it could be that the smallest loans carry somewhat lower rates than larger loans.

The subsidies depicted in the figure are not associated with "cheap credit" and all of the negative trappings that entails. Instead, they are strategically deployed and targeted to aid the poorest customers. While it may be possible to use cross-subsidization to cover the extra costs of small loans (using profits from larger loans to offset losses on smaller loans), cross-subsidization runs into trouble when competitors swoop in and steal away top customers with the lure of cheaper interest rates—a problem that happened most dramatically in Bolivia in the late 1990s. Thus it may be that smart subsidies are the most effective way to help programs focused on social transformation ensure outreach and affordability for their poorest clients.

Conning (1999) offers theoretical insight into the problem. He con-siders programs that have committed to covering their full costs, and argues that if reaching the very poor is impeded simply by high fixed costs associated with making small loans (e.g., having to put in the same paperwork and basic staff time for each loan, no matter the size), then raising interest rates and increasing scale could be a successful way to simultaneously cover costs and have both broad and deep out-reach. This, of course, assumes that borrowers can easily generate the returns to pay high interest rates. Subsidies might be used to defray costs for borrowers, justified perhaps in the name of fairness (if not in the name of efficiency). But, on the other hand, if the higher costs of lending to the very poor are largely a function of the extra monitoring costs entailed in working with borrowers without collateral, then raising interest rates could exacerbate incentive problems (as described in chapter 2). And in this second case, there is a possible efficiency-based argument for using subsidies. If subsidies are not forthcoming, Conning further shows that when monitoring costs are important (i.e., when incentive problems are important), microlenders that target poorer households must charge higher interest rates than other lenders if they want to break even. Such poverty-focused lenders will also have higher staff costs per dollar loaned, and they will be less leveraged: a finding that Conning tends to confirm with data on seventy-two microlenders. In this case, the costs per dollar lent are, in part, a function of the interest rates charged to cus-tomers, because interest rates affect borrower behavior and that in turn affects monitoring costs.

SUMMARY AND CONCLUSIONS

Critics of failed state-owned banks have formulated a devastating cri-tique of subsidies. The lessons should be taken to heart, but economic analysis shows that in principle subsidies in modern microfinance can be well-designed. And, if so, they can be part of efforts to achieve mean-ingful transformations in the lives of clients, without sacrificing the integrity of the institution. Doing it well in practice remains the ongoing challenge, but the growing number of subsidized programs that can boast impressive efficiency benchmarks and high repayment rates gives cause for optimism.

Some microlenders have found ways to achieve full financial self-sufficiency while serving very poor clients. ASA of Bangladesh, the example that led off chapter 1, is frequently cited for its achievements in achieving both financial and social missions. ASA's example is impressive, and we hope that it will be emulated.

At the same time, the fact that financial self-sufficiency can be attained while achieving an impressive depth of outreach does not mean that it can be done always. Some contexts, such as rural Africa and Latin America, are inherently more costly to work in than rural Bangladesh; other contexts offer less scope for internal cross-subsidization. Achievements such as ASA's don't mean that there are no trade-offs involved.

But even if the case for strategic subsidies is stronger than some microfinance advocates have let on, arguments for financially sustain-able microfinance continue to have power. One concern is with incen-tives. While subsidies can help outreach to poor clients, there is always a fear that subsidies make institutions flabby. By subsidizing costs, pressure is removed that would have otherwise pushed management to seek efficiency gains and to experiment with new procedures. Dynamic efficiency may thus be sacrificed in the cause of reducing inequality in the short term. Donors should be prepared to tackle the problem head on and condition receipt of future funds on the achieve-ment of realistic efficiency goals. The objective in principle is to maintain "hard budget constraints" rather than allowing constraints (and incentives) to soften, but this is easier to said than done. This is one reason that arguments for limiting subsidies to start-up funds with clear exit strategies, have appealed to donors.

Even programs that claim to make profits may in fact use subsidies as a systematic, ongoing part of their operations. Our concern is not with how profits are measured but with how the subsidies are used. In principle, there is nothing in herently wrong with using subsidies, even in an ongoing way. As the discussion of smart subsidies suggests, there are a range of possibilities for using subsidies to maximize the social and economic outcomes enabled by microfinance. But empirical evidence is in short supply, lays out an empirical agenda that can enrich conversations on how to use subsidies well, as well as how to avoid inadvertently undermining incentives.

Another concern is that relying on subsidies will limit the scale of operations. There are times when this is certainly so, and it is often better to serve more people with less (or no) subsidy per person. But, by the same token, there will be times when advantages flow from serving fewer people, and reaching out to the poorest and most under-served. In practice, the trade-offs may not in fact be so stark. BRAC's collaboration with the World Food Programme, for example, shows that using subsidies can actually *expand* the scale of outreach (and not just help with *depth* of outreach). A third concern is with innovation: The donors' strong push for financial sustainability has forced some microlenders to devise inno-vations to slash subsidies (a feat thought to be impossible before). Such "induced innovation," to borrow a term from the Danish economist Esther Boserup, suggests that the static framework of cost-benefit analyses may overstate the benefits of subsidies: When push comes to shove, some programs have shown that the subsidies are less vital than once thought.

A final concern emerges from a world in which donors (and the tax-payers who fund them) tend to grow restless and eager to move on to the next project and a new set of concerns. In the rational, analytical world where decisions are made according to cost-benefit analyses, there is no space for "donor fatigue." Instead, if a program is shown to be worthy of support year after year, it should get support year after year. But donors and practitioners are well aware that the actual world looks different, and their warning is that microlenders need to prepare for the day when subsidies disappear as donors choose to move on. In the end, options for using subsidy to maximize the potential of micro-finance may rest in greatest part on how seriously donor fatigue must be taken.

10

Managing Microfinance

INTRODUCTION

For the most part, economists cite contract design to explain microfi-nance successes. Group lending is especially celebrated, followed by the dynamic incentives described in chapter 5. International donors tend to focus on financial choices instead, celebrating lenders that min-imize subsidies and set interest rates at levels that promote saving and wise investment (as described in chapter 9). Both good contract design and pricing policy matter greatly. Still, they are necessary conditions for success, not sufficient conditions. A great deal of what distinguishes failed microfinance from successful microfinance ultimately has to do with management: Particularly with how staff members are motivated and equipped to do their jobs. In this, microfinance is no different from businesses that sell soft drinks or haircuts.

If one just read newspaper stories, it would seem that all microlenders can boast repayment rates above 98 percent and are making steady profits; management does not seem to be a big issue. But table 10.1 shows a wide range in levels of productivity indicators for the 147 leading microlenders surveyed by *The Microbanking Bulletin.* The first column and third columns give the range minus and plus one standard deviation from the mean. (If the indicators are distributed normally, the range should include about two-thirds of the observa-tions, so one-third of programs would be even further away from the average.) The programs vary by age, scale, and location. Were the data made accessible, we could control for these factors, but the raw numbers suggest the basic point: While all of the lenders employ at least some of the mechanisms described in the previous chapters, much of performance variation is left unexplained by the type of loan contract.

Table 10.1: Productivity indicators of microlenders by target market

	-1 Standard deviation	Average	+1 Standard deviation
Operational self-sufficiency (%)			
Low-end	59	106	152
Broad	85	115	145
High-end	109	130	151
Cost per borrower ($)			
Low-end	-2	56	114
Broad	26	128	230
High-end	35	268	401
Portfolio at risk > thirty days (%)			
Low-end	0.1	4.9	9.7
Broad	-0.8	5.8	12.4
High-end	0.2	5.8	11.4

Source: The Microbanking Bulletin 2002 and calculations by the authors. *The Microbanking Bulletin* calculates averages on the basis of values between the second and ninth per-centiles, leading to some of the negative values when calculating values one standard deviation below the mean. The low-end group includes microlenders with average bal-ances under $150 or under 20 percent of GNP per capita. The broad group includes microlenders with average balances between 20 percent and 149 percent of GNP per capita. The high-end group has average balances between 150 percent and 249 percent of GNP per capita. The operational self-sufficiency ratio is operating revenue divided by financial, loan provision, and operating expenses. Cost per borrower is operating expense plus in-kind donations divided by the average number of active borrowers. Portfolio at risk > thirty days is the outstanding balance of loans overdue for more than thirty days, divided by the gross loan portfolio.

Consider first the operational self-sufficiency ratio in table 10.1; it indi-cates whether lenders cover their operating costs (salaries, overhead, and the like). The ratio is a rough measure of efficiency, and the table shows that, on average, all programs are covering these costs. But there is wide variation, with some low-end lenders only covering 60 percent of costs, while others in the same category cover over 150 percent. Similarly, the amounts spent per borrower and the management of overdues varies widely; the latter range from near-perfection to delin-quencies greater than 10 percent.

The implications are investigated by Woller and Schreiner, (2003) who use a regression framework to analyze thirteen village banks in *The Microbanking Bulletin* data set in the period 1997–1999. By focusing only on village banks, they hold constant the social mission and target group of the institutions. Woller and Schreiner find "interest rates, administrative efficiency, loan officer productivity, and staff salaries to be significant determinants of financial self-sufficiency." The result should not be surprising, and it leads to a next set of harder questions: How can administrative efficiency be improved, loan officer produc-tivity be maximized, and staff salaries be optimally set?

It also leads to the question: How can incentives be provided that enhance financial bottom lines while not undermining social missions? Can institutions design better incentive schemes to meet their varied objectives? Managing microfinance is made particularly challenging by the fact that, unlike the soft drink and haircut businesses, most microlenders pursue multiple objectives in making decisions: financial sustainability on one hand and social impact on the other. The dual goals color hiring practices, compensation policy, and corporate culture in ways that can make being a microlender seem closer to running an educational institution than a bank.

Microlenders also work with pop-ulations that have traditionally scared away commercial banks for fear of excessive costs and risks. Thus, traditional banking modes (and man-agement practices) are up for rethinking as microlenders battle to keep costs down. Somewhat surprisingly, however, relatively little has been written on management in microfinance in general, and we know of nothing that brings in recent perspectives from the economics of incen-tives and contracts. In this chapter we highlight key principles and ten-sions, drawing in part on advances in the economic theory of incentives and in part on experiences in Latin America and Asia.

We start with a cautionary tale: the story of the rise and fall of Colombia's Corposol, an ACCION International affiliate based in Bogotá (Steege 1998). We state the multitask incentive problem formally, and discuss issues that arise in designing incentive schemes (e.g., avoiding myopia, promoting teamwork, and reducing fraud). We draw out the issues, using the example of incen-tive schemes at PRODEM in Bolivia and BRI—two microlenders oper-ating in very different economic environments. We review structural issues that affect incentives, including patterns of ownership and how much decision making is delegated to staff. The final section briefly considers lessons from incentive theory for product design.

THE RISE AND FALL OF CORPOSOL, BOGOTÁ

We start with the story of Corposol, an ACCION affiliate that started with great promise in 1988 (as Actuar Bogotá) but that collapsed in bankruptcy in 1996. The details draw heavily on Steege's (1998) account. At its peak, in 1995, Corposol served nearly 50,000 clients and had a loan portfolio of over $38 million. Corposol's managers aimed for aggressive growth, partly to reap economies of scale, partly to be able to extend their outreach, and partly as a matter of prestige. They thus rewarded their staff amply for signing up new clients and for renewing loans. The efforts were remarkably effective: At the end of 1990, each loan officer was responsible for 258 clients on average; and by 1992, the average number of clients per officer had risen to 368. The pace continued so that in 1994 and 1995 the dollar value of Corposol's loan portfolio increased by more than 300 percent.

The quality of loans was only a secondary concern, however, and staff members who aggressively expanded volume were given larger bonuses than those who were more conservative. A brewing crisis of borrower overindebtedness emerged in 1994 and 1995 when Corposol diversified the type of loans (or products) it offered, and began giving bonuses to staff based on the number of products (i.e., based on the variety of loans extended to clients), rather than on the number of clients. Then, in 1996, staff members were told to shift gears and expand lending volume rather than the number of products, again with secondary emphasis on the number of clients. The size of loans per client more than doubled in 1995, while the long-term health of the portfolio became ever more precarious. The expansion also brought a shift in orientation. In 1993, 86 percent of lending went to solidarity groups using ACCION-style group lending methods. By 1995, the frac-tion fell to 30 percent. Instead, loans were increasingly large and made to better-off entrepreneurs. Corposol's expansion goals were set by top management, and the goals were far greater than what middle management thought was fea-sible. Still, punishment for noncompliance was tough. In 1995, roughly two employees were fired each month for failure to meet performance objectives. Early on, the president's charisma had motivated workers to do the impossible; but as goals became tougher, motivation more fear-based, and management more arbitrary in its decisions, employ-ees became so disaffected that what had been valued as charisma was soon dismissed as theater.

Delinquency rates followed these trends. (Rates are defined as loans overdue for more than thirty days, as a fraction of the active portfolio outstanding.) Early on, delinquencies were below 2 percent, but they hit 8.6 percent by the end of 1994 and 35.7 percent by the end of 1996 (Steege 1998, 100). In 1996, the superintendency of banks stepped in to halt new lending by Finansol—one of Corposol's main divisions—and bankruptcy ensued.

Corposol originally looked like many other top microlenders in Latin America. Founded by a charismatic leader, Corposol received the backing of ACCION, and built a program around solidarity group lending. But in hindsight we can see that top leadership failed to appro-priately decentralize decision making, set realistic and clear goals for staff, create mechanisms for internal control and feedback, balance social objectives while pushing financial ends, and create a culture of openness and professionalism. How to simultaneously motivate staff, balance objectives, and cut costs (especially while trying to rapidly achieve scale) is the ongoing challenge for all institutions.

MICROFINANCE MANAGEMENT THROUGH THE LENS OF PRINCIPAL-AGENT THEORY

To put structure on the discussion of how failures like Corposol can happen (and how management successes like ASA of Bangladesh can happen too), we turn again to principal-agent theory (or simply "agency" theory), as used in chapters 2 and 3, to examine relationships between lenders and borrowers. But in applying principal-agent theory to microfinance management, we instead identify the top management as the "principal" and loan officers (and other field staff) as the "agents." The framework then focuses on difficulties that managers have in working with staff members to whom daily decisions have been delegated. The bargaining power of field staff is strengthened here since some of their efforts cannot be fully observed. Managers must then figure out how to adequately reward their unobserved effort in order to most effectively maximize the institution's objectives.

The concern with agents that can take unobservable actions that may not be entirely aligned with the interest of the principal goes back to Alfred Marshall's (1890) writings on sharecropping in the late nineteenth century. Much later, Mirrlees (1974, 1976) provided a framework that has been applied to a large variety of contractual relationships, including those between employers and employees, insurance companies and insured individuals, and politicians and bureaucrats. The framework describes the best possible contracts that principals can design to elicit maximal (unobservable) effort by agents. The contracts have to take into account that the agent may have outside options that have to be at least matched in order for the agent to voluntarily enter into a contract with the principal. A tough contract with harsh penalties for poor performance (a one-million-dollar fine?) may get agents to take the desired action, but in practice it would be hard to get anyone to agree to the terms. This is often called a "participation constraint" or "individual rationality constraint." The principal also has to give appropriate incentives to do the right thing, the "incentive constraint."

Assume that there is only one manager, and she is only concerned with profit, not with risk. She hires one employee who values expected pay and prefers that, all else the same, wages will be fairly predictable. In the first scenario, consider a fixed wage contract that meets the employee's participation constraint. The contract is great from the per-spective of risk since the employee is guaranteed a given wage regard-less of the outcome. But from the angle of incentives, it falls far short: The employee has no incentive to provide additional effort, since addi-tional effort is costly and goes unrewarded.

Next consider the opposite extreme. Instead of offering a fixed wage, the manager commits to making the employee a full owner of the microfinance institution, provided poverty is reduced and profitability is attained within a reasonable period of time. Otherwise the employee is fired. This contract gives full incentives for the employee to deliver maximum effort, but it obviously burdens him with a lot of risk. This is a "high-powered" incentive, and we return to it below.

The trade-off between risk and incentives is well-known, and the optimal contract lies somewhere in between the two extremes: that is, between a fixed wage contract with no incentives and a full ownership contract with no insurance. Sharecroppers around the world, for example, often split output fifty-fifty with landowners; but running a microfinance institution has more dimensions than basic farming, and there are not yet well-established rules of thumb for microfinance incentive systems. Instead, below we highlight concerns that should inform contract design.

THE MULTITASK PROBLEM: POVERTY REDUCTION VERSUS PROFITABILITY

The problem in designing incentives for microfinance is made more challenging by the multiple tasks that managers expect their staffs to perform. For simplicity, think of the principal as being the manager of a microfinance institution with the twin objectives of reducing poverty and achieving financial self-sufficiency. Mosley (1996b) investigates these two objectives and finds that, rather than being complementary, the objectives often conflict. His arguments draw on evidence from BancoSol in the early 1990s. Consider figure 10.1: Poverty reduction is on the vertical axis and loan size on the horizontal axis. The downward sloping "poverty reduction" curve indicates that the impact on poverty reduction decreases with loan size. On the other hand, financial per-formance improves with loan size as economies of scale are reaped. (This is seen in the upward sloping "profitability" curve). Mosley esti-mates that in the particular case of BancoSol in the early 1990s, loans larger than $400 improved financial bottom lines but had a negligible effect on poverty. Incentive schemes could push loan officers to make larger loans or, if designed differently, to focus on the low-end; the answer hinges on which objectives managers choose as priorities.

The extent to which the two objectives can be obtained also depends on employees' constraints. So, how should managers design a contract to maximize the possibility of attaining their goals, subject to employees' participation and incentive constraints? The bonus schemes attempted by Corposol satisfied the participation constraints, but they rewarded the wrong targets.

By rewarding loan volume, the Corposol managers gave employees little incentive to spend effort training and screening borrowers, and the contracts pushed the portfolio upmarket toward better-off customers. If managers had instead only rewarded the number of loans made, it might have pushed downmarket, but again would not have addressed loan quality. Suppose that instead the Corposol managers had offered bonuses to employees that were a func-tion of repayment rates only. Employees might then have favored bor-rowers that are less poor or live in economically affluent areas (so that they have alternative resources to cover loan losses). But this would have gone against the objective of poverty reduction.

A potential way to resolve this trade-off is by offering bonuses to loan officers based on both high repayment rates and a large number of clients. This strategy has been followed by most microfinance insti-tutions, a small sample of which is shown in table 10.2. In particular, by following such a strategy, lenders like ASA of Bangladesh have attained a high degree of financial sustainability while working with very poor clients, producing financial outcomes that compare favor-ably to that of BTTF of Kyrgysztan, which offers large and collateral-ized loans to relatively well-off borrowers.

This is a start, but in thinking about optimal incentives in microfinance, concerns go beyond risk versus incentives and beyond loan volume versus quality. There is also concern with enhancing teamwork, balancing short-term versus long-term objectives, discouraging fraud, and (holistically) creating an organizational culture of trust. The story of Corposol shows that each of these concerns can be undermined by incentive schemes that are too high-powered and inconsistently admin-istered. The rest of this section takes up these concerns in greater detail.

Unmeasurable Tasks

The multitask problem is made more difficult when performance is ill-defined or is measured by highly visible indicators that are nonethe-less noisy (Kerr 1975). In a seminal article, Holmstrom and Milgrom (1991) provide a framework to analyze contracting situations involv-ing a principal (employer) and agents (employees) who are asked to distribute their time among several activities. Employers can only directly assess and reward their employees on a subset of required tasks, whereas performance on the other tasks is unobservable. A typical example is that of teachers who have to divide their time between at least two activities, such as teaching and mentoring their students. Of these, only teaching is observed while mentoring is not. Teachers can only work for, say, eight hours per day. The principal of the school, on the other hand, wants teachers to undertake costly efforts on both tasks, but since the principal can only observe teaching (e.g., through teaching evaluations), school principals will offer a com-pensation scheme based on teaching only. Not surprisingly, teachers will end up teaching more than is efficient, at the cost of mentoring— even though school principals perceive both activities to be equally important.

To better understand the problem, consider the following exposition spelled out by Robert Gibbons (2002) in a recent review of the litera-ture. Suppose that meeting a desired objective y depends on agents taking two actions, respectively a_1 and a_2. The most simple example is the case in which $y = a_1 + a_2$. Suppose further that the only observable action is a_2, so bonuses can be based on a_2 only. But then the agent will have incentives to concentrate on a_2 only. With maximum performance, his bonus can be huge, but the bonus may make only a limited contri-bution to meeting the ultimate objective. Optimal outcomes can only be achieved if both a_1 and a_2 are observable.

Next consider a situation with two different objectives, y_1 and y_2 (car-rying forward the case at hand, suppose that y_1 = reducing poverty and y_2 = earning profits). Furthermore, consider a tradeoff between actions such that

$$y_1 \text{ -} a_1 \text{ -a } a_2 \quad (10.1)$$

$$y_2 = a_2 \text{ -b } a_1$$

where 0 < a < 1 and 0 < b < 1. Here, taking one action (say, working to reduce poverty by seeking out poorer customers and helping them develop business plans) promotes poverty reduction (y_1) but makes it harder to achieve profitability (y_2). Likewise, making larger loans may promote y_2 at the expense of y_1. If only action a_2 is easily observable, incentive schemes will necessarily bias against the objective of poverty reduction. Instituting high-powered bonus schemes with imperfect information is thus not necessarily a step forward.

So, why just reward staff for their effort? Perhaps in this case making pay contingent on outcomes would be better. If y_1 was indeed observ-able, it might be possible to reward performance based on outputs rather than inputs, but in practice outputs are not always observable either. In microfinance, social goals such as poverty reduction and female empowerment are notoriously difficult to measure in a simple, regular way. A similar tension runs through education reform in the United States under President George W. Bush, whose No Child Left Behind strategy provides schools with clear incentives based on how well children do on a battery of standardized tests—because those out-comes are fairly easy to measure. Meanwhile, a desired outcome like creative thinking, which may ultimately be more important, is hard to quantify. Critics argue that test-based incentive schemes can lead teach-ers "to neglect general education in order to train pupils exclusively for the purpose of doing well at the tests" (Dewatripont, Jewitt, and Tirole 1999). In this same way, rewarding loan officers based on easily collected financial indicators can lead them to neglect other, less tangi-ble social objectives. This takes us to the general issue of high-powered versus low-powered incentives.

High-Powered versus Low-Powered Incentives

Bonus schemes provide high-powered incentives. So-called low-powered incentives, on the other hand, are typically implemented by offering a combination of fixed wages and rewards such as promotions that are granted based on broad achievements. The hope is that employees are induced to balance objectives and not skew efforts too sharply in one direction or another.

The main microlenders in Bangladesh, for example, promise their staff members security of employment, reasonable salaries, and career advancement within the institution—as long as their performance is deemed satisfactory (Morduch and Rutherford 2003). These job char-acteristics have strong appeal given the severe underemployment in Bangladesh and the country's weak labor laws. Rather than leaning heavily on bonuses (although some are used), the institutions try to set clear, simple targets that help employees understand the behavior that leads to steady promotion. And employees receive nonmonetary awards that are used to publicly recognize the most successful indi-viduals and branches. Organizations have also been successful in making staff members feel that they belong to a special culture, espe-cially committed to serving the poor. Staff training programs en-courage this commitment; applicants for jobs at Grameen Bank, for example, are required to interview and write a case history of a poor rural woman.

PRODEM, a microlender operating in sparsely populated rural areas of Bolivia, has experimented with various incentive schemes and ended up with a balance of low-powered and high-powered incentives. PRODEM is best known as the organization out of which BancoSol emerged in 1992. But PRODEM has continued as a separate entity (now as a regulated "private financial fund" known as PRODEM FFP) and its Managing Director, Eduardo Bazoberry has paid close attention to how to create constructive incentives in the challenging environment in which PRODEM operates. Bazoberry (2001, 12) describes the impor-tance of low-powered incentives at PRODEM:

> To strengthen our hand in a competitive market, PRODEM FFP has developed a complex and creative matrix of incentives to help employees fulfill a variety of personal needs ranging from shelter and security to acceptance and self-fulfillment. The matrix includes financial as well as non-financial incentives, such as staff development, job enrichment and promotional opportunities, extensive health benefits, achievement awards, and the opportunity to take a sabbatical after ten years of service. As noted above, providing these kinds of low-powered

incentives may be superior even with regard to those tasks for which performance is relatively straightforward to measure, for example, financial self-sufficiency. In line with PRODEM, leading microlenders lean on low-powered incentives alongside higher-powered bonus schemes, and the experience of microlenders varies widely.

Consider the following data on thirty Latin American Microlenders collected by MicroRate. While MicroRate finds that bonus pay as a percentage of base salary varies from zero (not much risk for field staff and low-powered incentives) to 101 percent (high risk for field staff and high-powered incentives), the median percentage is 35 percent, with the twenty-fifth percentile paying bonuses of 13 percent, and the seventy-fifth percentile paying bonuses of 66 percent. These are not necessarily optimal contracts, but they are set at levels that balance risk and incentives.

Average loan size is a rough indicator of how poor clients are at a given institution, and a clear pattern is hard to detect, although the best-fitting curve appears to be gently U-shaped such that institutions serving the poorest households lean on incentive pay more heavily than institutions that serve less poor households, but high-powered incentives again prevail as institutions move to better-off households.

Cultural Implications: Lessons from PRODEM of Bolivia

A different kind of tension with regard to high-powered incentives involves the implications for institutional culture. Bazoberry's experience at PRODEM FFP is instructive, and he places great weight on ways that a positive culture can achieve outcomes that bonus schemes cannot (or may even diminish):

This entire discussion about financial incentives, however, detracts from the invaluable non-financial methods that PRODEM uses to motivate staff to achieve high levels of performance. The most important method is the institu-tion's mission. We hire people who are committed to making a difference in rural Bolivia by working with low-income families and microenterprises. We use our mission as a motivating tool. Managers regularly remind their employ-ees about PRODEM's critical contribution to the economies of remote com-munities, and how integral each staff member's performance is to the institution's accomplishments.

PRODEM's culture directly contributes to the performance of all employees. Through the orientation of new staff members, regular training opportunities and other communication channels, PRODEM inculcates employees into a culture of commitment, trust and excellence that is more powerful than finan-cial incentives.

Granted, an institution's culture does not put food on the table—that is why it is important to compensate all employees fairly. But finan-cial incentives cannot effectively encourage employees to be innovative, to embrace change, to constantly seek ways of doing things better, and to not be afraid to learn from their mistakes. Only the institution's culture can accom-plish these objectives, which contribute vitally toward improvements in pro-ductivity and efficiency that must occur for an MFI to remain competitive and profitable. (Bazoberry 2001, 12)

Experiences from other sectors are more optimistic than Bazoberry allows, and well-designed bonus schemes have been used to foster innovation and change. But it is not simple. An issue that concerns us here is not just whether bonus schemes are better or worse than non-financial incentives (such as creating a strong sense of mission). Our concern also encompasses whether (and when) bonus schemes may actively *undermine* nonfinancial, mission-based approaches. Indeed, Bazoberry's stress on the role of institutional culture here follows from his negative experience experimenting with bonus schemes (Bazoberry 2001, 11):

During 1993, after looking at the different incentives that MFIs were offering worldwide, we implemented an incentive system that rewarded loan officers for accomplishing goals set in the incentive program. These goals included: the targeted number of clients, the maximum percentage of loans in arrears, and the average portfolio per loan officer. In addition, since PRODEM had differ-ent types of branches, we had defined the goals in relation to the potential market and the location of the offices: in rural areas, at the country's borders, in major cities, or in secondary cities.

Rosy Preliminary Results. The incentive program worked as we had hoped. The loan portfolio grew rapidly, the portfolio at risk was under control, the number of clients increased steadily, and profitability improved... All of our indicators in 1994–1995 suggested that we made a wise decision in imple-menting the incentive program.

Things Start to Get Sour. By 1996, we sensed something disruptive occur-ring. We began to notice a high rate of turnover among our loan officers, includ-ing an increase in the number of staff fired because of corruption or for constantly breaking the methodology and rules of the institution. Obviously, we had not managed to gain the loyalty of these loan officers. Instead, we had staff members who were mechanically performing their functions without a real responsibility toward the institution or our clients.

One of Bazoberry's greatest frustrations was that the bonus system was pushing staff members to maximize their own self-interest at the expense of the unified effort of the organization. This was a function both of the direct incentives built into the bonus system and of the indirect, symbolic role that having a high-powered bonus system played in pushing staff members to think of themselves as participants in a competition where the goal was to come out ahead as an individual.

Economists so far have had more to say about the direct role of bonus schemes on incentives than on the indirect symbolic and psychologi-cal roles. But an intriguing recent study shows how important these latter issues can be. Gneezy and Rustichini (2000a, 2000b) make their arguments using two experiments (neither of which involve microfi-nance but which nonetheless hold lessons). The first study involves wages and bonuses and is most directly applicable.

Gneezy and Rustichini (2000a) created an experiment that involved high school children in Israel. One day each year high school children go from house to house, collecting charity for cancer research, assist-ing disabled children, and similar social causes. In the experiment, 180 high school children were divided into three groups. The first was a control group; they were given a speech about the importance of the day and of the charitable causes. The second group got the same speech plus the promise of receiving one percent of the day's proceeds as a reward. The third group got the speech plus the promise of a ten percent reward. It was made clear to participants in the second and third groups that the reward money would come from the researchers' pockets, not from the charitable causes. The most money that could be collected was 500 shekels.

It turned out that the group getting a ten percent reward managed to collect more money on average (219 shekels) than the group getting only one percent back (153 shekels)—and the difference was statistically significant. In this sense, monetary rewards seemed to work as expected. On the other hand, neither of the two groups per-formed as well as the first group (which had no financial incentives, merely a speech on the intrinsic value of the work). The control group averaged collections of 239 shekels, and the difference between this amount and the other amounts was also statistically significant. Gneezy and Rustichini find similar patterns in other cases, and they conclude the lesson by titling their study "pay enough or don't pay at all."

The results put a different interpretation on statements like that of Gonzalez-Vega et al. (1997, 102), who write, "The low levels of arrears observed [at PRODEM and BancoSol in Bolivia] are outstanding, par-ticularly in the absence of bonus payments to loan officers." Our dis-cussion suggests the opposite possibility: It may not be that the impressive repayment rates occurred *despite* the absence of bonuses, but rather that they occurred *because* of their absence. Like PRODEM, BancoSol built a strong culture through nonmonetary incentives like public recognition of successful staff members, development of a shared mission, and trusting loan officers with discretion in making choices about accounts.

In addition, "seminars and lectures by expert speakers are frequently offered to the staff [in order to build a com-monly held ideology], and a strong *esprit de corps* is encouraged" (Gonzalez-Vega et al. 1997, 111). The bottom line is that, given that financial incentives are used, individuals respond positively to stronger incentives. But providing monetary incentives can conflict with attempts to build social cohesion and a sense of shared mission within organizations. Thus, at low levels of monetary bonuses, outcomes are not clearly superior to situations with no financial incen-tives at all. So, as Gneezy and Rustichini argue, pay enough—so that the benefits of the bonuses outweigh their cultural costs—or don't pay at all.

Incentives in Teams

Bazoberry's frustration that the bonus schemes tried at PRODEM undermined teamwork is echoed by other microlenders, and below we turn to successful solutions adopted by Bank Rakyat Indonesia (BRI). First, though, we continue with the story of PRODEM:

At the same time, some staff members began demanding larger incentives amounts. They were under the false impression that PRODEM's good per-formance was due solely to their efforts, without realizing that everyone was part of one system of integrated departments, and that other aspects of the organization were also important for PRODEM's performance...

As a result, in 1996, PRODEM changed the incentive to an annual bonus awarded for branch performance. All members of a branch received a bonus if their branch met certain performance targets. The largest bonus was worth an additional month's salary...

This modification was generally successful in motivating staff and creating teamwork within a branch, but it still had negative side effects. It dis-couraged staff rotation and cooperation between branches. If employees agreed to transfer to a branch with problems, they reduced their chances of obtaining a bonus. Because some markets were riskier than others, some staff concluded that the bonus involved an element of luck, depending on where one worked. This conclusion generated tension between those who were perceived to have received a bonus because they worked in a good environ-ment and those who failed to earn a bonus even though they worked extremely hard. In such cases, the incentive system discouraged rather than encouraged staff...

We decided to eliminate the branch bonus program and instead reward the performance of the whole institution on an annual basis. The collective approach reiterates that we are all in this together. (Bazoberry 2001, 12)

Bazoberry's essay is titled "We Aren't Selling Vacuum Cleaners," pre-sumably because, if they were selling vacuums, teams would not matter so much. In running a microfinance institution, Bazoberry instead found a variety of layers of complication related to team efforts. First, the nature of high-powered incentives promoted an individual orientation among staff members. It was thus natural to shift the scheme so that branch-level performance was rewarded instead. But that created resentments and made employees reluctant to move from "good" branches. So, in the end, rewarding employees based on the performance of the whole institution was chosen as the way to reduce those frictions.

The trade-off, from our viewpoint, is that incentives are then made weaker since the free-riding problem that was evident at the branch level is even worse at the institution-level. Strong cultural norms are needed to overcome the tendency of employees to not pull their weight, and this, as noted above, seems to be the secret of PRODEM's man-agement success. Thus, in this case the gains from reducing resent-ments appear to outweigh the losses from dulling the incentive scheme. Other institutions have addressed these tensions in different ways, and we turn next to the example of BRI, a well-run, state-owned commercial bank. Their strategy has been to combine incentives at every level: individual, branch, and institutionwide.

COMBINING INCENTIVES: LESSONS FROM BANK RAKYAT INDONESIA

BRI started as a government-owned rural development bank in 1968, with the main mission of helping to spur agricultural pro-duction. To help both borrowers and depositors, the government mandated that borrowers pay interest rates of 12 percent while depos-itors received 15 percent under the national savings program. The pro-poor intentions may have been noble, but the negative interest rate spread was untenable, and by the late 1970s the bank was suffering huge operating losses. Indonesia deregulated banks in 1983, and BRI transformed itself with the aim of becoming financially viable without subsidies.

The heart of microfinance at BRI is the "units," small sub-branches set up throughout Indonesia to dispense loans and take deposits from low-income customers. (BRI also does corporate-scale lending through other offices, while microlending is done exclusively through the units.) Before 1983, there was no accounting of profit or loss at the unit level. So while it was clear that the system as a whole was suffering losses, there was no reckoning unit by unit. The 1983 transformation created accounts so that the units became individual profit centers. The key to the policy was to set a "transfer price" to value deposits gener-ated and capital used to make loans at each unit. The transfer price moves closely with the bank's costs of funds and provides a way to calculate profits for each unit.

In addition to yardstick competition as described later, the BRI uses three main mechanisms to provide incentives to staff. First, staff get a percentage of the profit of the unit for which they work, capped at 2.6 times monthly wages annually. Most employees get roughly twice their monthly pay through this incentive mechanism. (There is also a component that is, in principle, based on individual performance.) An important aspect of this bonus is that rules are clear, so staff can anticipate it—unlike the often arbitrary and changing bonus rules employed by Corposol.

Second, bankwide bonuses are also dispensed, and they are again roughly twice an employee's monthly pay. But since the bank's board of directors decides on bonuses each period and has full discretion, employees can not count on them as faithfully. Third, staff members are allowed to keep 2 percent of the value of total collections for loans that had been written off by the bank but that are then subsequently collected. This is gives a strong incentive to be vigilant in pursuing defaulters, and it lets customers know that staff are unlikely to let defaults pass without a struggle.

The decision to allow some workers to earn more than others in similar posts was controversial at first, but because incentives were designed so that everyone can in principle gain through hard work (there is no "zero-sum game"), the move has been both popular and effective within the system. The incentive system also works because BRI pursues clear financial objectives. While state-owned, BRI runs on commercial principles and tends to serve low-income customers, who are a few rungs up the economic ladder from the typical customers of the large Bangladeshi microlenders. Social objectives are secondary, freeing BRI from the balancing act faced by microlenders elsewhere. But BRI still wrestles with how to promote unmeasurable tasks (notably, teamwork), and the result is this somewhat elaborate (but clear and understandable) set of bonuses that balances individual and group efforts.

Yardstick Competition

The specific way that BRI deter-mines bonuses matters as well. The theory of incentives tells us that in situations where the range of individual performance is hard to measure, as is common in microfinance, yardstick competition can help. Contracts are then structured so that employees are rewarded on the basis of their performance relative to other employees. The optimal contract does not create a competition in which there are just a handful of winners. Instead, employees are rewarded when they exceed benchmarks that are set at levels determined on the basis of the past performance of other employees. In prin-ciple, if everyone surpassed the benchmarks, everyone would be rewarded. (And in subsequent periods, management may then choose to raise the bar a bit higher in order to induce even more effort.)

BRI uses this basic idea in its microfinance operations. At the end of 2002, BRI operated nearly 4,000 units throughout the country, whose managers enjoy a high degree of autonomy. Yardstick competition among these managers takes the form of unit performance contests. Each semester, the top management creates a list of targets to achieve (e.g., finding new customers, account growth, keeping arrears down, managing savings), and units compete to reach the goals.

The competition is not between units, but relative to the goals so that one unit winning doesn't affect another's chances. The aim is to have ambitious but achievable targets. As at PRODEM, the awards amount to roughly one month's pay or less, and about 30 percent of units win at one of the three award levels. Awards are given out at a large public ceremony, and the prestige of winning may be as rich a reward as the actual financial benefits.

Avoiding Myopia

An additional dimension to incentive schemes involves the time frame. Again we return to Bazoberry's (2001, 11) description of bonuses at PRODEM: The original scheme awarded a monthly bonus to individuals who met certain performance standards. We learned, however, that this type of incentive had a negative effect on team performance and encouraged a short-term outlook...

An annual payment encouraged a long-term perspective. It corrected the "delinquency lag," caused by new loans that go into arrears several months after they were issued. An annual payment also adjusted for the profound sea-sonal fluctuations that are common in Bolivian microfinance and it allowed PRODEM to complete our audit before issuing bonuses.

The lesson is clear: Bonuses that are based on short-term goals may bias employees away from maintaining the quality of loans over the long-term. Some outcomes, such as poverty reduction, are also achieved over a longer horizon and are best judged at wide intervals. Focusing on annual achievements addresses the issue of seasonality, but it can also be addressed by basing bonuses on year-to-year performance gains even when using monthly or quarterly incentives.

Discouraging Deception

One of the lessons from the experimental evidence of Gneezy and Rustichini (2003a) is "pay enough or don't pay at all." Our discussion earlier focused on what happens when you pay too little—and the advantages of low-powered incentives. Here we describe another problem that arises when you pay too much. The issue is that as incen-tives to perform to a given level get greater and greater, the incentive to cheat also rises. Not only is it vital to have accurate information on which to assess employees, it is also important to recognize that incen-tive schemes can themselves lead to biases in the information that gets reported to management. Problems emerge from an accounting stand-point when employees can easily hide default rates or increase the non-repayment period before considering a loan a defaulted loan. This can in turn make the microfinance institution appear more financially viable than it really is and set up managers for problems down the road.

Bazoberry comments on the scene in Bolivia, describing a consumer credit company that was paying the equivalent of $50 per month as average staff salary. But through bonuses, loan officers were actually earning nearly $900. This is three times what most other loan officers earned in competing companies. Bazoberry argues that this incentive scheme ended up encouraging deception on the part of loan officers. The kinds of unauthorized activities that emerged included the following:

- Frequent rescheduling of loans without much control
- Loan officers forming ROSCAs to pay for clients' arrears, which allows employees to maintain or increase their incentive levels despite worsening portfolio quality
- Creation of "ghost" loans to hide the fact that goals are not met
- Deduction of an arbitrary amount from the clients' loans during dis-bursement to create a fund to cover bad loans
- Pressure on loan officers to repay clients' arrears from their own salaries
- Utilization of inactive savings accounts to pay for outstanding debts. (Bazoberry 2001, 12–13)

These kinds of phenomena have been reported widely outside of Bolivia as well, and they provide microfinance skeptics with plenty of fodder. The straightforward solution is to institute greater internal con-trols. Public repayments, as we noted in chapter 5, can help by making fellow borrowers aware of transgressions of rules. Similarly, pushing for strong management information systems and timely reporting aids oversight and the ability to quickly identify looming problems. Com-puterization has facilitated the work, and by creating simple data checks, much can be accomplished even in situations where comput-erization is only partial. But, in the end, the answer may necessitate reducing the reliance on overly high-powered incentives and getting to the root of the problem.

UNBUNDLING TASKS: LESSONS FROM ASA OF BANGLADESH AND PROGRESA OF MEXICO

One solution to the multitask incentive problem is to unbundle tasks, so that different staff members are responsible for different jobs and can be rewarded accordingly. To take a term from Dewatripont, Jewitt, and Tirole (1999) the principal can avoid conflicts of interest by seeking "functional specialization" among agents. An example is the state-run PROGRESA program in Mexico, now renamed Oportunidades. Opor-tunidades's main task is to deliver grants to needy households on the condition that their children go to school and attend health clinics for regular checkups (see Armendáriz de Aghion, Rai, and Sjöström 2002 for an overview).

The government is also interested in microlending, so it launched a second program, FOMIN, to deal primarily with finance. Rather than nesting within Oportunidades, FOMIN is an inde-pendent entity that functions in parallel. Thus, staff members at Opor-tunidades can be rewarded for progress in education and health outcomes, and FOMIN staff can be rewarded for their financial suc-cesses. Problems will still arise when the two outcomes are linked, but one layer of complication is removed.

Another reason for functional specialization (and perhaps a more compelling one) is that it allows managers to hire staff that are best matched to particular tasks, rather than needing to hire employees that can perform well in a wide range of circumstances.

For example, by shifting its focus sharply onto providing basic financial services, ASA of Bangladesh, a world innovator in cost-minimization, is able to hire less-educated staff members who are still capable of carrying out the required transactions. Most of ASA's loan officers are thus young and lack college degrees—and therefore cheaper as well. Nevertheless, the job is perceived as a good one, and the staff members are highly moti-vated (for more on ASA's basic model, see Fernando and Meyer 2002).

ASA's loan officers had initially been responsible for a half hour of training sessions for customers each week, scheduled as part of weekly group meetings. Topics included health and social issues, and issues under discussion could touch on, for example, oral rehydration thera-pies, breast feeding practices, and options for divorce. Older, better-educated staff members appear better-equipped to take on these training tasks. So by focusing tasks (and removing training duties from loan officers), ASA can now hire loan officers better suited to their main duties. In addition, by simplifying their loan-making process through publication of a clear manual with a set of rules that govern all choices, ASA has taken away most of the loan officers' discretion (Ahmmed 2002). ASA thus relies on the professionalism of its staff members, but ASA does not need to lean heavily on their decision-making abilities.

Ownership: Commercialization versus Cost Recovery

Microlenders like ASA are interested in achieving financial sustainability (i.e., full cost recovery) because it allows them to serve more cus-tomers without relying on continual replishments of donated funds. But while it seeks to cover costs, ASA is an NGO and has no intention (as of this writing) of becoming a commercial bank.

The advantage of commercialization is that it would allow ASA to more easily obtain capital from the market, but the disadvantage is that it would leave ASA beholden to a board of directors whose main responsibility would have to be maximizing ASA's commercial success. ASA's management feels that commercialization would undermine its ability to balance its focus on reducing poverty and promoting social change.

In addition, as described by Hart and Moore (1998), outside owners will tend to disregard the average customer's preferences and concentrate instead on attracting the marginal customer (who, given the profit motive, will likely be richer than the average). The push toward commercialization is much stronger in Latin America and leading donors have joined the bandwagon, but the evidence is not yet in as to how business demands are being balanced against social progress there. And there is growing concern (and debate) about "mission drift" away from serving the poorest clients (Drake and Rhyne 2002).

Another advantage of pursuing cost recovery (even if it falls short of commercialization) is that it limits the scope for politicization that can occur when donors (and possibly the government if they are a major funder) intervene in setting priorities. The problem can be (partly) overcome if the microfinance institution decentralizes, spinning off decision-making authority to a large number of independent "profit centers" (i.e., branches). On the other hand, centralization increases the scope for cross-subsidization among different groups of borrowers and across regions. Cross-subsidization, in turn, may help to achieve overall institutional self-sustainability.

There are times, though, when accepting donor funds can help with incentives, particularly when business imperatives are crowding out social goals. In this case, reputational considerations and the need to look "good" for certain kinds of donors can act as a commitment device that pushes the institution to delegate some authority to professionals who are primarily concerned with social objectives. (Of course, accept-ing donor funds also has the direct advantage of providing sources of inexpensive finance that can be used to build institutions and push social missions.) In other cases, donors may help strengthen commit-ments to pursuing cost recovery.

A different ownership issue arises when ownership of part of the institution is ceded to employees, as is the case at PRODEM FFP. There, employees receive PRODEM shares as part of their annual benefits package. The hope is that by giving employees a degree of direct own-ership, they will strengthen their long-term commitment to the insti-tution's success. A tension, though, arises when employees are mainly interested in securing their financial futures, while management is also pursuing a social mission. Employee ownership in this case carries some of the same tensions as commercialization. If, on the other hand, employees have internalized the social message, employee ownership may provide a way to align all incentives appropriately. The employ-ees are then akin to "social investors" who invest part of their personal financial portfolio in institutions that deliver reasonable financial returns coupled with significant social dividends.

Forming a cooperative (or joint ownership) takes the idea of em-ployee ownership even further. A main advantage of cooperatives is that the preferences of group members are taken into account, but as suggested by Ward (1958) and Hart and Moore (1998), in order to max-imize their average revenues, incumbent group members may move to restrict entry. In the case of microfinance institutions, this means that older borrowers may restrict the entry of new borrowers—which would defeat the push for broad outreach and reinforce conservatism.

SUMMARY AND CONCLUSIONS

We have analyzed how the design of incentive schemes, ownership struc-tures and organizational forms can affect the performance and impact of microfinance institutions. Institutions tend to reward loan officers for making more loans, making bigger loans, and making higher-quality loans (i.e., loans that get repaid). Curiously, relatively few programs explicitly reward cost minimization or measures of poverty reduction.

Tensions in designing optimal incentive schemes hinge on the mul-titask nature of microfinance, in which institutions seek both profit and social impact. In principle, the task of managers is to give staff members incentives to pursue both ends, although in practice the goals are not always aligned. An important constraint arises when all inputs and outputs and outcomes are not observed. Rewarding only easily observed actions (like the number of customers served or on-time col-lection rates) can skew staff away from other important—but harder to measure—goals, like empowerment or reaching the particularly needy. As a result, low-powered incentives (generated through promises of promotions, training, and interesting assignments in return for steady performance) can dominate high-powered incentives that closely link salaries to observable performance indicators.

Another tension in using (overly) high-powered incentives is that it can undermine institutional culture by creating the sense that loan offi-cers are "out for themselves" as individuals, rather than working for the greater collectivity. The insight holds a lesson for product design, in which tough loan contracts used by microlenders can end up pitting customers against loan officers in what becomes a zero-sum game. Ten-sions can quickly mount.

But when loan officers can not seize the col-lateral of borrowers in trouble, cooperation is needed. The Grameen Bank, for example, found that their initial contract system created undue tension between loan officers and customers, and the bank has proposed moving to a more flexible system under Grameen II that aims to be "tension free" (Yunus 2002). While some tension no doubt helps by providing basic motivation to customers, the general insight is useful: Maintaining incentives needs to be balanced against the cre-ation of good will, a reserve that may be vital in later periods.

Overly high-powered incentives may also inadvertently increase shortsighted behavior by staff members, encourage fraud, and dimin-ish accurate record-keeping. The theory of contracts and incentives suggests alternative solutions like yardstick competition and the insti-tution of strong internal controls.

The discussion is a reminder that microfinance entails entwining social and economic relationships. While microfinance borrows lessons from successful commercial banks, the task for microlenders is more compli-cated, and there is still ample room for innovation and new visions.

Bibliography

Baran, Paul A.: *The Political Economy of Growth,* New York, Modern Reader Paperbacks, 1975.

Bardsley, N., Cubitt: *Assessing Experimental Economics*, Princeton, Princeton University Press, 2009.

Basu, Kaushik. *Analytical Development Economics, The Less Developed Economy Revisited,* Cambridge, Mass.: MIT Press, 1997.

Benería, Lourdes. *Gender, Development, and Globalization, Economics as if All People Mattered,* New York and London, Routledge, 2003.

Caplin, A. and Schotter, A.: *The Foundations of Positive and Normative Economics*, New York, Oxford University Press, 2008.

Commons, J. R., *Institutional Economics-Its Place in Political Economy*, The University of Wisconsin Press, Madison, Wisconsin, 1934.

Desmond, Glenn, and John A, Marcell, *Handbook of Small Business Valuation Formulas and Rules of Thumb,* Valuation Press, 1993.

Gowdy, J., *Coevolution Economics: The Economy, Society and the Environment*, Kluwer, Boston, 1994.

Granger, Clive W. J.: *Empirical Modeling in Economics, Specification and Evaluation*, London, Cambridge University Press, 1999.

Guala, F.: *The Methodology of Experimental Economics,* New York, Cambridge University Press, 2005.

Gul, F. and Pesendorfer, W.: *The Foundations of Positive and Normative Economics*, New York, Oxford University Press 2008.

Hausman, D. M.: *The Inexact and Separate Science of Economics*, Cambridge, Cambridge University Press, 1992.

Hayek, F. A. *Individualism and Economic Order*, The University of Chicago Press, Chicago, 1948.

Hunt, E. K. *History of Economic Thought, A Critical Perspective,* New York, HarperCollins, 1992.

Lindblom, C. E.: *A Strategy of Decision: Policy Evaluation as a Social Process*, New York, The Free Press, 1970.

Loomes, G.: *Current Issues in Microeconomics*, New York: St. Martin's Press, 1989.

Marris, R. L., and Wood, A.: *The Corporate Economy*, London: Macmillan, 1971.

Martin, Gerald D.: *Determining Economic Damages,* Santa Ana, CA: James Publishing, 1995.

Nelson, Judy A.: *Feminism, Objectivity and Economics,* London and New York, Routledge, 1996.

Ross, D.: *Economic Theory and Cognitive Science*, Cambridge, Mass., MIT Press, 2006.

Roth, A. E.: *The Handbook of Experimental Economics*, Princeton, Princeton University Press, 1995.

Santos, A.C.: *The Social Epistemology of Experimental Economics,* London, Routledge 2009.

Schumpeter, J. A., *The Theory of Economic Development*, Harvard University Press,Cambridge, Massachusetts, 1934.

Smith, V. L.: *Papers in Experimental Economics*, Cambridge, Cambridge University Press, 1991.

Throsby, David, *Economics and Culture*, Cambridge University Press, 2001.

Tietenberg, Tom, *Environmental Economics and Policy,* New York, HarperCollins, 1994

Tinbergen, Jan.: *On the Theory of Economic Policy*, Amsterdam, North-Holland 1952.

Towse, Ruth ed.: *A Handbook of Cultural Economics*, Edward Elgar, 2003.

Weber, M.: *The Theory of Social and Economic Organizations*, New York, Oxford University Press, 1947.

Woodward, J.: *The Oxford Handbook of Philosophy of Economics*, New York, Oxford University Press, 2009.

Index

□□□